New Political Economy

Edited by
Richard McIntyre
University of Rhode Island

A Routledge Series

New Political Economy

Richard McIntyre, *General Editor*

Political Economy from Below
Economic Thought in Communitarian Anarchism, 1840–1914
Rob Knowles

Structuralism and Individualism in Economic Analysis
The "Contractionary Devaluation Debate" in Development Economics
S. Charusheela

Encoding Capital
The Political Economy of the Human Genome Project
Rodney Loeppky

Miracle for Whom?
Chilean Workers under Free Trade
Janine Berg

Market Sense
Toward a New Economics of Markets and Society
Philip Kozel

The African-Asian Divide
Analyzing Institutions and Accumulation in Kenya
Paul Vandenberg

The African-Asian Divide

Analyzing Institutions and Accumulation in Kenya

Paul Vandenberg

LONDON AND NEW YORK

Published 2006 by Routledge
2 Park Square, Milton Park, Abingdon, Oxon OX14 4RN
52 Vanderbilt Avenue, New York, NY 10017

Routledge is an imprint of the Taylor & Francis Group, an informa business

First published in paperback 2012

International Standard Book Number-13: 978-0-415-97983-2 (Hardcover)
International Standard Book Number-13: 978-0-415-65439-5 (Paperback)

Library of Congress Cataloging-in-Publication Data

Vandenberg, Paul.
The African-Asian divide : analyzing institutions and accumulation in Kenya / Paul Vandenberg.
p. cm. -- (New political economy)
Includes bibliographical references and index.
ISBN 0-415-97983-8
1. Industries--Kenya. 2. Alien labor, Asian--Kenya. 3. Corporations, Asian--Kenya. 4. Investments, Asian--Kenya. I. Title. II. Series: New political economy (New York, N.Y.)

HC865.V36 2006
338.096762--dc22 2006010229

To Akiko, with love

Contents

List of Tables and Maps

TABLES

MAPS

Acknowledgments

While this book is mostly about men in Africa, it would not have been completed without the support of two women from Japan: my supervisor and my wife. Machiko Nissanke guided the doctoral thesis that eventually became this book. Her advice and suggestions throughout the thesis process were invaluable. Thank you so much. My wife, Akiko, encouraged me to undertake a PhD in the first place, supported me through the triumphs and frustrations and helped me see the degree and this book through to the end. I hope I have given you as much help with your thesis as you gave me with mine. This book is dedicated to you.

I would like to thank Janine Berg for advice on publishing, Richard McIntyre, the Series Editor, for helpful comments and Benjamin Holtzman, at Routledge, for guiding me through the publication process.

Financial support for the original thesis was received from the Committee of Vice-Chancellors and Presidents (CVCP) of British universities by way of an Overseas Research Scholarship. A Fieldwork Award from the School of Oriental and African Studies and a Central Trust Fund Award from Senate House, University of London were also received and are gratefully acknowledged.

My thanks also extend to Dr. E. Rathgeber who provided office space at the International Development Research Centre in Nairobi during the fieldwork. At the centre, George, Osita and Abwao extended their kindness and support to me and helped me to understand how Kenya works. I would also like to thank John and Terry Lobsinger who hosted me and my wife in the early stages of the fieldwork. Finally my thanks go out to the many entrepreneurs who filled in the questionnaire and explained to me how businesses operate in Nairobi.

Introduction

Anyone who conducts a field survey of manufacturing in Kenya will be struck by the fact that most formal sector firms are owned by Asians, while nearly all informal businesses are run by Africans.[1] It is possible to ignore this fact and concentrate on factors that affect the sector as a whole, such as technology use, credit access or tariff policy. It is also possible, however, to view this ethnic-economic cleavage as a puzzling anomaly in a country with a population that is overwhelming (black) African. Furthermore, if there is evidence that this cleavage is found in other developing countries, it may be possible to use the analysis of the Kenyan case to reflect more generally on the process of economic development. Instead of specific, but limited, suggestions about technology or credit policy, we may be able to uncover some of the longer term dynamics of the development process. It is an interest in such dynamics which provides the broad objective of this study which is pursued through an attempt to explain the specific problem of an ethnic-economic cleavage in Kenya's manufacturing sector.

THE KENYAN-ASIAN PHENOMENON

The predominant position of Asians (originally from the Indian sub-continent) in Kenyan manufacturing is not a new discovery, although it has been avoided or overlooked by the many analysts who have sought to understand the country's economic development following independence. The position of Asians was brought to the forefront of academic consciousness by a very blunt analysis of Kenya's manufacturing (and bureaucratic) situation by David Himbara (1993, 1994). His simple but arresting survey revealed that 75% of large-scale manufacturing firms (with more than 50 employees) were owned by Kenyan-Asians, while only five percent were wholly owned by Africans. While some attempts have been made to qualify the figures (arguing that they tend to ignore tea factories and other agro-processing units), the figures are not seriously in dispute. The far more important problem with his work is that it lacks an explanation for the Asian position. Indeed, Himbara took pains to argue against theoretical approaches, in part because he felt that they had blinded analysts in the 1970s and 1980s in debates about Kenya's economic development. By taking a non-theoretical position, however, Himbara was implicitly (and sometimes explicitly) providing an explanation which read simply: Asians are better at business than Africans. Because the two groups are of different races, it could be seen as a racist account, denigrating the capabilities of Africans. His blunt analysis attracted criticism, notably from Michael Chege (1997, 1998), and sparked a new debate about Kenyan development.

This *second* Kenya debate followed an earlier debate of the late 1970s and early 1980s which focused on the role of Africans in Kenya's economic development, including the manufacturing sector. In the first debate, Colin Leys (1975) initially argued that in the post-independence period from 1964 to 1971 Africans had gained control of some of the mixed farms previously owned by white settlers but that those settlers were still in control of the large agricultural landholdings known as the *estates*. Furthermore, white immigrants and foreign multinationals controlled most other sectors of the economy, including manufacturing. Following a classical dependency line of argument, Leys argued that Kenya was enmeshed in a neo-colonial relationship with foreign capital that limited its growth prospects and was leading to increased misery for the less wealthy classes. The first Kenya debate was sparked when Leys (1978) reversed his position and, based on new evidence, suggested that by the late 1970s the Kikuyu, heavily supported by the state, were now gaining ownership of trade, construction and real estate and were beginning an advance into manufacturing. Other analysts of Kenya then supported either the original or the revised Leys' position.[2] This intriguing debate petered out by the early 1980s with no definitive conclusion about whether Africans were or were not gaining control of their economy through ownership in manufacturing and other sectors. The positions of the debaters were often based on how one interpreted the facts and it was unclear whether the state was supporting an independent and competitive African business class or a state-dependent type of crony capitalism. In a 10-year retrospective on the debate, however, Leys (1994: 235) did admit that "Africans (as opposed to Kenya Asians) were still virtually unrepresented in the manufacturing sector."

The first debate focused on Africans and tended to ignore the Asian business community or implied that it was a relatively minor force that was being rapidly supplanted by Africans (Leys 1975: 256). In the 1990s,

Himbara brought this omission to light. He argued that dependency theory had overlooked the Asians because they did not fit into the neat categories of indigenous and foreign capital. He noted that many multinationals had closed or sold off their subsidiaries during the unstable and slow growth decade of the 1980s and that Asians had bought many of these firms or established and expanded their own enterprises. His simple survey provided some revealing results. Not only did Asians own 75% of firms with more than 50 employees, but 86% of large firms with more than Ksh100 million in invested capital were Asian. Kenya Asians were the country's true capitalists, according to Himbara. The second Kenya debate effectively began when Chege (1997, 1998) challenged Himbara's analysis.[3] The survey was biased, according to Chege, although subsequent analysis, using a larger sample of World Bank data, suggested that the results were a relatively fair representation of the ethnic split in manufacturing (Vandenberg 2003). At about the same time, Kenneth King's 1996 study on micro and small-scale entrepreneurs in Nairobi appeared. Although his work did not address the debate, King found cases in which African entrepreneurs had moved beyond micro-sized artisanal work into light industrial activities. His book suggested that the small (as opposed to micro) enterprise sector contained many African firms and that these firms might be part of a nascent African push into urban manufacturing. My own survey, in the late 1990s, covered the areas mentioned in King's book. However, in comparing these African firms with other small firms in the more formalized industrial areas, it became apparent that while Africans had penetrated into small-scale manufacturing, even this end of the size distribution was dominated by Asian firms. What Himbara had found at the level of large-scale firms, I found at the level of small, formal enterprises. In this regard, I accepted his evidence but agreed with Chege that an explanation was needed that was not based on racial categories, given evidence that Africans were successful in other sectors of the economy. This book is an attempt to provide that explanation.

PROVIDING AN EXPLANATION

It is obvious that the dependency framework, used in the first debate, cannot address the central issues of the second debate. Dependency focuses on international economic relations and the second debate is about differences in domestic patterns of accumulation. Nonetheless, the Marxism which inspires dependency theory might have been used to undertake the analysis. Indeed, quality political economy analysis, which accounts for class, can make a contribution to understanding Africa's development trajectory.

However, the second debate is about an ethnic difference, not a class one. There may be a class element to the ethnic difference (Asians employing Africans in manufacturing) but it is not the central issue. Furthermore, although the second debate is about patterns of accumulation, Marxism suggests that accumulation is based on the extraction of surplus value, a notion that I reject.[4]

A proper explanation of the African-Asian divide needs to account for several factors that either arose in the course of my survey of African and Asian businessmen in Nairobi or were evident from the historical record of Kenya's development. Three main factors are relevant here. The first factor is that Asians may have gained advantages through their connections with the British during colonialism and by being channeled into urban activities due to their exclusion from agriculture. The second factor concerns the strong informal networks that Asians used in conducting business with each other and whether they restricted entry into sectors (i.e. manufacturing) where they had become dominant. The third factor is that there might be what I call an ethnic-sectoral specialization in which Asians have concentrated in manufacturing and Africans in businesses more closely related to agriculture.

The question of informal networks derives from two sources. One is the increasing importance of information in development economics, which was borrowed from the new economics of information in mainstream analysis (see Bardhan and Udry, 1999). The other development is a growing academic interest in ethnic business (or trading) communities which is being pursued through empirical work in a variety of countries (Moore 1997). Kenya's Asians are like the overseas Chinese in parts of south-east Asia. In those cases, there is no racial distinction because Asians compete with Asians.

Basing the explanation of Asian success on informal ethnic networks and a quasi-supportive colonial environment resolves some issues but it raises others. If the explanation rests on the ability of Kenyan-Asians to operate informal networks, then it suggests that Africans are less adept at building such networks and we are back to Himbara's notion that Asians are better at business than Africans. More importantly, however, the literature on African credit institutions is replete with examples of the informal arrangements which Africans have devised to provide credit in rural, and in some cases urban, communities. Are the Asian networks somehow better or stronger than the African ones, or instead, are there reasons why Africans are less able or less inclined to use such institutional support to venture into urban manufacturing?

The latter question is prompted by a more general re-evaluation of the basis upon which Asian and African success can be characterized. Why has business success been equated with success in urban manufacturing and is this part of the post-war legacy in academic thought which has equated development narrowly with industrialization? A more fair comparison would be African success in agriculture against Asian success in manufacturing and urban trade. In addition, it prompts a further questioning of the supposition that Africans should be venturing into manufacturing, when in fact they have traditionally developed their expertise in agriculture and when it is agriculture (and tourism) and not manufacturing which provides the bulk of the country's foreign exchange. These issues and questions are important for the broader questions of the study because they highlight the relationship between the ethnic cleavage in manufacturing and the activities of Africans in other sectors. (The relationship is sketched out in this book but it requires a more detailed examination of surplus generation and the investment decisions of Africans which goes beyond the current study.)

This leads us to the possibility that the difference in firm size is related not to the activities of Asian and African firms *in* the manufacturing sector, but to differences in the African and Asian communities regarding *who has entered* the sector. Many of the African entrepreneurs who operate micro businesses are urban migrants with little money, with little access to people who have money and thus with limited capacity to invest in the technology needed to set up proper formal sector businesses. The Africans who enter urban manufacturing are not successful farmers who decided to liquidate agricultural holdings and self-invest in manufacturing by setting up their own shops. Nor have they pursued a diversification strategy by investing their surplus into manufacturing while maintaining their agricultural operations. As suggested in subsequent chapters, diversification from farming tends to involve investment in trade, transport, real estate and agro-processing and that the leap from farming to urban manufacturing is large, risky and uncommon.

By contrast, the Asians who enter manufacturing often come from families with a background in urban business. In many cases, the family has been involved in trade and thus the move into manufacturing is a natural progression into more complex business activities. In other cases, the family has been involved in manufacturing for one or two previous generations. Asian entrants also tend to come from relatively wealthy segments of the community and thus have access to the capital needed to start proper manufacturing firms in the formal sector. They may be using informal networks to obtain starting and working capital but they can do so not so much because the networks exist but because the networks connect to people who have money to lend. African migrants develop similar networks but they link people who are relatively poor and have little money to channel into new businesses.

These three factors (formal institutions under colonialism, informal networks and sectoral specialization) provide a rather diverse explanation. Fortunately, those issues are all, in one way or another, addressed in the theoretical work on institutions by Douglass North (1981, 1990). His work is intriguing because of the importance it places on the relationship between economic development and the institutions that support property rights and inter-temporal contracting. Furthermore, by separating the *institutional environment* (the broad macro level) from the *institutions of governance* (at the micro level) and by distinguishing between formal and informal arrangements, North's work suggests a possible explanation for Asian success. Such success might be based on both their favorable treatment under the formal institutional environment, notably during colonialism, and their propensity to develop strong informal institutions to screen transactors, enforce commercial agreements and channel investment and credit within the community.

The above explanation comes closest to answering the question of why the micro firms are all African-owned while the small and medium sized firms are predominantly owned by Asians. A statement which sums up the conclusions might be the following: *Asians used strong informal networks and the benefit of formal institutions (notably during colonialism) to amass funds which have allowed them to enter urban manufacturing with higher levels of starting capital than most Africans.* Furthermore, *successful African entrepreneurs in the agricultural sector have tended not to shift investment into urban manufacturing due to the lack of expertise and experience.* Thus the explanation is based on: formal institutions (the state), informal institutions (networks) and sectoral specialization (urban manufacturing and trade versus agriculture and rural activities).

AN OUTLINE OF THE CHAPTERS

The line of argument is pursued through seven chapters. The theory of institutions is provided in the first chapter, followed by three chapters of history (pre-colonial, colonial and post-colonial) and then three chapters on institutions and accumulation in Nairobi's metal manufacturing sector. This combination of historical and contemporary analysis is required to demonstrate how past patterns of accumulation have produced the African-Asian sectoral divide.

The first chapter sets out the institutional approach of Douglass North and shows how it combines elements of both the more neo-classical new institutional economics and the old institutionalism. The distinction between the institutional environment at the macro level (state) and the institutions of governance at the micro level are highlighted as a holistic approach to the topic. The distinction between formal and informal institutions is relevant to an analysis of Africa given the problems of governance (at the state level) and the resilience of informal institutions at the local level. The third part of the chapter discusses the general characteristics of ethnic business (or trading) communities, of which Kenya's Asian community is an example. A key feature of such communities is the use of thick and low-cost information to support the informal enforcement of commercial contracts. The discussion provides a general framework for the empirical work in subsequent chapters.

The three historical chapters trace the fortunes and the patterns of economic activity among the African and Asian communities. The pre-colonial chapter highlights the division between interior and coastal communities and how Asians traders worked along the coast of East Africa for centuries under Arab and European rule. In the interior, African pastoralists (herders) and settled cultivators developed distinct institutions to protect property and gain the benefits of exchange. The Asian experience along the coast put that community in a much better position to benefit from the British move inland at the end of the 19th century. Under British colonial rule, the Asians were barred from farming and concentrated on urban trade and manufacturing. African communities, meanwhile, struggled against the British for control of land in the White Highlands and elsewhere. The formal institutions of the colonial state reinforced a sectoral division between Africans and Asians. At independence, Africans gained control of the state and tried to use that power to enter urban trade and manufacturing. While many Asians fled the country, their experience and network capital allowed others to resist and continue in business. The ban on non-African trading in certain areas and certain commodities encouraged the Asians to move more into manufacturing. The change of presidents in 1978 from Kenyatta to Moi resulted in a rapprochement with the Asian community. African ethnic competition and a sluggish economy prompted multinationals to sell off subsidiaries. Many of these were bought by Asians.

The three subsequent chapters are based on a survey of over 120 metal manufacturing firms in Nairobi. The results support the notion of an African-Asian divide in urban manufacturing with Africans owning almost all of the micro and more informal firms while Asians own the bulk of the larger, more established firms. The first of these chapters provides an overview and feel for the four main metalwork sites in Nairobi. Chapter 6 then reviews the evidence on a number of key institutions regarding property and credit transactions, making distinctions based on both size and ethnicity. The final chapter considers a network effect among Asian enterprises which may give them a contemporary advantage over their African counterparts. Such an effect is hard to prove but instead it is clear that Asians begin with much higher levels of starting capital. This suggests that past processes of capital accumulation in the Asian community may account in part for its dominance in urban manufacturing.

RELEVANCE FOR POLICY IN OTHER PARTS OF AFRICA

Kenya is not alone in possessing a foreign ethnic business community. Asians are engaged in business in other parts of eastern and southern African, while the Lebanese constitute an important community is several West African countries. Furthermore, in many places people of European origin stayed on after colonialism and constitute a similar foreign business community. South Africa and Zimbabwe are two important examples in this regard. In many cases, it is now not fully appropriate to refer to these groups as *foreign* given that members of these groups have lived in Africa their entire lives. Nonetheless, the arguments and analysis applied to the Asians in Kenya can inform our understanding of these other groups.

The analysis of Kenya that is provided in this book is not particularly focused on policy. Instead, an effort has been made to provide an explanation for a phenomenon, the African-Asian divide, rather than to determine the effectiveness of specific government legislation or action. Nonetheless, governments across Africa have grappled with the fact that following independence a small elite of non-indigenous Africans were in control of manufacturing and formal business (Collier and Gunning 1999: 68). Kenya's political leaders have taken a fairly benign approach to the Asian community, although restrictions were placed on trading activities in the 1970s. President Daniel arap Moi (1978–2002) subsequently developed a closer relationship with elements of the Asian community to support the rise of his own ethnic group in urban business. By contrast, in neighboring Uganda, President Idi Amin expelled the Asians from the country in the early 1970s. The current leader, President Yoweri Museveni, has invited them back, promising the restitution of land and buildings. The move recognizes the important contribution that Asians may be able to make to the economic revival of that country. Meanwhile, in Zimbabwe, President Robert Mugabe is forcing an exodus of white farmers through a sudden denial of existing landed property rights. The move has precipitated a disastrous decline in the country's fortunes. Neighboring South Africa has been following a more gentle approach, encouraging the buy-out by blacks of white farms on the basis of willing-seller/willing-buyer. It is not clear that this voluntary approach will be successful in effecting a substantial transfer of land between the two communities and a more forced approach is envisaged by the government. Since the end of apartheid in 1992, the state has also supported a program of black empowerment in the business sector. A key question for these and other governments is how to redress historical inequalities in business ownership while not undermining the contribution that ethnic business communities make to the economy.

Part of the answer to this question relates to the nature of institutions and thus to the institutional perspective used in this study. Ethnic business communities operate on the basis of strong informal networks that allow for the transmission of new ideas and technologies and for the enforcement of trade, credit and other types of contracts. These networks are necessary when formal institutions are weak, as they are in many parts of Africa. Thus, part of the solution to expanding black African participation in business is the shift from informal, ethnic-based institutions to trusted formal institutions managed by the state. Recent international proposals to address Africa's economic problems, notably those of the *Commission for Africa* chaired by Tony Blair, the British prime minister, have highlighted the importance of institutions in securing a trusted investment climate for the continent. The connection between institutions, ethnic business communities and current reform efforts is an interesting and complex one. We address it in the Conclusion so as not to undermine our explanation of Kenya's African-Asian divide, which is our central theme.

Chapter One

Institutional Theory, Africa and Ethnic Business Communities

Institutional economics provides a framework for understanding economic growth by focusing on the formal and informal institutions that support investment and trade. When applied in an historical manner, institutionalism can focus attention on the bias and corruption of formal institutions that lead to distinct patterns of capital accumulation. In this regard, the colonial state contains a particularly biased set of formal institutions. Moreover, the efficiency of informal institutions can help to explain the sectoral concentration of ethnic communities. An important part of the explanation of the African-Asian divide in Kenya is the historical process of urban accumulation for Asians and rural accumulation for Africans.

A key institutional theorist who has focused on both formal and informal institutions and has taken an historical perspective is Douglass North. While his early work has been criticized as being narrowly neo-classical, his writings from the mid-1980s onward have incorporated many non neo-classical elements. The first part of this chapter thus explains how North's later approach to institutions combines elements of two schools of institutionalism, the new institutional economics, which is more neo-classical, and the old institutionalism, which is decidedly not.[1] The second part of the chapter then explains how his institutionalism is useful for the study of African economic development and ethnic business communities. Through this two-part discussion (of North and of Africa), the chapter provides the theoretical framework for the six chapters on Kenya that follow. It is North's later approach to institutions that is adopted and used for this empirical analysis.

COMBINING TWO APPROACHES TO INSTITUTIONS

Over the past three decades, two schools of institutionalism have competed for prominence in the field of economics. One, the self-styled *new institutional economics* (NIE), has attempted to work within the logic of mainstream, neo-classical economics which derives from the capacity of rational, self-interested individuals to make choices between competing alternatives. This work has drawn on the pioneering insights and questions raised by Ronald Coase (1937, 1960) and is commonly thought to include the work of Alchian, Demsetz, Barzel, Williamson, North and others. A second branch is often referred to as the *old institutional economics* (OIE) because it was developed in the early part of the 20th century and received considerable attention, notably in the United States, until just after the Second World War. Its key proponents included Veblen, Commons, Mitchell and Ayres.[2] The increasing dominance of neo-classical economics after the war, as well the descriptive nature of much of the old institutionalism, tended to relegate the latter to a fringe discourse from the 1950s until the early 1980s. More recently it has been revived and developed in European economic circles (and to a lesser extent in North America) by such writers as Hodgson, Rutherford, Bush and Tool (Rutherford 1994). Both the earlier and the more recent theorists working in this vein have been critical of neo-classical theorizing because of its narrow focus on rationality, choice and utility maximization in explaining human behavior. In contrast, the old institutionalism focuses on how economic action and activity is influenced by social norms, habits, culture and, in some variations, unequal political and economic power.

In dividing institutionalism in this way, one encounters the common difficulty of analyzing a sub-field of economics by placing its various contributors into respective schools. While certain authors may fall squarely within—and indeed define—a particular school, others are not so easy to place. As in many disciplines, these not-so-well-placed writers are often the more interesting ones because, in attempting to combine the strengths of competing schools, they force us to compare their underlying assumptions. They require us to ask whether these assumptions can be integrated in a new synthesis or whether they are inherently contradictory. One author who prompts such questions is Douglass North, an economic historian who has made an important contribution to the theory of institutions.[3]

His early work is not difficult to define: it is an attempt to apply transaction costs, contracting and property rights to produce a neo-classical institutional approach to economic history. As a result, in the 1970s and early 1980s, he and Oliver Williamson came to define two different but related strands of the new institutional economics which were based largely on the precepts of neo-classical economics. While he continued to work within the mainstream, by the early 1980s North's attitude toward the neo-classical school was undergoing some important changes. His 1981 book, *Structure and Change in Economic History*, contained important deviations from the approach, notably on the nature of human behavior and on the notion of an inevitable evolution towards greater institutional efficiency. With the publication in 1990 of *Institutions, Institutional Change and Economic Performance*, the deviations from neo-classical analysis were more fully presented with prominent roles given to uncertainty, inefficiency and cognitive constraints. While a number of analysts have noted the shift (Samuels 1995; Dugger 1995; Rutherford 1995; Groenewegen *et al.* 1995; Hodgson 1998), there still exists no detailed treatment of North's work in relation to the two main branches of institutionalism. In addition, a lingering misperception within the discipline (caused by the association of new institutionalism with neoclassical economics) results in his work being classified with other neo-classical theorists (i.e. Field, 1994; Stein 1994). One of the main purposes of this chapter, therefore, is to situate North's work in relation to the two main branches of institutionalism and to determine the extent to which his work is based on neo-classical theory. Following a first section on definitions, this will be done in the second section by comparing his work against several of the central postulates of neo-classical analysis (rationality, opportunism, relative prices and universalism) and will include comparisons with Williamson and several 'old' institutionalists. The third section considers his view of history and suggests that while it represents an advance over the ahistorical analysis of mainstream theory, it is not truly *historical* in nature. The fourth section then argues that North's shift in thinking over time can best be understood in the context of recent trends within the social sciences and notably a breakdown of the traditional division of labor between economics and sociology. This has resulted in attempts to reconcile the rational choices of neo-classical economics with the socialized actions of modern sociology. While North attempts such a reconciliation, he is only at the initial stages of designing a fully integrated approach.

DEFINING INSTITUTIONS, TRANSACTION COSTS AND PROPERTY RIGHTS

Given the variety of types of institutions, it is difficult to provide a definition which is clear and precise (and thus possesses analytical value) but which is also encompassing. Generally, an institution governs interaction between separate units; in this way the notion of a relationship is fundamental. Negotiating, monitoring and enforcing that relationship are, therefore, the key aspects of institutional analysis. This definition is different from common understandings of the term such as 'financial institution' (bank) or 'government institution' (ministry or department). North refers to these units as organizations and thus institutions govern the relationships between organizations, between people and organizations or, in simple exchange, between people. In economic matters, a key organization is the firm.

The difficulty with this strict definition is that there are relationships within a firm or a government organization which are structured by institutions. These would include either relationships between workers and owners/mangers (principal-agent issues) or between divisions. Generally, North pays limited attention to these relationships while for Williamson they are of prime importance, notably those between corporate divisions. Williamson's definition of institutions is, therefore, quite specific: they are the mechanisms which govern transactions and a transaction occurs "when a good or service is transferred across a technologically separable interface" (1985: 1). Thus, there are three principal institutions in capitalism: the market, the firm and supply (or relational) contracting. The firm is an institution because transactions between divisions represent interaction across that separable interface. The institutional choice of firms—of whether to make or buy a component—involves a choice between whether the interaction takes place between firms or between departments within a firm. The choice is based on a number of factors, but notably "asset specificity," which is the degree to which assets used in production are specific to producing a particular product or, instead, are readily redeployable. The make-or-buy (or buy on supply contract) decision is the key and indeed almost the sole problematic of Williamson's work, and it is analyzed with reference to a limited number of well-specified concepts (bounded rationality, opportunism and asset specificity). Williamson's principal works, *Markets and Hierarchies* (1975) and *The Economic Institutions of Capitalism*(1985), focus on these questions in the context of industrial firms in developed markets.

North's work is broader in that it includes political decision-making and activities in civil society, as well as changes which occur over long periods of history. As a result, his definition of institutions is consciously broad: "a framework within which human interaction takes place" (North 1990a: 4). It can encompass both inter- and intra-organizational issues of private transacting, as well as the development of the legal and regulatory environment which requires an understanding of the political system. Furthermore, it includes the cultural, social and cognitive processes which provide a norm structure and thus also guide human interaction. The old institutionalism tends to focus on this cognitive-behavioral aspect which is based on the insight of Veblen, a key figure for the OIE, who defined institutions as the "settled habits of thought common to the generality of men" (Veblen 1994: 239). In turn, this helps to explain the old school's incorporation of insights from sociology and psychology. Thus, institutions include habits, cultural characteristics and routinized behavior which may not involve the type of deliberative-rationalized action which is the motivation behind neo-classical behavior.

The NIE relies heavily on the concept of *transaction costs*, which are the costs of *specifying* what is being exchanged and *enforcing* the subsequent agreement. These costs are distinct from the traditional production costs of capital, labor, technology and natural resources (which North calls *transformation costs*, 1990a: 6). The basic institutional critique of neo-classical economics is that transactions costs are assumed to be zero. The two aspects of transaction costs—specification and enforcement—are related but distinct. Enforcement relies either on a set of informal constraints and norms which tend to be fairly low in cost but limit exchange to a small group of known participants or it depends upon a set of legally enforced rights which apply to a large number of economic agents who interact through impersonal relationships. Usually there is some combination of formal and informal constraints. A strong and efficient enforcement regime lowers the cost of transacting because it screens out those who might have no intention of fulfilling the terms of a contract and it encourages those who have entered into a contract to follow through and fulfill their obligations.

Specification costs are more difficult to define. They involve the cost of measuring what is being exchanged and they are closely linked to technology for two reasons. First, improvements in the quality of goods and services are often based on investments in more advanced technology. Secondly, however, such improvements will only be encouraged if the producer can reap the rewards of that additional investment. To do so, the buyer must be able to discriminate between different goods on the basis of quality and this will require technology which can measure such quality differences. A good example is steel. Investments in processes which make steel stronger will only be worthwhile if buyers, who are willing to pay a higher price for stronger steel, can ensure (measure) that the steel is indeed stronger. While private agents may retain measuring equipment, the state can play an important role in reducing these specification costs through credible systems of weights and measures. At a developed level, the activities involve grading (common to agricultural produce, but also commodities such as steel) and inspection (for example, for health standards in food and technical standards in engineering work).

Property rights are important in North's approach because they also help to reduce transaction costs by providing a system of ownership, enforcement and adjudication which fosters increased transactions (because of lower costs) and thus greater specialization.[4] The movement to broader based, formal systems are important to economic development because without them exchange and specialization are governed by personal relations and knowledge, and by local enforcement mechanisms at a lower, and less specialized, levels of output.

NEO-CLASSICAL ASSUMPTIONS AND THE CRITIQUE

To assess North's approach, his work can be compared against the central tenets of the neo-classical school (Table 1.1). That school is based on a particular analytical approach and on a number of key assumptions regarding human behavior. Upon these foundations is developed a system for analyzing economic phenomenon. At its core, the neo-classical approach is based on an *ontological* individualism in which the basic economic actor is the individual, as opposed to groups, classes, governments, etc. Furthermore, an individual's actions are based on rational deliberation—even if that rationality is often bounded—with the aim of maximizing personal utility. Rightly or wrongly, these assumptions of rational maximization allow the neo-classical economist to model individual responses in an environment of incentives and, through a process of *methodological* individualism, to aggregate those responses to explain economy-wide behavior. The environment of incentives is based largely on the role of relative prices such that for a given economic activity, either production or exchange, individuals will seek to reduce outlays and maximize benefits. These relative prices, furthermore, play a fundamental role in ensuring that goods supplied and goods demanded are equated and that the market clears so as to avoid oversupply (and wastage) or undersupply (and scarcity). Relative prices, working through the market in this way, ensure that the economy is at or moving toward a long-run equilibrium which represents an efficient situation. In this rational functioning of individuals and markets, there is little attention to habitual, cultural or historical processes and little recognition of how power and coercion might affect the operation of markets. The strengths and weaknesses of neo-classical economics lie in just such a distinction: the approach is clear, logical and precise but narrow. Furthermore, the extent to which this approach provides a realistic conception of how economies work is what divides neo-classical from alternative theorists.

Table 1.1: Standard neo-classical theory and North's institutionalism

Aspects	Standard neo-classical theory	North's institutionalism
unit of analysis	individual	transacting parties
objective of actors	self-interested utility maximization	utility maximization within a framework of institutional constraints to reduce transaction costs and secure property
cognition	rational	rational within a framework of mental models and culture
information	full	limited, subjectively processed
approach	universalistic	universalistic, with some attempt at historical
method of analysis	mechanistic	combination of deductive use of neoclassical analytical tools with reference to history
change	movements around equilibrium based on changes in relative prices	through periods of prosperity and stagnation, based on efficiency of institutions in lowering transaction costs and securing property rights
equilibrium	efficient solution	no pre-supposition of movement to equilibrium
central concept	optimize efficiency	explain the rise of the West and current regional economic disparity
econometrics	well-adapted	ill-adapted
modeling	highly developed, equational	informal, general framework
extent of market: determines specialization	limited by government barriers to the free movement of capital, people, goods	determined by efficiency of institutions in lowering transaction costs
approach to development	market liberalization, getting prices right	institutional refinement leading to lowering of transaction costs and security of property over wider areas
role of prices	central	important but incremental impact over time

Source: By the author, based on North, 1981, 1990a; format from Paarlberg, 1993, 824.

NEO-CLASSICAL ECONOMICS AS NON-INSTITUTIONAL

Both the NIE and OIE concur that neo-classical economics has avoided or denied the importance of institutions. In a neo-classical world, exchange takes place between buyers and sellers without reference to institutional arrangements which have developed over time. Markets arise spontaneously and even the Walrasian auctioneer, with his unlimited—and unrealistic—matching abilities, is recognized as a fiction, carrying out the job as an all-knowing automaton. Thus, for North neo-classicism has failed to provide a theory of institutions just as it has also failed to provide adequate theories for the growth in the stock of knowledge and demographic change (North 1981: 7). Hodgson, working in the old institutionalist tradition, is similarly critical and derives his critique from the neo-classical assumptions of methodological individualism which include a "refusal to examine the institutional and other forces which are involved in the molding of individual preferences and purposes" (Hodgson 1988: 54).

Thus the attempts by the OIE to critique neo-classical theory from an institutionalist perspective may be quite valid but such a critique can be shared by proponents of the NIE. The critical question, then, is whether the OIE can muster a valid critique of the NIE or in fact whether the new institutionalism is a useful modification and extension of neo-classical theory. This ultimately concerns the extent to which institutional analysis can be grafted onto neo-classical theory or whether such an attempt is doomed to fail due to an essential incompatibility between neo-classical theory and institutionalism. The OIE would need to argue that they are incompatible while the NIE would need to prove that they are not. This critical distinction is not always clearly defined and thus the otherwise excellent alternative institutional analysis of Hodgson (1988) is for the most part a critique of neo-classical theory and only incidentally a critique of the NIE. Furthermore, his critical comments of the NIE are directed at Williamson (not North) and it is the former who receives both praise for understanding the importance of institutions, and criticism for remaining within a neo-classical framework. In subsequent work, however, Hodgson (1992) does stress the ultimate incompatibility of institutionalism with neo-classical theory and thus the impossibility of producing an institutionalism based on neo-classical analysis. The ability to both praise and criticize the new institutionalism is less a contradiction and more an understanding that neo-classical institutionalists stand part way between standard neo-classical theory, which has not incorporated institutions, and the OIE, which takes a non-neoclassical approach not just by its acceptance of institutions but by its approach to them.

In terms of logical method, (a)historical approach and the reliance on (un)changing postulates of human behavior, however, Williamson is more neo-classical in his approach (than North) and thus it is usually his work which is criticized by alternative approaches (Granovetter 1985; Hodgson 1988).[5] For our purposes, what is important is the extent to which one can move from the standard neo-classical pole and still be considered neo-classical. This requires an investigation into how different schools treat the issue of human behavior and economic activity. These issues are considered in the sections which follow.

RATIONALITY, COGNITIVE CONSTRAINTS AND IDEOLOGY

Neo-classical assumptions regarding behavior are based on Enlightenment notions that humans are rational (we can calculate possible outcomes to a course of action) and purposive (we have will and thus are unlike animals which are guided by instinct). More recently, social scientists have amended these broad statements by adding that actions might not be strictly rational under several conditions: if full information is not available; if it is too costly (and thus not available to the decision-maker); and/or if it cannot be adequately processed. Thus, *bounded* rationality denotes a situation in which decisions are rational within the context of available and processable information. Thus, Williamson expresses current neo-classical thinking in borrowing from Kenneth Arrow the notion that people are "*intendedly* rational but only *limitedly* so" (Williamson 1985: 45). That is, they want to make fully informed rational decisions but are limited by the knowledge which they can utilize. Limits on rationality are also recognized by the OIE, for which the "rationalistic, utilitarian calculus is limited and constrained within everyday acts of exchange" (Hodgson, 1988: 167). For institutionalism, the main question is the extent of these limits and the degree to which people are also guided by habit, culture or structure.

The importance of habits and established patterns of behavior is critical to the OIE and is a central aspect of Veblen's famous critique of marginal utility and the assumptions of neo-classical theory (1909). For Veblen, institutions condition human action in a manner which is different from the immediate response to altered incentives, notably prices, which guides marginal analysis. It is important to note, however, that Veblen's often-cited definition of institutions—that they are "settled habits of thought common to the generality of men" (*ibid.*, p. 626)—is part of a larger view of human nature which includes a basic "instinct" to engage in purposeful action (Veblen 1899: 15). While purposeful is not the same as rational, rationality or "intelligence" is employed to achieve the purposeful end (Veblen 1914: 30–32). Taken together, Veblen suggests that individuals operate within a culture of habits and established patterns of thought, that they are instinctively engaged in purposeful action and that such action is guided, to some degree, by intelligence. While the purposeful aspect of his theory has been under-appreciated (as noted by Hodgson 1998: n. 10), it does appear that habitual behavior takes precedence over rationality. This emphasis provides a critical distinction between the OIE and neo-classical theory. Indeed, it has been argued that old institutionalism's main contribution to economic theory lies in providing a "radically different perspective on the nature of human agency, based on the concept of habit" (Hodgson 1998: 167). Furthermore, the relative importance of these factors is significant in developing an approach to institutional stasis and change. To what extent do people follow habits of behavior and to what extent do they defy habits when confronted with an altered environment of incentives? This question can never be answered absolutely in the abstract because the influences of new incentives and old patterns are specific to circumstance and setting.

North is aware that behavior will not change immediately, even as a result of a one-off price change or a change in formal rules (North 1981: 50). He is also aware that human conduct, including adherence to institutions, is guided by a perceived understanding of the world embodied in ideologies or "mental models" (North 1981: ch. 5; 1995a: 18). Ideology provides a guide to behavior in a world of uncertainty by allowing people to "economize on the amount of information" they must have to make decisions and take action (North 1984: 35). In the early 1980s, North suggested that ideology both, i) allowed individuals to overcome cognitive constraints; and, ii) provided them with a sense of what is right. The sense of what is right (or fair or legitimate) involves both outright altruism and a sense of justice (which can include a variety of acts from honoring a contract to rebelling against a change in property rights). In this earlier work, the emphasis was on this second element (the sense of right) and both how it helped to account for those activities in which people risked their well-being for political and economic change and how it provided social stability. As discussed below, this sense of what is right also helps to reduce the tendency for people to engage in opportunistic behavior.

In 1990, North provided an explicit distinction by dividing behavioral assumptions into: i) deciphering the environment, and ii) motivation. While the distinction was similar to that made earlier, the emphasis shifted to the cognitive problem of deciphering the environment. Motivation did not receive detailed treatment but was divided, rather simply, into altruism and self-interest, with the emphasis on the latter. Thus, he argued that, "we can build more elaborate models of complex human behavior *within* the individual expected-utility model, incorporating certain aspects of altruism" (North 1990: 21, emphasis added). The focus here on self-interest, even if supplemented with a notion of altruism, is similar to the neo-classical emphasis. However, the argument is somewhat disjointed, as the discussion on informal constraints in a following chapter explores the importance of moral codes and the sense of what is right—clearly issues which affect motivation but are not specifically altruistic in character. He notes that these ideas are important in explaining, for example, the movement to abolish slavery in the U.S. (*ibid.*: 43).

There is much more focus, in his later analysis of human behavior, on the cognitive problem of deciphering the environment. In effect, North realizes that economic actors do rely on habits to make a large portion of their decisions and in this regard, he comes very close to the position of the old institutionalism. He notes that "the existence of an imbedded set of institutions that has made it possible for us not to have to think about problems or [how] to make such [routine] choices" (North 1990: 23). Furthermore, organized ideologies provide a subjective view of how the world works which allow for decisions in more complex, uncertain situations. For North, ideologies are sometimes group-specific but they can also be specific to the individual. Thus for example, he argues that, "Individuals make choices based on subjectively derived models that diverge among individuals and the information the actors receive is so incomplete that in most cases these divergent subjective models show no tendency to converge" (North 1990a: 17).

While these individuals may be rationalizing within a given mental model subject to an information constraint, the models they employ are so subjective that it will hardly be possible to define what is rational behavior. The importance for neo-classical economics of postulating a certain uniform rational behavior across individuals stems from the desire to build models with which to predict the human responses to changes in economic variables. If A occurs, then given the presumed rational calculation of individuals, we can assume that they will respond by doing B. This process of theorizing breaks down, however, if the rational calculation which connects A with B is filtered through an infinite number of subjective mental models and results in a great variety of responses.

FREE RIDING, OPPORTUNISM AND LEGITIMACY

Because neo-classical theory is based on the notion of individual welfare maximization, it has recognized that some individuals will attempt to gain benefits without incurring the costs. This sometimes involves a free rider problem (often associated with not joining a pressure group but benefiting from its lobbying) but can also take more immoral forms such as shirking or fraud. Problems also arise in an exchange context in which information is withheld to benefit a particular party—an idea that was developed by Akerlof (1970) in the context of the "market for lemons" (used cars). It is also an important aspect of principal-agent issues in which principals seek ways of ensuring that their agents are acting honestly on their behalf. Williamson groups these issues together under *opportunism* which is defined as "self-interest seeking with guile" and is a central element of his institutionalism (1985: 47). As noted, North disagrees with the neo-classical assumption that individuals are always motivated by self-interest. Instead he argues that individual welfare maximization does not account for such things are blood donations, voting or support for certain lobby groups which involve acting on altruism or moral codes. In each of these cases, it is better to avoid the individual costs of making the effort (in terms of time, energy and money) and free ride on the efforts of others. This is so even if the individual may desire an adequate supply of blood, the election of a certain party, etc. (North 1981: 10, 46). North, along with the OIE writers, rejects the pervasiveness of opportunism because it is unable to explain group dynamics in which free riding is possible but not acted upon (North 1981: 11; Hodgson 1988: 265). He does recognize that game-theoretic approaches which involve repeated games offer some explanations as to how opportunism is reduced but that is only part of the answer (North 1981: 35). The other part comes from ideology and the support it can lend to feelings of legitimacy, loyalty and trust:

> Individuals may . . . obey customs, rules and laws because of a . . . deep-seated conviction that they are legitimate. Change and stability in history require a theory of ideology to account for these deviations from the individualistic calculus of neo-classical theory (North 1981: 12).

North demonstrates these concepts with reference to his weekly purchase of a bag of oranges. When he returns home, he does not find a few rotten oranges at the bottom of the bag. While this may be partly due to the vendor's wish that Mr. North will buy more oranges the following week (repeat dealing), it is also due to the vendor's ideological commitment to the values of honesty and fairness. For his part, Mr. North's own sense of honesty constrains him from slipping a few extra oranges into his pocket while the vendor's back is turned (North 1981: 35–7).

A legitimizing ideology is critical to North's institutional analysis because it allows for the reduction of opportunistic behavior and thus the lowering of transaction costs associated with monitoring and enforcement. North recognizes this concept as a central difference between his approach and that of Williamson. While the latter may fully recognize the importance of opportunism and the enormous (and probably unsustainable) costs of total enforcement, he provides no suggestions for how those costs might be reduced through norm reinforcement (North 1990a: 54–5). For North, the importance of norms is not to be underestimated: "Strong moral and ethical codes of a society are the cement of social stability which makes an economic system viable" (North 1981: 47).

These ideas have been developed by Platteau (1994A, B) who has extended North's analysis by stressing the economic importance of moral norms and how they are reinforced through primary and secondary socialization (in the family, at school, in the workplace) and through regular religious attendance. He argues that while the rise of the West is commonly attributed, in part, to the expansion of an individualistic ethos, it was supported coincidentally by a pan-Christianity which emphasized honesty and morality in human interaction. The issue of moral norms is also closely related to the growing literature on 'social capital,' including the importance of trust in underpinning economic and social relations (Bourdieu and Coleman 1991; Fukuyama 1996). This work focuses on the 'good' side of human behavior which helps to reduce enforcement costs and both the threat and incidence of opportunism.

THE RELATIVE IMPORTANCE OF RELATIVE PRICES

From the central behavioral postulates of individualistic and rational utility maximization, neo-classical theory constructs a framework centered on the importance of relative prices. These are the main economic incentives to which individuals respond and it is this automatic response to prices that gives the approach its predictive potential. Even with the incorporation of concepts such as stickiness, lagged responses and expectations, prices are the central allocative instrument that guides the equalization of supply and demand. Because institutions are patterns of interaction and because economic interaction is responsive to prices, they would naturally be accorded a central place in a neo-classical theory of institutions.

North's *Structure and Change* is based on a foundation of changes in factor scarcities, which result in changes in relative prices and which, in turn, prompt changes in institutions (see in particular: 1981: ch. 7). This same dedication to the neo-classical approach of price changes is not at first apparent in *Institutions, Institutional Change and Economic Performance* (1990) which, instead, tends to focus on co-operation and cognitive constraints. It remains, however, the central means by which change is induced. Halfway through the book, North states:

> Institutions change, and fundamental changes in relative prices are the most important source of that change. To the non-economist (and perhaps for some economists as well), putting such weight on changing relative prices may be hard to understand. But relative price changes alter the incentives of individuals in human interaction, and the only other source of such change is a change in tastes (North 1990: 84).

By itself this statement would lead us to place his work in the neo-classical camp, as Dugger does (1995: 457) in focusing particularly on North's approach to prices and institutional change. There are, however, three important qualifications to the statement quoted above. Firstly, North is not talking about the immediate responses to price changes, which is the focus of neo-classical analysis. Thus, he notes that, "A single change in a relative set of prices by itself may not alter an individual's perspective and therefore decisions, but persistent changes that run counter to an individual's set of rationalizations or a change of fundamental consequences for his well-being will induce him to alter his ideology" (North 1981: 50).

This suggests that one-off price changes will not alter behavior but that changes must be persistent to have any real impact. Secondly, North deviates from traditional price theory because for him the reaction mechanism is affected by ideology, which, as noted, is the framework for making sense of information. How ideology operates to affect the influence of prices is not well specified. Its importance is not to be doubted, however, as indicated by the following statement: "changing relative prices are filtered through pre-existing mental constructs that shape our understanding of those price changes. Clearly ideas and the way they take hold, play a role here" (North 1990a: 85).

Thirdly, and most critically, in North's work it is not clear that the changes in factor scarcities, which lead to altered prices, are not themselves affected by institutions. For some, the question of whether prices affect institutions or institutions affect prices is the key issue distinguishing neo-classical institutionalism from old institutionalism. For the OIE, "relative price changes are the result, rather than the cause of institutional change" (Dugger 1995: 455). It is this distinction which leads Dugger to argue that North is working mostly in the mainstream. Stanfield (1995) takes a different view by arguing that because North is cognizant of the importance of power and how power affects the design and operation of institutions, he implicitly accepts that institutions affect prices. Indeed, there is evidence that this interpretation is justified. North notes that formal institutions are "are created to serve the interests of those with bargaining power to devise new rules" (1990a: 16). Moreover, he argues that while relative factor price changes (between land, labor and capital) sometimes occur as a result of exogenous change (i.e. the plague in medieval Europe), "most will be endogenous, reflecting the ongoing maximizing of entrepreneurs (political, economic and military) that will alter relative prices and in consequence induce institutional change" (North 1990: 84). If the entrepreneur's means of maximizing is based on a pre-existing (unequal) distribution of power embedded in the formal rules, then changes in institutions may induce price changes which, in turn, may result in institutional change. North does not, however, specifically elaborate such a pattern of causality.

EFFICIENCY AND EVOLUTION

Much of neo-classical theorizing takes as a central tenet the idea of efficiency. If the market mechanism is not obstructed, competition between economic agents will result in a more efficient use of scarce resources and this will benefit the economy as a whole. Institutions which encourage greater efficiency will be retained while less efficient ones will be abandoned. North and Thomas (1973: 11–12) originally applied this rationale in developing an institutional explanation for the rise of the West. Economies in this region grew because inefficient institutions were replaced by efficient ones. However, the regional and relatively recent focus of their study introduced a sample bias—they were dealing with a success story. In his next major work (1981), North's canvas was much larger, covering human history from the earliest times and across diverse regions. As a result, he was forced to confront and provide an explanation to account for both growth and stagnation.

To do so, he begins with neo-classical theory, noting that "competition in the face of ubiquitous scarcity dictates that the more efficient institution, policy or individual action will survive and the inefficient ones perish" (North 1981: 7).

However, economic activity takes place within a political environment of rulers and competing interest groups. This environment of "non-market decision-making" can mean that "inefficient forms of political structure do persist for long periods of time" (*ibid.*). While rulers may wish to structure property rights to increase national output (and therefore tax revenue), they must also ensure their own political survival.

They achieve the latter by altering rights to the advantage of their supporters. These altered rights (such as the granting of monopolies) are often economically inefficient, even though they are beneficial to the parties involved. Despite this understanding, North (1981: 81) still attaches great importance to the idea of an efficient evolution of institutions, notably in his explanation of the movement from hunting-gathering to settled agriculture, which he calls the first economic revolution.

In his later work, he clarifies the issue by making a distinction between institutions (property rights structure) and organizations (notably firms) (North 1990a: 7). While organizations will compete and the more efficient ones will survive at the expense of the less efficient, there is no reason why the overriding property rights structure will evolve in a similar manner. It will, however, set the criteria for what is deemed "efficient" behavior but the criteria may lead to unproductive outcomes. In describing the situation of many Third World countries, he argues, "The organizations which develop in this institutional framework will become more efficient—but more efficient at making the society even more unproductive" (North 1990a: 9).

While institutions still do ultimately change as a result of relative prices and factor scarcities, such change is often "overwhelmingly incremental," taking place over centuries. Conversely, political factors may be a more immediate cause of abrupt, discontinuous change (North 1990: 86–89). In any event, the notion of a natural evolution to higher, more efficient forms of property rights institutions is rejected but replaced with the notion that organizations survive if they are more efficient at exploiting a particular rights regime. Such efficiency will only in some cases lead to greater social welfare and encourage economic growth.

Hodgson, as a key OIE exponent, also considers an evolutionary approach to understanding institutions. While he rejects a specifically Darwinian application, he does accept a more generic view which emphasizes a gradual process of change and patterns of behavior which are passed down through institutions. Thus, he argues that firms do not pass on a genetic code to future firms which make them more or less likely to survive in a changing environment. Indeed, in economics and "in contrast to Darwinian biology, the inheritance of *acquired* characteristics is possible" (Hodgson 1988: 141). Furthermore, evolution is not relevant to institutionalism if we consider the idea as a movement to more efficient stages of "greater and greater perfection" or associate it with the fierce and even mean-spirited competitiveness contained in the notion of 'social Darwinism' (North 1992: 760).

Instead, Hodgson suggests that institutions might be better understood through Lamarck's (discredited) theory of biological evolution in which *learned* behavior is passed on from parent to offspring. In a similar manner, the term is relevant once it is relieved of its strict genetic meaning. Evolution then emphasizes process and change—qualitative as well as quantitative—and evolving patterns of behavior. In this way, Hodgson (1992) contrasts the evolutionary notion implicit in the OIE with the comparative statics and mechanistic postulates of neo-classical theory which, he argues, appear to have more in common with 19th-century physics than biology. Indeed, it is the mechanistic quality of neo-classical theory which, for Hodgson, would stifle any attempt to expand its relevance to include behavioralist elements such as ethics or broader social phenomenon.

Thus North first accepts and then rejects the idea that over time institutions promote greater economic efficiency. He replaces it with the idea that organizations become more efficient at exploiting a property rights regime but that this often does not lead to economic progress. In any event, he maintains an adherence to the notion of on-going incremental change. Hodgson rejects an evolutionary approach based on a strict genetic interpretation or on fierce competition, but he accepts a more general understanding of evolution centered on the notions of process and change which, he argues, are relevant to human institutions.

HISTORY VS. HISTORICAL

A major criticism of neo-classical economics is that it is ahistorical; that it does not account for an economy's level of development and the particular structures and patterns of production and exchange which have emerged. This is especially relevant to institutions because they are human constructs particular to specific human endeavor and are influenced by demography, geography, technology and politics as well as economic and social factors. That neo-classical theory has traditionally been both ahistorical and a-institutional is therefore not coincidental because history would tend to highlight the importance of institutions while institutionalism would exert a tendency to consider the history of institution formation and evolution. As an economic historian, North is well-placed to produce an institutionalism grounded in the realism of history. In contrast, Williamson's work, which focuses largely on the modern industrial corporation, is highly ahistorical and it is to that aspect of his work that Lazonick (1991: 206, 214) directs much of his criticism of Williamson. While Lazonick (1991: 306–318) is also critical of North, it is not for his ahistoricism but for his specific historical approach, which focuses on society's contracting rules and norms instead of the dynamism of entrepreneurs and firms which Lazonick sees as the real engine of industrial development.

Even if North is an historian who has attempted to provide a theory of economic history, it is not clear whether his approach is truly *historical*. Properly defined, that term denotes a methodology in which specific processes and social configurations of the past are analyzed, compared and categorized and then used to develop theory through an inductive process. In North's case, while it is clear that he possesses considerable knowledge of Western (notably American) history, his approach to the larger canvas of human history often appears to proceed more from a deductive application of the central concepts of property rights and transaction costs. His detailed examination of specific historical problems (piracy and the cost of ocean shipping, 1968; forced loans and the Glorious Revolution, with Weingast, 1989) are interesting applications of theory but are too narrow to support a general theory of economic performance. When he does attempt to provide a general history (1981; and Thomas 1973), centuries are condensed into short passages and the evidence tends to illustrate rather than substantiate the theoretical arguments. Commenting on the thin layer of evidence in North's 1981 book, a sympathetic reviewer remarked: "this book is, emphatically, too short" (Tullock, 1983: 231).

North does provide two very broad schema of history. In the first, he suggests two economic revolutions (North 1981: chs. 7, 13). The first revolution involves the development of property rights in the transition from hunting-gathering, which employed a common property regime, to settled agriculture, which required a private property regime so that farmers could reap the gains from investments in land. This change likely occurred in some areas of the world about 10,000 years ago. The second revolution occurred about 150 years ago and involved the development of a property rights regime to protect and encourage the use of scientific research in commercial production. While this analysis is somewhat historical in its attempt to define two key transition points, the intervening period is analyzed through the deductive supposition that the rise and decline of regions depended upon the efficacy of property rights in reducing transactions costs. Moreover, it is based on the neo-classical approach of relative factor costs as determined by relative scarcities, notably the land/labor ratio. In this manner, North has sought to endogenize institutions on the basis of other (exogenous) factors. This approach is at odds with the OIE approach to history which suggests that institutions should be treated as exogenous (along with endowments, technologies and preferences) and used as a dependent variable to explain output and prices (Field 1981: 184).

In his recent work (North 1990a), the emphasis is on how institutions support the co-operation needed for exchange, with much less attention to investment. In line with this new emphasis, he suggests a three-stage process of institutional evolution from personalized, local exchange with informal contract enforcement to impersonal exchange and state enforcement covering broader, national territories (*ibid.*: 33–35). What drives this process is an increased volume of activity which encourages—and is encouraged by—a greater degree of specialization. The suggestion of a three-stage process which is applicable across regions and time periods is decidedly ahistorical, but North makes limited use of this model. This reluctance appears to be part of a larger tendency in his recent work to avoid making general statements about institutional development. While he provides a strong and plausible argument for the importance of institutions in determining economic performance, the attempt to explain how institutions are formed and develop is much less neo-classical—but also much less clear—than in his earlier work (Clark 1993: 877).

A SHIFTING EMPHASIS

The above analysis suggests that North's work deviates from the neo-classical tradition in a number of important respects. It is also true, however, that this deviation is a function of his later work. Indeed, in 1989 Hodgson argued that North applied a "standard, mechanical version of maximizing rationality" to institutions, but he has suggested more recently that North's work now exhibits a "degree of convergence" with the old institutionalism (Hodgson 1989: 252; 1998: 185). A number of others have also noted the shift (Dugger 1995; Rutherford 1995) with closer analysis revealing that it had begun in the late 1970s and early 1980s (Groenewegen *et al.* 1995). In this regard, *Structure and Change* (North 1981) marks an important turning point but one which does not reach its full expression until 1990. In the earlier work, he rejects the notion of efficient outcomes, places greater emphasis on power in stifling efficiency and introduces the importance of ideology in shaping human behavior. These are additions to neo-classical theory, however, and are not fully integrated into the history which makes up most of that work. By 1990, ideology and cognitive constraints take on much more prominent roles but, as we have seen, several of the central tenets of neo-classical theory remain albeit with subdued emphasis (the importance of relative prices, self-interest are a motivator, and even the notion of organizations becoming more efficient even if they do not promote economic development). This combination of a shift in thinking combined with a continuing adherence to some of the central ideas of neo-classicism prompts two important questions. One, why has he made this type of half-shift between theoretical schools? And two, does he actually reconcile the underlying differences between them? This section briefly considers these questions.

The cause of North's shift can likely be ascribed, in part, to his own intellectual evolution and an effort to provide explanations which are personally more plausible and satisfying in accounting for historical process. At the same time, however, theorists are influenced by the intellectual developments of their time. This appears to be particularly true for North when we consider his work in the context of trends within the social sciences which began in the 1960s and are continuing today. These trends have involved a breakdown in the traditional division of labor between economics, sociology and political science and have included some attempt to provide a more realistic approach to what motivates and constrains human behavior. Important elements of this debate have focused on the agency-structure question, as provided below.

While North provides no detailed discussion of these developments, there are amble clues that he is both aware of them and attempting his own reconciliation of different theoretical perspectives. In the introductory chapter in 1990, he states that an underlying purpose of his institutional analysis is "reconciling differences between economics and other social sciences" (North 1990a: 5). This attempt involves allowing for individual agency within a structure of institutions. As he argues, "integrating individual choices with the constraints institutions impose on choice sets is a major step towards unifying social science research" (North 1990: 5). Furthermore, he is aware that a key barrier to such a unification is the conception in mainstream economics of what motivates and conditions behavior. Further into this book he sets out the neo-classical behavioral conditions and then notes that over the past twenty years, this model "has come under severe attack and also had strong defenders" (North 1990: 18). He notes that this attack has come from some elements within economics, notably the experimental sub-field, as well as from outside the discipline by psychologists and others (*ibid.*).

These unelaborated statements only possess real meaning in the context of developments within the social sciences. While the debate includes political science,[6] its behavioral nature has focused attention on the relations between modern economics and sociology. A division of labor was set down between the two in the early 20thcentury whereby the ascendancy of marginal analysis pushed economics towards a more narrow conception based on rational choice (*homo oeconomicus*). Meanwhile, sociology concentrated on how behavior is determined by the social environment and left the individual with hardly any room at all to exercise such choice (*homo sociologicus*). In the much quoted phrase from Duesenberry, "economics is all about how people make choices; sociology is all about how they don't have any choices to make" (quoted in Granovetter 1984: 485). For a number of reasons,[7] the traditional division began to break down in the early 1960s and led to the development of both the new economic sociology (Granovetter 1985; Ingham 1996: 265), as well as support for a revival of institutionalism. It also influenced—and was influenced by—the work of those like North who sought to develop a new institutionalism which combined emerging economic concepts, such as transaction costs and property rights, with a more sociological and less rationalized approach to behavior.

While North's theory does contain an appreciation of the various factors which affect economic behavior, there remains the separate issue of whether he has actually reconciled these elements. Do we gain from his work a coherent view of how humans behave and how they affect and are affected by the structures of society? Or do we have, more simply, a range of elements (self-interest with altruism and moral codes, mental models to overcome complexity, property rights to reduce transactions costs or maintain exploitation, etc.) all of which, in different ways and in different historical circumstances, impinge upon action and the potential for economic progress? There is a strong case to be made for this latter interpretation. Indeed, Clark (1993) suggests that North's increasing deviation from the hard and fast parameters of neo-classical analysis has led him to assemble "a noisy rabble of all the pet concepts and theories of a variety of disciplines and sub-disciplines" (p. 877). While this assessment may be harsh, it does contain a large element of truth.

In considering the totality of North's work, we might agree that institutions are a critical factor in economic progress, but we are not likely to be closer to an understanding of why some societies have devised strong institutions which support technologically advanced activity while others have not. We might agree that an increasing population with deepening factor scarcities creates pressure for more complex property rights, but we do not know why this has led to legitimate institutions and broad-based growth in some regions and to gross economic disparities and corruption in others.

Interestingly, this combination of setting forth a more complex approach to economic activity without developing a specific theory has been a persistent problem of the OIE. Its post-war existence as a more minor, alternative approach to mainstream economics stems in part from its failure to "agree upon, let along develop, a systematic theoretical core" with the result that an "integrated system" of the same stature as that of Marshall, Walras, Pareto or Marx has not been achieved (Hodgson 1998: 167). Moreover, the experience of the OIE and of North may suggest that in broadening our approach to economics to include social structure and complex behavioral notions, it may be more difficult to design consistent theory.

INSTITUTIONALISM: A SUMMARY

The previous sections have sought to explain the extent to which North's work is based on neo-classical precepts or, conversely, the degree to which it has incorporated alternative elements. While his narrative style, along with a shift in emphasis over time, inhibits any simple interpretation, a number of conclusions might be drawn. North argues that individuals often do behave rationally and can make choices but that what is rational is conditioned by ideology and circumstance. In addition, while opportunism can be minimized through institutions so as to encourage exchange and investment, monitoring and enforcement costs will be unsustainable unless supported by a culture of trust and fairness. At a broad level, more efficient organizations, including firms, will tend to survive but the institutional environment will not necessarily evolve to encourage greater overall efficiency. Instead, organizations may become increasingly efficient at socially unproductive activity. While relative prices are a critical factor in changing institutions over time, automatic responses are unlikely and, instead, change can be exceedingly incremental. In short, North's institutionalism combines elements from different theoretical schools and thus is best placed between neo-classical institutionalism and the old approach. At a deeper level, if North's goal was to suggest the importance of institutions to the process of economic growth and stagnation, he has likely been successful. In addition, he has provided a realistic view of the vagaries of economic progress, highlighted the importance of politics to economies and focused attention on informal mechanisms.

RELEVANCE OF INSTITUTIONAL ANALYSIS FOR AFRICA

Development economists, like historians, have long been interested in the institutions that support economic activity, notably in terms of property rights in land and the informal arrangements used in rural communities. Two pioneers of development economics, Gunnar Mydral and Dudley Seers, considered themselves institutionalists, notably of the old school as the new school was not developed in the 1950s and 1960s when they were producing their work. Mydral (1978) was an institutionalist in part because he rejected the narrowness of neo-classical economics, which was based on uni-causal explanations that lacked value judgments. He argued that the central element of institutionalism was the recognition "that even if we focus attention on specific problems, our study must take into account the entire social system" (ibid.: 774). Institutionalism was capable—as neo-classical economics was not—of accounting for "circular causation" and "cumulative effects," two central themes of this approach (ibid.). As new institutional economics, based on transaction costs, developed from the mid-1970s, it slowly began to influence development issues. It was particularly suited to understanding micro-level information asymmetries and enforcement mechanisms related to informal institutions in the rural economy (Bardhan and Udry 1999). Elements of the newer approach are discussed below.

Institutional analysis is relevant to the study of Africa for two reasons. First, the region's formal institutions are often ineffective. This is part of the wider problem of the African state and is based on the low quality of public administration and the tension created by political competition. The weakness of formal institutions may be an important explanatory factor in the region's disappointing growth record. Second, economic activity is supported by strong, informal and community arrangements operating in both rural and urban areas. Informal institutions have the legitimacy and effectiveness which is commonly lacking at the formal level. For example, informal property rights continue to secure land and other resources where the state is unable to do so effectively and at low cost. Inter-temporal trade and credit contracting are supported by low-cost information networks, systems of reputation and community level enforcement. The existence of these two systems of institutions, operating simultaneously, gives rise to a number of intriguing questions. To what extent are or can the two systems be integrated so as to draw on the strengths of each? Can informal arrangements be semi-formalized to expand their operations? What are the root causes of formal institutional failure and can they be remedied?

In addition to its general relevance for Africa, institutional analysis is used to address the central problematic of this book: explaining differences in the relative success of Asians and Africans in urban manufacturing. A key aspect of those differences may be access to credit, an issue which is at the heart of inter-temporal contracting and the role of institutions. Furthermore, the methodology of some approaches to institutions (notably that of Douglass North) is historical analysis. In the case of Africa, the relative economic positions of African and other ethnic business communities (i.e.

Kenya's Asians) stem in part from historical developments and the influence of the formal environment during colonialism.

These issues are analyzed in two main parts. The first deals with the problems of the formal institutions of the African state and with the operations of informal arrangements developed by Africans. The second part seeks to unpack the operations of informal networks in ethnic business communities (notably among Asians) and show how they are based on information and reputation effects. This is combined with an appreciation of the advantages which such communities often obtained in the colonial period.

THE WEAK STATE AND AFRICAN INFORMAL ARRANGEMENTS

At a general level, there are two aspects of the economic activity of Africans which are amenable to—indeed require—institutional analysis. Together these relate to the use and misuse of institutions by Africans. The first is the disappointing condition of the formal institutions of the state. Economic performance is undoubtedly being constrained by the lack of a well-organized, efficient and supportive institutional environment. The second issue is the importance of informal arrangements, whose origins mostly pre-date colonialism and which currently operate 'underneath,' alongside or in the absence of formal institutions. The extent to which these informal institutions can support large increases in economic activity or can form the basis for building stronger semi-formal or formal arrangements is a key question for African development and related policy initiatives.

Regarding the formal environment, Africa's institutions are generally seen as weak and ineffective in supporting transactions and, in many places, securing basic property rights. As the data in Table 1.2 highlight, the general level of efficiency of Africa's formal legal system is well below that of fast-growing regions and more on par or below that of other slow-growing ones. These data are supported by detailed studies of specific countries which suggest that the court system offers only "protracted and uncertain recourse" for businesses (Levy 1993: 71; see also Coldham 1990; Degni-Segui 1995). The immediate causes are several. A lack of properly trained judges reduces the speed of the process, while an insufficient number of judges trained in commercial law further undermine confidence. Inadequate court provision, especially in hearing appeals above the local level, also contributes to long delays. Many of these problems are manifestations of a more general problem with African public administration and highlight the need for improvements in personnel, resources and bureaucratic systems. There are, however, deeper factors which affect public administration which are not so easily remedied by institutional support.

Part of the problem does appear to stem from the political environment, including the structure and functioning of political institutions, and the nature of political norms which set the parameters for the behavior of politicians. The formal structures have been mostly inherited from the colonial period and either added to, altered or reduced depending on the latest development approach to the state.[8] The norm structure and actual pattern of behavior are often based on a patrimonial tradition which predates the colonial period. It has been given new and greater significance as a result of the national fiscal resources which are available to the group which can secure control of political power.

In many countries, this combination has led to a misuse of fiscal resources, interference with bureaucratic procedures and the political manipulation of technocratic decision-making. The nature of the African state is now often depicted as 'rentier,' 'parasitical,' 'predatory,' 'crony,' or 'kleptocratic' (see Mkandawire 1998), although there is some evidence that the current group of leaders is less prone to using the state in this manner (Ellis 1996). Because we employ a definition of institutions as those arrangements which secure property and reduce the costs of transacting, our focus is on how these activities are affected by the general misallocation of state resources and the corruption of technocratic decisions. When the misallocation of fiscal resources reduces the flow of funds to those departments and agencies which do support property rights and transacting, then the political problem is also an institutional one. For example, the underfunding of, and political interference with, the legal system are critically important for the proper functioning of institutions. In a review of judicial systems in Anglophone Africa, Coldham (1990) has noted that:

> The notion that a judge could be apolitical is difficult to defend in those countries where politics is organized on a tribal/ethnic basis, in one-party systems or where the regime is confronted with large economic and political instabilities. (1990: 32).

The number of African states which fall outside of the parameters listed here is likely to be rather small. As indicated in Table 1.2, African judicial systems are less efficient that those in other regions of the world. Underfunding and interference with the processes which secure landed property rights is another example in which formal institutional failure is linked to political problems.

Table 1.2. Efficiency of the Judicial System

Region	Mean for The region (10=most efficient)	No. of countries in the regional sample	Percentage of countries above the overall mean (7.10)
Sub-Saharan Africa	5.40	10	10
Latin America—Caribbean	6.34	15	27
South Asia	6.50	4	25
East Asia	6.53	8	38
Middle East—North Africa	6.95	9	44
Western Europe	8.77	16	75
North America—ANZ	9.05	5	80
Overall	**7.10**	**67**	**45**

Source: Calculations by the author from Business International risk assessment data as provided in: Mauro (1995: Appendix 3). The data indicate: "the efficiency and integrity of the legal environment as it affects business, particularly foreign firms." East Europe/Central Asia not included because data available for only one country (Iran, 2.0).

Efforts to explain the sources of the political problem have recently focused on the region's accentuated ethnic diversity. Combined with acute poverty, the situation of a national state covering a multiplicity of competing ethnic groups has resulted in a winner-take-all approach to politics. Economists have recently begun to look more closely at the possible impact of ethnic diversity on institutions, resource allocation and ultimately growth. Mauro (1990) has shown a negative correlation between such diversity and the perceived efficiency of the legal system and the state bureaucracy. These in turn are negatively correlated with growth. Easterly and Levine (1997), noting that 14 of the 15 most ethnically diverse countries in the world are located in Africa, have also found that such diversity negatively affects growth and does so through ethnically oriented policies. While ethnic diversity is a demographic fact that is diluted only very slowly over time, the problems which it causes may be dampened by a move to broader political representation at the centre, or conversely, moves to implement real federalism.

If the problem of formal institutions is deeply rooted in politics then simple efforts to improve the quality of personnel or upgrade systems may have little impact in the short term. In the longer term, however, technocrats may be able to use their technical knowledge to build restraints and safeguards into bureaucratic procedures which, together, may act as a countervailing force against a narrowly political approach to economic policy, resource allocation and the functioning of institutions.

In addition to the problems of formal arrangements, new institutional economics is also helpful in understanding the use of informal arrangements by individuals, households, farms and firms. At one level, this involves simply understanding how these institutions function and, more specifically, how they overcome traditional problems of asymmetric information which can lead to moral hazard and adverse selection. At a second level, such analysis should address questions of how change comes about, including how informal arrangements might interact with or develop into semi-formal or formal arrangements. These two levels of analysis are dealt with in turn in the remainder of this section.

Institutional analysis is particularly useful for not just describing but for understanding the rationale behind informal credit relations in rural (and also urban) environments. In the absence of formal screening and enforcement mechanisms, communities have developed their own low-cost means of fulfilling these functions, which are based on the ease and costlessness by which information flows in these communities. Information flows are backed up with a norm structure and community level systems of adjudicating disputes. These institutions are limited in their scope, however, and thus are not able to support transacting over wide areas and between communities.

The study of informal rural credit in Nigeria by Udry (1990) provides one of the clearest examples of institutional analysis in this regard. Because households have good information about each other, they find it easy to assess creditworthiness. They also have on-going knowledge of their debtors' activities which allows them to distinguish between the willingness and the ability to repay. The ability to repay may be predicated on such factors as adverse weather and other cropping factors, health mishaps, exceptional outlays for funerals and other shocks to the household which may impair cash flow in the short term. With this knowledge, creditors are able to incorporate an element of 'state contingency' into the informal credit contract and lengthen repayment terms or reduce implicit interest charges. In doing so, credit can act as a form of insurance against idiosyncratic shocks. In the event of disputes, village elders adjudicate between parties, using their own knowledge of the two litigants' past records of trustworthiness. Restitution orders can be applied and litigants will be eager to comply with the elders' decisions because failure to do so can result in the loss of reputation in the community. This can seriously impair future efforts to access credit or to engage in other commercial transactions within the village.

In addition, Shipton (1995) has highlighted the variety of credit contracts which a household may maintain simultaneously and how obligations for repayment are felt most strongly with those to whom the debtor has the greatest social bond. Outside aid or national credit programs receive the least priority and will be paid last, if at all. Failure to understand this pecking order of obligations can undermine the effectiveness of the most well-intentioned credit programs. Furthermore, work by Bouman (1995) and others on rotating savings and credit associations (ROSCAs) has shown the importance of reputation, peer-monitoring and enforcement through social bonds on savings and credit behavior. Such activity can often take place in urban settings among waged or salaried employees at their place of business or among members of church or other social groups.

But understanding how informal institutions operate provides only half of the value of the new institutional economics. Institutions also change and develop over time as a result of the opportunities and pressures emanating from more primary economic forces and from interaction with formal institutions. The focus of the old institutional economics on established patterns and norms—with little reference to change—tends to limit its relevance for understanding institutional change and indeed the larger question of economic development. This dynamic element is overlooked in the otherwise perceptive analysis of institutions and economic reform in Africa presented by Stein (1994). He has argued that while institutional analysis provides an advance over standard neo-classical analysis, the old rather than the new institutionalism is more suited to Africa.

Incremental and evolutionary change can come about as a result of demographic increase, resource scarcity and commercialization. These are the three main factors behind the evolutionary theory of property rights to land (cf. Platteau 1995). According to that theory, changes in population and in particular in land-labor ratios can exert pressure over time on the development of more defined rights to landed property and on alterations to labour contracting. This is particularly relevant to Africa where, prior to the 20th century, much of the region was land-abundant and people-scarce (Iliffe 1995), which inhibited the development of more advanced institutions, related to land but also generally to all institutions. Over the past century, population levels in some areas have risen considerably and their impact on institutions needs to be closely scrutinized, including the evolution of informal or community-based land rights from common to more individualized property. Commercialization and the development of a more intensely capitalist economy, stemming in part from more direct access to foreign markets, are also important elements. The problems of institutional development in Africa may be prompted in large part by more fundamental changes in the relation of people to resources. The lack of accurate long-term data about such informal arrangements makes it difficult to plot changes over time. Interesting puzzles also arise when Africa is compared with other regions. Why, for example, is there so little inter-linked contracting between credit and standing crops in Africa, compared with parts of Asia? (Udry 1990).

While evolutionary change is generated from within the economy, more discrete changes in institutions may result from policy and program decisions by governments. One of the key questions for institutional analysis is the extent to which policy changes, notably those designed to introduce formal structures, can be effective when adopted in sectors where informal institutions are used widely and well understood. This is no better illustrated than in the debate about the adoption of formal, Westernized systems of individual land tenure. This less evolutionary and more explicit change has allowed for a rather direct comparison between informal and formal tenure. Much of the research has highlighted the problems of introducing formal property rights in areas where informal, community regulated rights are legitimate and well-understood, especially when formal systems are poorly administered and under-funded (Platteau 1996, for a summary). A highly nuanced interpretation, provided by Carter *et al.* (1994), suggests that formal property rights are most useful for larger farms which stand to benefit from increased land transferability. Smaller farms, with only traditional holdings and not in a position to buy, sell or use land as collateral, gain relatively few benefits from formal rights. This interesting approach to the issue is considered in more detail in the fifth chapter where Kenya's land-titling experience is reviewed.

It is not only in regards to land, however, that the debate about change and formalization is relevant. A key question regarding credit is whether informal arrangements can support villagers in the event of major shocks and whether they can finance higher levels of investment, beyond consumption smoothing. It may be that Udry's Nigerian villagers could benefit from access to formal credit to mitigate not only idiosyncratic shocks but village-wide ones as well. Furthermore, formal finance might allow for investment to support greater use of animal or mechanized traction or better irrigation. If formal finance needs to be introduced, then the lessons from institutional analysis suggest that it must be able to address the screening and enforcement problems which are easily handled at the local level by access to high quality and inexpensive information.

Current research and programming efforts have focused on how to combine the advantages of informal monitoring and information networks with the benefits of formal finance (notably size transformation). Recent programming has focused on peer-monitored credit programs, along the Grameen Bank model, in which NGOs provide finance to the poor by relying on social pressure among peers to encourage repayment. Meanwhile, recent research has looked at whether informal money lenders are linking in with formal banks to deposit savings and to access loans for on-lending to small borrowers (Nissanke and Aryeetey 1998; Aryeetey *et al.* 1998). This process would combine the informal screening and monitoring information of the moneylender with the benefits of security and size transformation offered by the formal banking sector. The evidence suggests that there is in fact very little interaction between the two and further effort needs to focus on understanding the reasons why and possibly in finding ways to encourage such a link. In a similar vein but at a much broader level, Dia (1994, 1996) has suggested that the cultural dissonance between African and Western approaches to organizing businesses and other economic activities means that Western models are difficult to transplant into the region. The author suggests that formal, colonial-inherited institutions need to be re-designed to take into account African norms and a more collectivist approach to economic activity. While plausible in many respects, it is not clear whether the formal institutions must adapt to the informal, or vice-versa.

More germane to the central problematic of this study is whether the informal institutions which are prevalent among Africans in the rural sector can be used to challenge the dominance of ethnic business communities in urban sectors. Indeed, the informal arrangements of these ethnic communities represent another example of the importance of institutions in explaining economic behavior. The analysis of such communities is the subject of the following section.

EXPLAINING ETHNIC BUSINESS COMMUNITIES

Ethnic business communities are comprised of immigrants who concentrate their business activities in trading, and in some cases manufacturing, in countries to which they are not native. In East Africa, the Asian (mostly Gujeratis and Khoja Ismailis) and Arab (Yemeni) communities are important examples, while in West Africa such communities are comprised mostly of Lebanese. In some cases, European communities left from colonialism play a similar role, such as in Zimbabwe. The presence of such communities is not specific to Africa, however, and many groups in Asia occupy a similar position, notably the overseas Chinese and Hadramaut Arabs in most of south-east Asia. Other examples include: Chettiars in Burma; Marwaris in Bangladesh and Nepal; and, in more minor numbers, Dawoodi Bohras, Memons and Khoja Ismailis in a variety of places (Moore 1997). Armenians in central Asia and Jews in Europe provide yet further examples. These groups are considered foreign because they come from outside of the country in which they have established themselves. There are also examples of ethnic business communities whose members come from within the country or region but are considered separate communities and in some ways 'outsiders.' In Africa, these include the Hausa, Yoruba and Mossi in West Africa, and Somalis in parts of East Africa. In south Asia, such groups include: Punjabis Marwaris, Dawoodi Bohras, Memons, Khoja Ismailis, Khoja Isnasheris, Banias, Jains, Sindhis and Parsis. While they are often referred to as ethnic *trading* communities, in many cases their members have accumulated capital, become more permanent residents and expanded through the generations into manufacturing and other aspects of industry. As noted by Moore (1997: 309), "there is no serious evidence, from south Asia or elsewhere, to indicate that a history of specialization in trade or finance is any serious obstacle to expansion into industry." The Asians in Kenya expanded into industry during the colonial period.

The challenge for economic analysis is to understand how they have become successful in business, especially because they have operated under the same formal institutions as the local populations since independence from colonialism. This might suggest that they have strong informal institutions. As noted, however, Africans and local populations in other regions, have long developed and used informal arrangements to structure and support their economic activity. While it is possible that institutions are not transferable across sectors, the basic question remains: what is specific about ethnic business communities that has led to their prominence in trading and urban activities?

Institutional analysis, as part of a larger change within the economics discipline, has increasingly stressed the importance of transactions costs and information in explaining economic behavior. If information is important, then it is likely that it travels better and at lower cost within ethnic groups than between them. A tight, closely knit ethnic community, especially one specialized in specific sectors, may enjoy considerable advantage over less cohesive local groups. The information passed on through ethnic networks may relate to a variety of aspects of business activity but its key function may be to support inter-temporal contracting. To ensure that a contract is honored, it is necessary that agents are able to effectively screen other transactors and that they can enforce the contract to deter opportunistic behavior. Such deterrence, which works through the threat of a damage to reputation (information which circulates about non-performance) can be highly effective in close ethnic communities. While economists have generally understood the importance of such issues of reputation and information flows, it is not always clear why this has developed so well in ethnic business communities and why it might be a barrier to local people attempting to enter certain sectors.

One of the best attempts at providing an explanation has been put forward by Greif (1993) and his notion of a "multilateral punishment system (MPS)." His research has focused on the Maghribi (Jewish) traders in North Africa in the 12th century. At that time, the larger Maghribi traders needed to establish links with trading agents in the various ports in North Africa and to rely on them to sell their goods and to send return shipments of local goods. Because of the distances involved (and thus the difficulty of direct monitoring), it was vital that such agents could be trusted not to pocket a proportion of the trading profit in excess of the agreed payment for their services. To support this trust there needed to be strong incentives to deter opportunism. Greif has suggested that this can be explained by distinguishing between multi-lateral and bilateral punishment systems (MPS and BPS). Under the latter, an agent acting opportunistically and thus against the interests of his principal will, if caught, forego any potential future gains from *that* bilateral relationship. In short, the principal will not contract with him again. Under a multilateral system of punishment, however, the loss from opportunistic behavior extends beyond the bilateral relationship to affect the agent's current and more importantly potential future transactions with other principals who have learned of his bad behavior. The damage to reputation has downgraded his reliability within the ethnic community. Knowing that this will happen if he acts opportunitistically, the agent will be deterred from doing so. Furthermore, only if one ethnic group dominates a trading or commercial activity will it be difficult for the agent to find other people with which to trade. If commercial activity is spread more widely and if information channels are not too closed then the loss of reputation from one bilateral transgression will be less critical. For example, Greif shows how it was difficult for Maghribi traders to expand into Italy because agents there would have a variety of others with which to trade who were outside of the Maghribi community.

The value of this interesting historical example is Greif's ability to distinguish between MPS and BPS and to show the importance of reputation as an enforcement and deterrent mechanism. It can be applied equally to other historical and contemporary situations where ethnic communities appear to dominate specific sectors of the economy. It suggests both how transactions are secured in the absence of efficient formal institutions and how it is that local populations find it difficult to establish themselves in areas of trade and business dominated by others. While it is often surprising that such a small minority controls such a large proportion of trade or wealth, it is, as Moore (1997) suggests, precisely because they are a small group that they can monitor each other informally. The system works less effectively with larger groups.

The screening of transactors can take place either by knowing the person or his family directly through the social and business community or by being able to discuss the person's reliably with other members of the community. Screening becomes relatively costless when conducted in this manner. In addition, the monitoring of others' activities can also take place through the free flow of information between members of the community. Enforcement takes place through the MPS as explained above in which reputation is a strong deterrent against opportunism.

OTHER ELEMENTS OF THE EXPLANATION

While central to the operations of ethnic business communities, the informal institutions provide only part of the explanation of their relative success. Formal institutions also play an important role in the existence and development of these communities. The political authorities, which control the institutional environment, can either have a negative or a positive impact.

On the negative side, the ethnic community does constitute a visible minority at which official discrimination can be easily targeted. In addition, members' legal status, as foreigners, may be precarious and subject to the whims of political leaders. Greif's Maghribi traders lost influence after being banished by political authorities in many North African cities. More recently Asians were forced to emigrate from Amin's Uganda. Aside from outright banishment, authorities can impose discriminatory policies against business activities. They can do so because the political power of the ethnic community is often weak and there may be general support for such negative discrimination by local people who resent the commercial influence of the foreigners. At the same time, there may be positive discrimination in favor of local populations in an effort to build a local business elite. In the 1970s, the Malaysian government required domestic companies above a minimum size to reserve a portion of their shareholdings for Malays, as an attempt to rebalance the business positions of ethnic Chinese and Malays

(Vandenberg 2000). As we shall see, Kenya instigated similar laws to reduce Asian influence in trade and, to a more limited extent, in manufacturing.

Ethnic business minorities are often under threat from changes in the formal institutional environment because they are a minority and have limited political influence. The success of an ethnic community thus stems from both the efficiency and effectiveness of its informal institutions and the extent to which there is a liberal or neutral formal environment, as opposed to one which is discriminatory. In many instances, the ethnic community is able to withstand some level of discrimination because it has the advantage of its networks. If discrimination becomes too onerous, however, its members may be prompted to immigrate to more liberal environments.

Their position vis-à-vis rulers may, however, work to their advantage, especially under colonial regimes. In many cases, their numbers may not be sufficient to challenge for political authority, and as a result their presence may be tolerated by the authorities. This is especially true under colonial/imperial regimes in which the political threat to foreign rule comes from the local population, not principally from the ethnic business community. Indeed, European imperial powers tolerated and indeed benefited from the presence of an ethnic community (whose ethnicity, it should be noted, was different from that of the colonial rulers). These ethnic communities may be much better acquainted with local business customs and have or are able to develop supply networks with members of their ethnicity living outside of the colony. As middlemen, they have often played an important role in provisioning the colony and its ruling group, and even providing credit. The imperial power may also provide a level of protection and security from the local rulers and people, as was the case regarding Asian migration inland in East Africa. Thus, an ethnic group's separateness can aid its position if it is not interested in political matters and instead focuses on collaborating with the regime in commerce.

Apart from political matters, another important aspect is whether these communities are by their nature or by their circumstances inclined to work harder, to invest more time and energy in their businesses and to re-invest a greater portion of their financial surplus. They often appear to take a longer view of their investments than local people. Because the community is of a different ethnicity, it is easy to assign these behavioral differences to ethnicity. For example, the overseas Chinese in south-east Asia might be seen as better at business than local populations by the very fact of being Chinese. In east Africa, the differences take on racial tones because the foreign ethnic community is in fact of a different race. Chege (1998), for example, has deplored Himbara's (1994) use of "race as a variable" in debates about the development of local capital in Kenya. An analysis which is based, explicitly or implicitly, on notions of inherent ethnic or racial differences in entrepreneurial ability or work attitudes are superficial and miss the real factors affecting differences in business success.

There often are noticeable differences, however, between local peoples and ethnic businessmen which cannot be accounted for fully by informal screening and enforcement arrangements, or by the political situation. There may be pressures emanating from the experience of emigration and the concentration in certain business activities which may generate within the community more knowledge of certain types of non-agricultural business practices and a greater competitiveness in those activities. Local people who attempt to move from agriculture into urban based activities in trading, finance or manufacturing may be at a definite disadvantage if ethnic communities are more established and have greater experience. This does not mean that local people cannot enter these sectors but it does mean that it may be much more difficult for them to survive without the norms and culture prevalent in the ethnic community.[9]

This behavior may be supported by pressures on the immigrant which make it more critical for him to concentrate on his business. When the immigrant arrives there is considerable pressure to succeed. Not wanting to return home a failure and having little to fall back on in the new land, it may be critical that he succeed and do so by channeling all energies into the business. Collectively, this may generate norm structures within the new community which heighten aggressiveness and competition. Furthermore, these issues and characteristics may be passed from one generation to another, notably if they remain distinct from the local population. Even the act of immigration itself is quasi-entrepreneurial in that it involves a risky decision to venture to a foreign land in search of economic gain. Those less willing to take on the risks and challenges are likely to stay at home.

While their informal institutions are important, ethnic communities also use formal institutions to advance their economic activities. They rely on the property rights system for the purchase of urban land and the rental of business premises, they resort to court action for unpaid bills and they secure credit from the formal financial system for operations and expansion. The advantages of formal institutions in broadening the transacting possibilities within an economy remain and North's argument that growth is supported by modern, efficient formal institutions is relevant even for these ethnic communities. Their advantage may in fact stem from the judicious use of both formal and informal institutions.

The ability to take advantage of the formal system is fundamentally related to transaction costs. Formal arrangements are by their nature usually more expensive to access and operate, and thus are only possible for those firms whose size and level of business activity are sufficient to underwrite the costs of using the formal system. For example, a firm must be able to provide the collateral required to secure a bank loan. The firm must also request a loan of sufficient size to cover the administrative costs for the bank in transacting that loan. Likewise, if a firm is to settle disputes through the court system, the amounts in dispute must be of sufficient value to justify the time and legal costs involved. Very small firms will not be in a position to access formal institutions because of the transaction costs involved.

Thus, instead of considering how institutions might change and become more formalized, it may be better to see the institutional environment as comprising different informal and formal institutions which firms are in a better or worse position to make use of, depending on their size. Instead of institutions evolving over time, it may be that firms and business communities evolve over time to expand their ability to access existing formal institutions. The advantage which ethnic firms may have is that their informal networks, colonial advantages and the pressures emanating from the immigrant experience have combined to allow them to amass the capital and grow above a size threshold which makes access to formal institutions possible and cost effective. At a given point in time, notably in the years following independence, such firms may have a double advantage over local entrepreneurs in that they can access both informal and formal institutions.

Furthermore, the apparent disparity in success in urban activities between local and ethnic minority populations may be as related to the problem of amassing capital as it is to differences in access to informal and formal institutions. Local populations generally have developed in the rural sector and those who are successful in agriculture may not be inclined to venture into urban business. Rationally, it may make more sense to expand within a sector in which one is already successful than to branch out into activities in which one lacks expertise and connections. Those who enter the urban sector may be those with less success in rural areas and as a result have less access to starting capital. This may bar them at least from access to formal arrangements and makes it more difficult to enter formal business activities on par with established firms. This line of analysis is pursued in more depth in the context of the empirical work on urban manufacturing in the latter chapters. Here we need to simply highlight that a comparison between local and ethnic business success in urban activities may be less 'fair' than a comparison between local entrepreneurs in agro-related sectors and ethnic minorities in urban activities.

CONCLUSION

Institutions provide the rules and mechanisms that guide trade and investment. They lower transaction costs and thereby reduce uncertainty and opportunism. Institutional economics is a theoretical approach that can be applied to both micro-level phenomena, such as credit transacting, and to the macro-level structures of the state. Two schools of institutional economics currently compete for attention: a newer school that relies heavily on concepts from neo-classical economics (choice, prices and equilibrium) and an older school that gives importance to regularized patterns of thought and behavior. Douglass North's approach blends concepts from the new and the old schools. It is particularly suited to analyzing growth and stagnation in economic history due to its attention to vested interests, path dependence and culture. These elements also make his approach suited to analyzing contemporary problems of economic development.

An institutional approach is useful for the study of African economies both historically and in a contemporary setting. Africa is undergoing a long-term evolution from informal, localized institutions, to a system of formal institutions. The African state, however, is constrained by the influence of ethnic competition, poor administration and corruption. These limitations prevent formal institutions from playing a more effective role. The existence of ethnic business communities, such as the Asians in Kenya, can be explained with reference to both formal and informal institutions. These communities often occupied a special place in colonial society, having local knowledge and a special relationship with rulers. In addition, they were often barred from acquiring rural land and thus concentrated on urban activities. Their small size, as a community, gave them advantages in developing tight informal institutions based on reputation. A failure to honor obligations could mean ostracism from the business and social community. The six empirical chapters which follow apply institutional analysis to the development of the Asian and African business communities in Kenya. The story starts in the pre-colonial era.

Chapter Two
Institutional Diversity Prior to 1900

Kenya's population is—and always has been—comprised primarily of Africans. For centuries, however, small but influential groups from outside of Africa have settled along the coast and influenced the area's economic and political development. Those other groups have included Arabs (from the southern Arabian peninsula), Asians (from the Indian sub-continent) and Europeans (Portuguese and British). All of these groups, foreign as well as African, sought ways to enhance their economic well-being but did so in different ways and by developing different institutions. In this chapter, we explore those differences by applying North's institutionalism to African and non-African communities prior to 1900 in the area that is now known as Kenya. This analysis of the pre-colonial era draws a basic distinction between African communities, primarily in the interior, and non-African groups along the Indian Ocean coast. Further distinctions are then made between Africans who were herders and those who were cultivators and between foreigners who controlled political power and those who did not. The analysis highlights how Asians (Indians) settled along the Kenyan coast for centuries prior to 1900 and engaged in trade and finance. They developed informal networks and worked within the formal structures of various rulers (Arab, European or local). Africans in the interior had much less experience operating under foreign rulers and were thus more affected by the major changes wrought by British colonialism in the 20th century.

THREE BASIC APPROACHES TO ORGANIZING ECONOMIC ACTIVITY

How communities come to organize economic activity is based on a variety of factors. It is partly based on the natural environment in which they live, especially for food-growing cultures, and partly on the human environment,

Table 2.1 : Typology of economic cultures in pre-colonial Kenya

Economic culture	Main groups	Sub-groups	Origins	Time of pre-eminence	Property rights system
Interior					
Hunter-gatherer			Indigenous	Prior to 3,000BC	Limited territoriality
Pastoralism	Cushitic		Southern Ethiopia, Somalia	Prior to 1 AD	Communal land, private livestock
Pastoralism	Nilotic	Luo, Kalenjin Maasai	Sudan	500 AD to present	Communal land, private livestock
Cultivation	Bantu	Kikuyu, Luhyia, Embu, Meru, Kamba, Mijkenda	Inter-Lakes region	1 AD to present	Private land, with private livestock
Coast					
Trade	Swahili		Africans with incoming Arabs	1,000 AD onwards	
Trade-finance	Indian/Asian	Hindus, Muslim	Western India	17th century onwards	Strong intra-community networks, varying political support
Trade with political control	Arabs European	Omanis Portugese British	Muscat, Oman Portugal, Britain	17th-19th century 1490-1700 1880-1964	Taxation and trade Taxation and trade Colonial control

Source: author, see text for specific references

especially when there is intense competition and larger social structures. But activity is also influenced by economic culture, which may be defined as the type of activities and the institutional mechanisms which are prevalent in the homeland and which migrants carry with them to new areas. This was true for non-Africans who came to trade and rule along the coast of East Africa. It was true also for the Bantu and Nilotic groups who migrated from other areas in Africa, or otherwise spread their food producing cultures to existing people in Kenya's interior. While it is difficult to provide precise comparisons because of the diversity of groups and activities involved, several basic patterns are discernible. Africans developed economic cultures based on *land and livestock* in which investments in working and protecting landed property (for food production) and in expanding livestock herds were of prime importance. In the absence of larger political structures, conflict between groups for access to land and control over livestock were particular concerns.

By contrast, the situation for Asians along the coast was quite different and in some ways more complex. They never sought direct political control and thus had to reach an accommodation with contemporary rulers to ensure the protection of property and the enforcement of contracts. Their fortunes rose and fell with their ability to negotiate such protection and the propensity of ruling groups to grant it. Their economic culture of *trade and finance*, coupled with a non-ruling political culture, developed over centuries of Asian trading activity in the Indian Ocean basin. The groups which did rule the East African coast (Arabs, Swahili, Portuguese and British) tied economic welfare to political control, which allowed them to earn income from trade directly, from the taxation of trade carried on by others and from the arbitrary seizure of property. With the loss of political control, they were marginalized economically and often retreated from the area.[1] The ability to maintain political control and reap its economic benefits was based in large measure on military skills and technology. This economic culture of *military power, trade and taxation* was often lucrative but was susceptible to intense competition from similar rivals. Thus, these three types of economic culture structure our analysis of the pre-colonial era:

- land and livestock—Africans in the interior,
- trade and finance—Asians along the coast
- military power, trade and taxation—Arabs, Europeans and local rulers on the coast.

Each of the communities is analyzed in turn for the nature of its economic environment and economic culture, and for how these were important in determining economic activity and the design of supporting institutions. An overview of the various ethnic and racial groups, their cultures and their institutions is provided in Table 2.1. It deserves at least a few minutes of study, especially by those not familiar with Kenya's ethnic makeup.

Institutions were devised to overcome two central problems inherent in economic competition. The first was the protection of property so that the value of investments (including investments of labor) was not lost to outsiders. This is known as *the property rights problem* and is handled through defensive community protection and, internally, through legal structures. While the property rights problem involved an attempt to exclude outsiders from access to property, societies could also gain considerable benefits from trade and interaction with those same outsiders. Because opportunistic behavior was possible in the context of trade, institutions were developed to reduce the risks and lower the costs of engaging with outsiders. This is known as *the transactions problem*. Taken together, the security of property and the reduction of risks (and costs) in transacting are the two central problems which societies seek to overcome through the development of economic institutions. As noted, the development of these institutions is affected both by the physical and human environment and by economic culture.

Given the long time-period covered and the number of groups and activities involved, it is not possible to provide a detailed history. Instead, what is attempted is a comparison of institutions which societies have used to overcome the two central problems noted above. This chapter is divided into two main parts based on geography and peoples. The first part considers African communities in the interior and provides a three-way distinction between hunter-gatherers, pastoralists and crop cultivators. The second part considers activity along the coast which involved Swahili and hinterland Africans, along with various traders and invaders—Arabs, Asians/Indians, Portuguese and British. It considers the basis of political and economic power for each group and the institutions which supported their activities. The importance of this comparative analysis can be best seen in the context of a larger attempt to understand the later economic successes and difficulties of African and Asian communities during colonialism and in the independence period.

FOOD PROCUREMENT AND INSTITUTIONS

Whether a society procures its food by hunting and gathering (foraging), by herding livestock (pastoralism) or by growing crops (cultivation), it will seek to overcome two central problems related to economic competition. The first involves making an area of land—and with it game, plants, crops or livestock—secure from outside encroachment so that the society can gain the optimum use of those resources and an adequate return from its investments (of labor) in that land. This represents the property rights problem. The second problem is to structure exchange relations to gain the benefits from trade and interaction while reducing the potential for opportunistic behavior. This is also a property rights problem but is, more specifically, the transactions problem. Together they represent the prime issues of the new institutional economics.[2] In pre-colonial Africa, property rights systems varied based on which of the three types of food procurement strategy was used. In turn, the strategy was based on a number of factors, notably the local ecology, population densities and the food producing cultures brought by African settlers to new areas.

Hunter-gatherers engaged in direct procurement of the natural flora and fauna with little investment in land. The main concern was having access to areas which could sustain livelihoods with minimal effort, notably travel time from camp sites to foraging locations. The extent of land control was based on the relative availability of food resources. In cases where human population densities were low and resources abundant, there was little need to define property rights. Such conditions likely exerted a general tendency for the population to rise, however, and for competition to increase and rights to develop. Furthermore, the basic perception that population densities were low when foraging was prominent may reflect the fact that they were low relative to the human carrying capacity of the land for cultivation or pastoralism, but may have been adequate (and possibly just adequate) for hunting-gathering. Thus areas which, for African settlers (and later Europeans) seemed to be sparsely populated, may not have appeared that way for hunter-gatherers. In any event, it is likely that rights developed gradually over time as population densities rose due to natural population increase.

Pastoralists also required access to land, not for its game, however, but specifically for water and for grasses suitable for grazing. Investments in land included burning vegetation to encourage new growth (which possessed a higher nutrient value) and the maintenance of water holes in areas with inadequate natural sources. While land had to be occasionally defended, the main labor requirements were not protection of land *per se* but herding and defense of livestock on that land. Because rainfall can be erratic, pastoralists adopted communal rather than exclusive land rights to increase the opportunity for individual farmers to graze herds where grasses were available. The care of livestock, however, needed specific attention and thus was held privately within family groups. Thus, communal rights to land co-existed with private rights in livestock. It must be clear however, that communal rights are not the same as common property rights. Communal rights are for members of a community and may not extend, more commonly, to members outside of that group.

The third type of food procurement, crop cultivation, required a more intensive use of land and direct investment of labor to clear trees, till soil, weed fields and harvest produce. Because of more intensive land use, less extensive (but more fertile or better watered) areas were needed to support a given population. This land also needed to be more secure to ensure the return from the investments in soil preparation. In this situation, landed property was held more privately. In most cases, however, such land was not given formal legal title and could not be sold as in Western society. Instead, land was held privately within the lineage group and was transferred between generations of the same lineage (Muriuki 1974). In terms of enforcing property rights, strong defensive capacities, in cleared areas of forests, in forest fringes and often in mountainous environments, were necessary to protect property and investments.

While the exclusion of outsiders was beneficial to the group, interaction with outsiders could bring important benefits. Societies able to produce a food surplus beyond their immediate needs could supplement the variety of foods and other goods by engaging in trade. Because the aim was to secure *different* goods, societies were likely to trade with people occupying different ecological zones (Ambler 1988; Hakansson 1994). For example, a pastoralist from the savanna would offer goats in exchange for millet from a cultivator who lived on the ridge. Along with trading food and other goods, interaction could also result in learning about new methods of growing food or managing livestock. The benefits from such interaction, however, had to be balanced against the risks inherent in allowing outsiders access to a group's area (Hakansson 1994). These risks arose from the absence of a shared legal framework and the common practice of livestock raiding which was one element of a diverse food procurement strategy. The problem could be overcome by several means, notably through developing long-term friendship/brotherhood relations and restricting the movement of outsiders to those less likely to engage in opportunistic behavior.

In the following sections, this basic framework is applied to food producing cultures in Kenya's interior. The country provides an interesting case because it includes a varied ecology which has been used for pastoralism and cultivation. In addition it includes three of the major ethno-linguistic groups of Africa (Bantu, Nilotic and Cushitic). These groups brought with them different food producing cultures, tended to settle in different ecological zones and developed different approaches to property.

Map 1: Ethnic groups of Kenya

EARLY INHABITANTS AND FOOD PROCUREMENT: HUNTING-GATHERING

In East Africa, hunting-gathering was the only form of food procurement practiced until about the beginning of the second millennium BC. It was still widely employed in the second millennium AD, but was overtaken by herding and cultivation as the predominant food procurement strategy. The early hunter-gatherers may have been composed of early Khoisan peoples and others referred to in the literature as *autochthons*. Initial population densities were likely very low and allowed different groups to live with little competition over resources. As populations increased, however, competition began to rise. This was particularly true for areas in the south-west quadrant of what is now Kenya (Lake Victoria, Rift Valley, west and central highlands) and along the coast. In these areas, the climate was moderate and game and wild plants were in abundant supply. Riverine areas (the Tana and those near the lakes), where water was plentiful and fish could supplement the diet, were particularly coveted. Over time, the people's knowledge of local plant and animal life became quite developed, as did their familiarity with the local terrain and neighboring peoples.

Pre-colonial histories of East Africa, which focus on pastoralism and agriculture, tend to suggest that foragers lived in small roving bands, with the implication that they had little sense of rights to landed property. This depiction is somewhat speculative, however, because much of the evidence of human existence in these periods is derived from archaeological evidence and thus focuses on technology and physical remains rather than social institutions. Evidence from oral tradition suggests, however, that forms of property rights existed in a number of areas. Many incoming Bantu and Nilotic groups have histories which recount battles against hunter-gatherers for control over settlement areas (see, Muriuki 1974; Spear 1976, 1981). New settlers also used methods such as partnerships to obtain the use of land from hunter-gatherers in a friendlier manner. Thus, the Kikuyu of the central highlands acquired land from hunter-gatherers through several different means which consisted "partly of alliance and partnership and partly of adoption and absorption, and partly by payment" (Muriuki 1974: 70). The specific method employed was likely based on the nature of relations (friendly or not) and the relative strength (in numbers) of new versus existing inhabitants.

Furthermore, the ethnography on hunters-gathers in other parts of the world suggests that "no society has a laissez-faire attitude toward spatial boundaries" (Kelly 1995: 185) and that complex hunter-gatherer societies do have a sense of territoriality which will often be marked and defended

(Burch and Ellana 1994). It usually involves two central elements. One is to indicate to neighboring groups specific areas of jurisdiction that should be respected, through tree or stone markings for example, with permission required to cross or otherwise gain access to such land. The second element is military organization within the group, allowing members to work together to defend the territory against outside encroachment.

SPREAD OF FOOD-PRODUCING CULTURES: PASTORALISM AND CULTIVATION

The development of techniques for renewable food production, in the form of either crops or animals, had a fundamental impact on economic activity. In time, they gave pastoralists and cultivators advantages over hunter-gatherers by their capacity to produce a larger and more stable food supply which allowed them to increase populations. As a result, their economic culture, and the institutions which went with it, came to dominate the areas of settlement in Kenya. The three main groups which influenced food production were Nilotes and Cushites from the north who emphasized pastoralism, and Bantu cultivators from the west and south.

The Bantu ethno-linguistic group originated in western Cameroon. Its peoples developed a settled agriculture based on root-crop cultivation and fishing, but heavily supplemented in the initial stages by hunting and gathering (Vansina 1995). From about 2,000 BC, Bantu influence began to spread to other parts of sub-Saharan Africa, often adding cereal cultivation and livestock-keeping to its food producing repertoire (Ehret 1967; 1968; Schoenbrun 1993).[3] It is likely that Bantu influence resulted from eight or nine slow outward expansions that used assimilation as much as migration to spread its language and economic culture (Vansina 1995). Bantu culture reached Kenya from the east and south by about the beginning of the first millennium AD. The Gusii and Luhyia groups in the west were likely some of the earliest Bantu groups in Kenya (Ehret 1988). From the south, Bantu culture spread to the central highlands around Mount Kenya, with the settlement of land and the differentiation of current ethnic groups (Kikuyu, Meru, Embu and Kamba) likely occurring from about 1500 onwards (Spear 1981). The Mijikenda, along the Indian Ocean coast, settled as far north as the Juba River (modern-day Somalia) but were pushed backed and settled the higher areas of coastal Kenya from about 1600 onwards (Spear 1976). As cultivators, Bantus sought out well-watered areas, often in the highlands, and thus settled areas with a minimum of 900 mm of annual rainfall (Ehret 1988: 624).

While renewable food production brought long-term advantages, it also required additional attention. Large investments of labor were required to clear and weed fields. Furthermore, it required much better protection to ensure that labor investments were not wasted by the theft of produce by opportunistic gatherers or raiders. Thus Bantu societies relied on dense human settlements to protect crops and other property. Economic and social life centered on the house; an extended family often augmented by other dependants which were collectively engaged in food procurement. However, a single house was usually not strong enough to defend itself against outsiders and thus joined with other houses to form villages. Thus it was that "every house needed a village to feel secure, [t]he village was therefore the very foundation of society" (Vansina 1988: 78).

Nilotic influence in Kenya also likely began in the middle of the first millennium AD (Ehret 1988). The areas of Nilotic origin were flat, riverine areas of the central Nile in modern Sudan. From that environment, they developed a cattle and cereal culture, in lowland areas which were either dry (with the emphasis on livestock) or well-watered. Western Nilotes, ancestors of the Luo, settled in the lowland areas around Lake Victoria while Plains Nilotes, notably the Maa-speakers, came to control much of the Rift Valley and today include the Maasai in the central sections of the valley, along with the Samburu and Turkana to the north. They engaged mostly in pastoralism, although some groups have adopted more settled cultivation. The earliest groups were likely southern Nilotic who settled around Mount Elgon and adopted a varied culture. Today they include a number of tribes (notably the Nandi and Kipsigis) who make up the Kalenjin ethnic group. This group has combined cattle grazing in open areas with cultivation on the hillsides.

The third major ethno-linguistic group in Kenya is the Cushitic group of Oromo-speakers including the Orma, Boran and Somali. They migrated from the lowland areas south of the Ethiopian highlands and from Somalia. The Southern Cushites initially inhabited a much larger area than they do today, extending into the inter-lakes region and including central Kenya (Oliver and Atmore 2001: 135). Today, their areas are more confined to the harsher, arid margins of the northern and eastern areas where they practice pastoralism, which is sometimes nomadic and includes the use of camels near the Somali border. They are a more marginal group in the Kenyan economy, producing a minimal surplus. Like cultivators, Nilotic and Cushitic pastoralists also had an advantage over hunter-gathers in that their economic livelihood was based on a renewable food source. In this case, however, that food source was mobile, with livestock herded to grazing areas and the need for communal rights to landed property and private rights to herds, as noted.

How did the new groups and/or their economic cultures expand? The current approach is based on assimilation and is considered in rather benign terms (Vansina 1988). Hunter-gatherers were gradually incorporated into food producing cultures because of the latter's superiority in generating food. However, from a less benign point of view, there is also evidence that groups with different food producing cultures clashed over the use of landed resources. Hunter-gatherers may have had the option of assimilating or being banished to less favorable areas.

In the assimilation scenario, prestige is considered to have been an important factor in gaining adherents to a new and expanding culture. For example, Bantu settlements were rather permanent and in many cases encompassed up to 500 people in a district. Hunter-gatherer bands may have involved only about 30 people. The size and excitement of the large villages may have encouraged hunter-gatherers to adopt the Bantu language over time and become incorporated into their societies (Vansina 1988, p.191–2). Partnerships also likely played an important role. The incoming culture was always partly hunter-gatherer and thus there was some similarity in occupation. As well, the settlers had food crops with which to trade with hunters-gatherers for mutual advantage. The Kikuyu and other groups also formed alliances with the autochthons in order to gain their acceptance and obtain, there from, the right to settle land which was included in traditional hunting territory.

At times, however, the interaction between existing and incoming groups was much less civil. Kikuyu history records major battles with the Gumba, a foraging community in the central highlands (Muriuki 1974). Likewise, the Meru fought major battles against their neighbors for settlement space. Conflicts may have arisen, in part, from the fact that settlers cleared forest and altered the vegetation and the natural habitats of wild animals. Thus, the "clearance of bushland for agricultural purposes was in itself a direct threat to the Gumba way of life and, more specifically, often their livelihood" (Muriuki 1974: 42). The decline in forest cover caused the retreat of some animals to denser forest at higher elevations. In the plains, the practice of burning vegetation to induce new grass growth likely upset the ecology of foragers in those areas.

CONFLICT BETWEEN SETTLERS

As herding and cultivation expanded and populations increased, conflict with hunter-gatherers was succeeded by conflicts between more settled groups. The histories of ethnic groups since about 1500 are replete with references to such conflict and they are reflected in the current settlement distribution of these groups. At a general level, an interesting pattern emerged regarding Nilotic, Cushitic and Bantu settlers. As noted, Nilotic groups migrated from areas in which protection of property on open plains was more critical to survival. Thus they developed property protection capabilities well-suited to such terrain but generally ill-adapted to the forest and highland areas (Lawren 1968). Conversely, the Bantu culture originated in forested areas, with limited livestock (Vansina 1988). As a result, it was less capable of defending moveable property in the open.

The Mount Kenya Bantu groups were wary of settling or venturing out onto the open plain for fear of the Maasai, who were interested in controlling the widest possible area for their herds. Thus, "greater defense was necessary the nearer the [Kikuyu] immigrants approached the Maasai border." As they did, only those family groups (*mbari*) with "many warrior sons" or which had "attracted a clientele of fighting followers" could muster the defense necessary to settle these new areas (Muriuki 1974: 71). Settlements were built with the greatest attention to defense. Indeed, the "villages along the frontier were in effect forts" and were built for maximum protection. The ingenuity is described thus:

> When the site of a new village was earmarked, the ground was cleared but the larger trees and undergrowth of the primeval forest surrounding the site were left intact. The trees ringing the site were felled in such a way that the trunks were not completely severed from their roots; they were felled outwards where they were left growing in their fallen position. A hedge of tangled branches and trees was thus formed, and after some time the growth was covered with thorny creeps . . . making it impregnable (Muriuki 1974:121).

It was so well concealed that Europeans found they could be walking only metres from the settlement without knowing of its existence (*ibid.,* p. 122). Communities also developed very organized age-set systems which included a warrior set of young men trained to carry out raiding and defensive functions. The Kikuyu likely adopted this system from Nilotic groups and borrowed military tactics from the Maasai (Lawren 1968).

For the Mijikenda, a Bantu group near the coast, the situation was similar. As noted, they retreated south as the result of Somali expansion. In the hillsites where they settled in Kenya they were under constant threat from Cushitic pastoralists, the Boran and Orma, in the lowlands. They developed specific defensive settlements, called *kaya*, to protect people and property from lowland raiders. In western Kenya, the Gusii, a Bantu group, originally inhabited the lower, well-watered areas near Lake Victoria but were unable to defend themselves on the open areas against Nilotes. Over several centuries of contact and conflict with various Nilotic groups (Luo, Maasai and Kipsigis), they were finally forced to move into forested highland areas. In the initial years there they faced serious hardship in clearing land and making it suitable to cultivation. They survived, however, to develop a strong economy based on cultivation of this fertile area of high rainfall (Ochieng' 1974) and used strong defensive capabilities against neighboring groups.

CO-OPERATION AND TRADE

Along with the need to protect property, the settlers also could gain considerably from trade with other communities. To a great extent, this entailed trade between groups which occupied different ecological zones and thus produced different food items. Relations between groups likely ebbed and flowed, at times being more friendly and at other times more acrimonious. Because of the ever-present *potential* for raiding and others types of opportunism, the movement of outsiders had to be monitored and sometimes prevented. As a result, a number of mechanisms were developed to reduce the risks of inter-community interaction. For example, markets were established at border areas between communities, where the threat from raiding was minimized (Ambler 1988). In addition, longer-term partnerships between men were developed, based on personal bonds, and if open hostility erupted between communities, women could carry on trading nonetheless.

In central Kenya, considerable interaction and trade developed between the Kamba-Mbeere, on the one hand, who herded cattle and cultivated some crops in less fertile areas, and the Kikuyu-Embu, who were more specialized crop cultivators at the higher elevations. These contacts allowed communities a greater variety of foods and it allowed those with limited grazing space in highland areas to obtain animals. Such animals were important as a form of currency in the absence of minted coins or fiat money. Thus sheep, goats and cattle acted as a store of value and a medium of exchange, and were essential, for example, in bridewealth payments. Likewise in Western Kenya, the Gusii are known to have traded considerable quantities of grain with the Luo in exchange for cattle that were used for bridewealth and other social purposes (Hakansson 1994). In areas where soil was less fertile and rainfall less reliable, trade allowed people to exchange livestock for food crops in times of drought. The quantities exchanged may have been quite substantial; in some cases suggesting considerable surplus production. For example, during the famine of 1918–19,[4] the Gusii may have traded between 37,000 and 57,000 tons of grain for 75,000 to 115,000 head of cattle with the Luo (*ibid.*: p. 268). When rains failed repeatedly, the trading relationship allowed people at lower elevations to migrate and work temporarily in the households of their agriculturist trading partners at higher elevations. The Mbeere, in the lowland area south-east of Mount Kenya, employed this strategy with their upland Embu partners to survive the great famine of 1897–99 (Ambler 1988: ch. 1). In times of less severe food shortage, lowland communities might lend a family member (often a girl or young woman) to an upland community in exchange for quantities of food. When the rains resumed, the woman might return but might also be adopted or marry into the new community (*ibid.*: 61–2).

Trading relationships did not develop spontaneously however if animosity or unfamiliarity existed between potential traders. Men often did not have free access to the communities of others because of the potential for opportunistic behavior, such as theft. Venturing onto others' land could be dangerous because a community might not trust the intentions of the foreigner and might seek to expel him. As a result, institutions were developed to reduce the risks inherent in such interaction. In the absence of an overarching politico-judicial framework covering various communities, two types of institutions arose to govern these transactions. One was the establishment of specific market days at border areas between ethnic/ecological zones. This eliminated the need to travel in the territory of another community and thus it reduced the risk of raiding livestock and other goods (Hakansson 1994). Much of the 'small quantity' trade in food and tools was conducted in this manner. The other, more complex institution, involved the development of friendship-trading bonds or "fictive kinship" which combined economic exchange with a notion of adoptive brotherhood. It was a lasting partnership which could also be relied upon in times of hardship, as discussed above. In several central Kenyan communities, this relationship was known as *giciaro* and was usually practiced by men (Muriuki 1974). The process often involved an initial exchange of gifts to demonstrate goodwill. It allowed trade between settled communities in large-sized or large quantity items (such as cattle for grain). In this way, personal networks were built up which cemented trust and allowed trade to take place. *Giciaro* is likely to have "pervaded the commercial life" of central Kenya in the 19th century and probably in earlier times as well (Ambler 1988: 82–86).

While intense animosity or a state of war could seriously disrupt trade between communities, it could also be by-passed through the trading activities of women. Raiding and military activity were conducted by men while women were engaged in much of the regular trade. Because of this gender division, the two activities could be conducted simultaneously. Thus, trade between the Luo and Gusii communities could continue because "[w]omen were not affected by men's feuding and enmities and could therefore move unmolested within Gusii and Luo territories" (Hakansson 1994, p. 262). Similarly, Kikuyu women traded with Maasai women, even as the men were engaged in raiding each other's livestock.

INSTITUTION BUILDING WITHIN ETHNIC GROUPS

While institutions were developed for groups to better resist threats from outsiders as well as to benefit from trade with them, considerable institution-building also took place within societies to combat the potential for opportunism. Village life was organized by village councils (e.g. Gikuyu *kiama*) and the "most significant function of these councils was the administration of justice" (Muriuki 1974: 128). The council settled disputes between lineages, while disputes within the lineage were settled by its leader. Procedures were established for the giving of evidence and the right of appeal. For inter-village disputes, an *ad hoc* court might be established with joint representation from the villages. For more established areas, formal arrangements were developed to cover a number of villages within the same ethnic group to deal systematically with such disputes.

European ethnographers in the 19th and early 20th centuries studying these systems could detail quite specific punishments for a variety of offences (Tate 1910). Theft was treated very seriously, notably when it included such important assets as livestock or natural produce, such as honey. In terms of compensation, under the Kikuyu legal system it was treated similarly to bodily harm and judgments could be severe: theft of a single goat required 10 goats and a ram in return. The penalties were normally set in terms of compensation payments, with little use of imprisonment. Those who did not provide compensation (and therefore disobeyed the ruling) could be cursed or ostracized—serious matters in these close-knit communities. They might also have their crops uprooted. Thus, it was rare that a "culprit deliberately disregarded the judgment of the elders" (Muriuki 1974: 130). Capital punishment, in the form of a public stoning or burning, was used only against repeat offenders of serious crimes.[5]

The legal system also provided for the settlement of disputes regarding borrowing and lending. In the absence of currency, these activities involved livestock, produce, seeds, implements and other physical assets. This type of borrowing has a long tradition in most communities but its practice has often defied Western analysis which is based more on financial assets with standardized, written agreements (Shipton 1995). In many of these credit transactions, like had to be returned for like (i.e. seeds borrowed, seeds repaid). In some cases, this could mean that repayment was not eagerly demanded if the need did not exist. As in the case of livestock repayment, the risk that cattle would die would thus be borne by the holder of the unpaid debt. The duration of a 'loan' could range enormously from brief periods of a day or a week to a generation. Repayment was usually contingent upon the needs of the lender and the capacity for repayment of the borrower, indicating that these truly were personalized, not impersonal, transactions (ibid.). Keeping track of loans which spanned a generation was accomplished through oral tradition. Thus, Kikuyu youths in their second stage of education were taught "basic things about the *mbari* [family], for example, the family genealogy, the boundaries of their land, their debtors and creditors" and other important matters (Muriuki 1974: 9).

While detailed legal systems and inter-village institutions were emerging, larger structures were not in evidence. Kenyan communities in the interior did not develop into kingdoms as in other parts of Africa and there were no pan-Kenyan institutions, much less a proto-Kenyan state. By the end of the 19th century, it was still true that people "lived out their lives in small, independent communities—beyond the power of an indigenous state" and that the "effective reach of social and political institutions scarcely extended beyond a neighborhood" (Ambler 1988: 4). Even the extent of ethnic solidarity was limited. The notion of a Kalenjin ethnic group with a common identity was only developed in the 1950s and, likewise, the term 'Mijikenda' was coined only in the colonial period to identify nine distinct communities in the hills near the coast. Instead, ethnic solidarity developed much later, often in the effort to organize the struggle against British imperialism (see: Sutton 1976: 22).

Corporate forms of economic enterprise also were quite limited. Given the lack of fiat or metal-based currency, accumulation took the form of physical assets, notably livestock. With labor in short supply, lineage heads also needed to attract new members to work the land and tend the livestock. Thus, the notion of wealth was indicated, in part, by the size of one's human following. This was achieved through marriage (often polygamous) and subsequent offspring, and the use of temporary labor or the incorporation of poor or destitute individuals and families from neighboring areas.

In some instances, commercial organizations did develop with the expansion of foreign trade into the interior. This occurred for example in parts of Akamba-land at the height of the ivory trade in the mid-19th century. The Kamba acted as middle-men or caravan provisioners supporting the trade between the Swahili and Arabs on the coast and the Africans who hunted elephants and traded tusks in the interior. While some Kamba traders benefited greatly and accumulated large herds, their 'enterprises' had a limited life. They were based on and controlled by a single trader and tended not to survive his death. Thus, it was true that in the interior, Kenya "had no indigenous equivalent to the corporate commercial houses which existed on the Indian Ocean coast or in many areas of West Africa" (Ambler 1988: 74).

Why larger economic and political forms did not develop in the Kenyan interior is probably best explained by the low ratio of people to land. The process of African colonization of new land was only reaching its limits when the Europeans invaded at the end of the 19th century. This relative people- (labor) scarcity and land-abundance allowed for the dispersion of social pressure. It resulted in outward, frontier expansion, not the development of broader economic and social institutions to manage disputes and competition and support greater capital accumulation. This applies at the level of both independent enterprise and the political-judicial structures needed to regulate property rights and exchange relations. However, this should not downplay the importance of the institutions which did develop and which allowed for increased food production and higher population levels which were central achievements of the African population. It is true, however, that their land-based economic culture and its supporting institutions were quite different from the systems of the Swahili, Arabs, Asians and Europeans. We now turn to an analysis of these other groups.

COASTAL TRADING AND POLITICAL CONTROL

The Kenyan coast had a very different history from that of the interior. Indeed it was only from the mid-19th century that the interior was significantly affected by foreign influence. By contrast, coastal areas had been part of the Indian Ocean trading economy since as early as the first century AD. Along with Africans living on or near the coast, the economy was shaped by the trading, conquest, settlement and political activities of a number of foreign cultures. These included the Arabs from the southern end of the Arabian Peninsula (Oman and Hadhramaut), but also Persians (from the Gulf) and Indians (from Cutch, Surat and other areas of the north-west).[6] Chinese and Indonesian ships also visited different sections of the coast long before Europeans first explored these areas at the end of the 15th century. The contact with the Arabs resulted in the development of a distinct cultural group, the Swahili, who played a key role in the trade between the African hinterland and the sea merchants who ventured along the coast.

As a nexus of trade, the coast developed a trade-based culture that was distinct from the land-based culture of the interior. In this culture, the connections between the key players in the trade chain were critical, because it was seldom that trade took place directly between inland producers/procurers and ship-based traders (Middleton 1992). The two key groups of players were traders, including the Swahili and Asians, who had trade connections but limited political power, and the rulers, notably Arabs and later Europeans, who hoped to reap economic gains by controlling and monopolizing that trade. It is in seeking to understand the trade chain and the relations between traders and rulers that we come to understand the real importance of institutional mechanisms along the coast.

Many of the goods exported from Africa were not found along the coast but were procured in the interior and transported to the coast. This was true of ivory and also to an increasing extent over time of slaves, the continent's two prime exports. Indian Ocean shippers needed port-based intermediaries to obtain these goods, to store, hold or process them and to be willing to engage in trade. To capture the trade, foreigners sought to establish direct political rule over coastal towns. But direct control was not sufficient because it did not guarantee that the rulers could connect into the trade chain and thus obtain goods from the hinterland. Foreign rulers who did not develop such connections were much less successful in reaping the benefits of trade. In other words, political power did not translate into economic benefits if the nature of intermediation was not adequately understood and managed. To manage such interaction was to engage in institutional development. What was the nature of this development?

At a primary level there was intermarriage, which solidified the relationship between foreigners and indigenous people. The Arabs practiced this and the Swahili people and culture developed as a result. This approach involved an African-Arab combination that linked the two ends of the trade chain: African producers and procurers in the interior and Arab rulers and traders along the coast. Other foreign groups, such as the Asians, did not inter-marry and were more dependent on others such as the Swahili in the trade chain and were much more susceptible to arbitrary acts by rulers. Asians did develop strong information networks among themselves, posed no political threat to rulers and sought accommodation with the rulers of the day. The Europeans who came at different times to control the coast were better or worse at developing trade relationships.

The Portuguese were unsuccessful and both their commercial and political activities were always unstable and largely unprofitably.

EARLY COASTAL TRADING: INTERMARRIAGE, THE SWAHILI AND ARAB OVERLORDSHIP

The first written mention of contact by Arabs or Asians with the East African coast is contained in the *Periplus of the Erythrean Sea*, which dates from the second century AD. It is likely that contact before that time also occurred. The gains to be made from trade were based on regional differences in the goods available. From Asia, the Persian Gulf and Arabia, sea vessels brought wheat, rice, butter, sesame oil, cotton, cloth and sugar. These items were exchanged for the African products of ivory, gold, slaves, iron, gum copal,[7] ambergris,[8] incense and other items. The activity was seasonal, based on the Indian Ocean monsoons, which allowed easy wind-powered sea voyage from north-west India to Africa from mid-December to the end of February and return voyage with the winds from April to September (see Hollingsworth 1960: ch. 2; Mangat 1969: 1).

Arabs tended to both integrate with the local population and to impose political and military rule over coastal towns and sea traffic. Both of these efforts were designed to increase their economic benefits. The Swahili culture, which developed out of an inter-mingling and the intermarriage of Arabs with Africans, was a direct result of this economic objective. Marrying into local African lineages was a prime practice of Arabs to establish their influence in local economic and political matters. The major myths of Swahili origin attest to the importance of this practice (Middleton 1992: 29ff). It was also used later by Arabs who married not into African lineages but into the Swahili patrician families which had become established. This culture developed a more settled society and a coastal town civilization, from about the 11th century onwards, which was often governed by the overlordship of south Arabian rulers in alliances with local Swahili leaders. It was from this period until the coming of the Portuguese at the end of the 15th century that Swahili civilization likely reached its peak. Afterwards it was subjected to strong outside influence, conquest and foreign empire-building.

Compared with Arabs, the Asian contact with the African coast was likely not as long in duration and was definitely not as intense in terms of interaction and control. Asians from the north-western portion of the Indian sub-continent established themselves in many of the trading centers around the Indian Ocean (African and non-African) as an ethnic trading diaspora. The period in which Asians first established such trade with the

African coast is not known but, as noted, the earliest written evidence is from early in the first millennium AD. It does not appear that Asians established trading agents in these early centuries; instead trade was often conducted directly from their ships lying at anchor off the coast (Hollingsworth 1960). With the greater development of coastal towns in the second millennium, however, Asians began to station agents at the key ports. They would purchase from those who traded with the interior, notably the Swahili.

There is no evidence of Asian attempts to conquer African lands or build up major immigrant settlements, although Muslim Indians were more inclined to settle (under Muslim Arab rule) than Hindus. Despite a long history of Indian trading activities along the African coast, "nowhere [did] they show a particular hunger for political power" (Subrahmanyam 1995: 768). They seldom married into local families and retained strong links with their homelands. As a result, their fortunes were based on the property rights structure developed by others and their success in gaining access to local trading connections.

THE ERROR OF PORTUGUESE CONTROL: 1498 TO 1729

Portugal's error was to try to reap economic benefits from East Africa through conquest. They failed to understand the importance of the trade chain into the interior and thus failed to establish their own means of making friendly relations with the Swahili, Arabs and Asians who were connected to this chain. The result was a period of rule that was unstable and largely unprofitable.

The Portuguese began to challenge local and Arab control following Vasco da Gama's rounding of the Cape of Good Hope in 1497 and the seizure of Mombassa and other areas in the following year. They employed superior military technology to subdue Arab rulers and within a decade had gained control of the coast. The problem with their rule was that they tried to monopolize trade to the detriment of other communities, including the Swahili and Asians, their prime contact points in the trade chain. Denied rights to engage in trade, the economic activities of these other groups declined and therewith the prosperity of the towns. Few voyages were made from Asia and Arabia to Africa during Portuguese predominance because of the insecurity of sea travel in the Indian Ocean and the lack of trading rights. As a result, the Portuguese "in the their inability to co-operate either with Arab or African [or Asian], were their own greatest enemies" (Freeman-Grenville 1963: 135). Overall their governmental activities lost money, running a deficit as high as 40% of expenses over revenues (*ibid.* p. 142). Their power was always precarious and subject to local revolt. It was doomed to decline because of the lack of economic roots and the low number of Portuguese stationed there. Some 900 men were stationed along the coast and were required to control a combined population of about 100,000 people spread along the coast (*ibid.*).

After a series of raids and revolts, the Portuguese were ousted in 1729 by a combination of Omani Arabs and local rulers, who restored some semblance of the traditional trade chain. However this did not substantially revive trade around the Indian Ocean because property was not secure on the seas. After the Portuguese had mapped a sea route from Europe to Asia, other European powers were eager to capture the lucrative trade with China, India, Indonesia and other areas, resulting in intense competition for control of the seas. During the 18th century, Dutch, French and British ships competed, through piracy, thus making the seas "very unsafe to all but the large and well-armed vessels" (Hollingsworth 1960: 15).

EMPIRE BUILDING BY THE OMANI AND BRITISH, 18TH AND 19TH CENTURIES

By the early 19th century, increased Omani and British control combined to create security on the seas and along the coast. This led to the revival of trade generally and of Asian trading fortunes in particular. The Asians worked closely under Arab but notably British rule to strengthen their position and gain the protection and benefits necessary to expand their commercial activities. This British-Indian connection, along with the eventual demise of the slave trade and of plantation agriculture based on slavery, led to the decline of Swahili-Arab influence and their joint economic fortunes.

Omani trade and political control in East Africa was considerably strengthened under the rule of Seyyid Said (1806–56). In expeditions from Muscat he defeated Swahili and other local rulers, including the Mazuri of Mombassa in 1837. These victories gave Oman control of the coast from Mogadishu to Delgado Bay. The perceived importance of the region and its economic potential were underlined in 1840 when Said moved his capital from Muscat to Zanzibar, where he lived until his death. He established important trade treaties with France and the United States but most importantly signed the Commercial Treaty with Britain in 1839. At the same time—and decidedly after the Indian mutiny of 1857[9]—the British imposed increasing control over India and extended that control over Indian traders along the East African coast. They established a consulate at Zanzibar in 1841.

The Commercial Treaty between the Omanis and the British was important for the security of Asian trading because, as citizens of British-controlled and British-protected areas in the Indian sub-continent, Indians in Africa were afforded the rights of British subjects. The treaty thus granted protection in several critical areas including: the right to live in and trade in Omani areas; the right to own land and houses; and the right to protection against theft and trespass on private property (Hollingsworth 1960: 22). In addition, Asians had recourse to British authority in the settlement of commercial and other disputes. Any dispute between an Asian and an Arab in which the Asian was the complainant was decided by the British Consul. If an Arab was the complainant, Arab authorities had jurisdiction to settle the dispute but British authorities had the right to attend the proceedings.

The greater security which the Asians gained from Arab and British control did not extend to the interior where these sea powers had only limited control and the slave trade excited animosity between Africans and foreigners. While a few armed Muslim Indians did penetrate to the interior, they were the exception. Those who tried to do so without arms were often robbed and sometimes murdered (Hollingsworth 1960: 25). Instead, it was mostly armed Arabs who made ventures inland in search of slaves. It was no coincidence that Indian traders only moved inland later under British protection beginning with the building of the Mombassa-Uganda railway at the end of the 19th century. Only with British protection did the Asians feel that they and their goods were safe.

It is also interesting to note that the Asian played a dual role. In private commerce, they worked as traders and financiers in the towns. At the same time, they played an important role in the public finances of the Omani rulers. Key financial posts in the empire were held by Asians (Indians), mostly Hindu. For example, Seyyid Said always entrusted the key post of Customs Master to an Indian. He contracted it out to Zanzibari Asian firms for increasing sums during the first half of the 19th century. His successors, from 1856, did the same. When the position was awarded to the Hindu trader, Jairam Sewji in 1881, he paid the sultan £110,000 for the right. (After the British established a protectorate over Zanzibar in 1890, the customs were reorganized under European stewardship.) Arab leaders tended to find Asian, especially Hindus, more trustworthy with finance than they found other Arabs (Hollingsworth 1960: 19–22). The growth of Indian trade and finance during this period also meant that Asians became bankers to the sultan and were often owed large sums of money by the court. In other words, senior Asians at Zanzibar had direct access to Arab rulers.

This development did not mean, however, that Asian always received adequate protection for themselves and their property. They petitioned the Arab rulers as they did the British Consul, complaining that their commercial bills were not paid by local Arabs or that the protection of the Indian community was inadequate, notably for those who lived far from Zanzibar (Hollingsworth 1960: 25). If the historical record shows that Asians were not always pleased with Arab or British rule, the evidence of petitioning suggests that they were on good enough terms to think that it might bring results.

Another change which took place under increasing British control involved the abolition of slavery—a major change in property rights affecting Swahili and Arab plantation agriculture. Areas near the coast which supplied produce for the coastal towns and for the provisioning of foreign vessels relied on slave labor. Along with the Swahilis and Arabs, some Asian had large retinues, with reports of one Indian businessman owning as many as 400 slaves. Indians were considered to be under British protection even in non-British areas (such as East Africa in the mid- to late 19th century). Thus, the position of Asian slave-owners in East Africa became difficult as Britain moved to eliminate the practice throughout the empire. The slave trade was abolished in British possessions in 1803 while slavery itself was banned in 1833, although not in India until 1843. Because the Asians in East Africa were from British-protected areas of India they too were obliged to follow these laws. Indians at first resisted these efforts but after more forceful efforts, they relinquished their slaves, many of whom returned as wage-earners. In the 1860s and 1870s, successive British Consuls at Zanzibar enforced the laws, freeing almost 3,000 Indian-owned slaves between 1860 and 1875 (Hollingsworth 1960: 31–34). While particular owners may have lost from the change, most Asians supported abolition because they felt that slave-trading was discouraging more legitimate forms of commerce along the coast but notably with the interior. The real losers, especially when Britain wrestled overall control from the Arabs at the end of the 19th century, were the Swahilis and Arabs. British influence along the African coast gradually increased and a protectorate over what is modern day Kenya was established in 1896.

CONCLUSION

Institutional economics provides a valuable tool for analyzing economic history, including differences in economic culture. Ethnic and racial groups develop and evolve distinct institutions based on their economic, demographic and ecological environments. Moreover, people carry institutions with them and adapt them to new places and new situations. We have explored how various ethnic and racial groups brought ideas and institutions to Kenya from their places of origin, within and outside of Africa. Pastoralists brought herding techniques and military tactics that allowed them to defend moveable property. Cultivators used defensive mechanisms to protect land, crops and harvested produce. While both groups developed the means to protect property, they also evolved institutions to gain the benefits of intra- and inter- group trade and borrowing.

The Asians who settled along the coast engaged in trading and finance and also in plantation agriculture before the banning of slavery. They did not gain political control but instead sought accommodation with the rulers of the day, be they Arabs, Europeans or locals. Contact between the coast and the interior was arranged through middlemen traders. For their part, Asians lacked the support of a secure personal and property rights framework to protect themselves and their goods inland. The situation changed fundamentally near the end of the 19th century with the building of the Mombassa-Uganda railway and the establishment of British colonial control. The British banned Asians from rural land ownership and thus the latter concentrated on trade, finance and eventually manufacturing in towns and villages. The British established new formal institutions which were often designed to control African economic activity. The details of this colonial experience are provided in the following chapter.

Chapter Three

Discrete and Evolutionary Change during Colonialism

Colonialism brought the three main racial groups into more intense conflict, cooperation and interaction in the interior of East Africa. Economic relations were governed by colonial laws and regulations, as set down by British officials, but the structure of the economy was determined by the needs of the various groups and the intense interdependencies which developed. Europeans needed Asian labor to build the railway and African labor to operate their farms, Africans produced and sold commodities into new urban markets, Asians facilitated commerce under British protection. The influence of British control did exert itself more heavily on Africans, as opposed to Asians, both because colonial settlers feared competition from African producers and because colonial officials were concerned that social unrest would develop if African areas became too unequal. Asians had a much freer hand, worked more closely with the British and had greater opportunities for accumulation.

To focus solely on the formal constraints to economic activity, however, is to miss important aspects of the colony's institutional development and its impact on economic activity. Asians built strong informal networks for trade and credit in which easy access to high quality information supported a system based on reputation, trust and community censure. Combined with more equal relations with the British and their concentration in urban centers, Asians used these networks to increase capital accumulation and develop strong urban enterprises. They emerged from colonialism in a preponderant position with regards to retail and wholesale trade, real estate and, increasingly, manufacturing.

In providing this institutional interpretation of Kenya's colonial history, there is no attempt to refute the major themes presented in several excellent histories of Kenya's colonial period (Throup 1987; Berman 1990; Mangat 1969). Instead the current analysis draws upon, and is mostly consistent with, that literature but provides a distinctively institutional approach. It also contains the added feature of bringing the three prominent groups (Europeans, Africans and Asians) together for a more complete picture of the period. Most historical accounts analyze the tensions and interactions between Europeans and Africans, while the history of the Asian community is treated in a more limited number of specialized accounts. The chapter is divided into two main parts. Following a brief overview of colonial dates and events, the first part focuses on trading and transacting with specific sections on labor contracting, trading restrictions, Asian networks and credit transacting. The second part analyses landed property rights in the content of European settlement in the White Highlands, African developments in the reserves and Asian exclusion from rural land ownership. Because white settlement under colonialism was intrusive it disrupted existing patterns of rural property rights. As a result, such rights evolved only partially in accordance with the evolutionary theory of property rights as articulated by Plateau (1995). A final section briefly concludes.

BRITISH COLONIALISM: AN OVERVIEW

From the middle of the 19th century, Britain gradually extended its control over Zanzibar and the East African coast while individual European traders and explorers made journeys into the interior. These developments intensified following agreements at the Berlin Conference in 1886 regarding spheres of European influence and a further agreement, four years later, defining the areas of British control (Uganda, Kenya, Zanzibar) and those claimed by Germany (Tanganyika, Rwanda, Burundi). The British government sought to develop the interior by granting a trading monopoly in 1888 to a private concern, the Imperial British East African Company. The company subsequently established a number of posts but the costs of supporting them and developing trade proved daunting. By 1895 the company's unprofitable operations were taken over by the Foreign Office, which established the East African Protectorate. Most of this area officially became the colony of Kenya in 1920. Along with the trading interest at Mombassa, Britain was interested in controlling Uganda because it included a section of the Nile and thus might provide an alternate route to India if the Suez Canal was blocked. The British also wished to put a final end to the Arab trade in African slaves. Uganda's distance from the coast and the lack of navigable east-west rivers prompted the building of a railway. Construction began in 1896 and reached its midway point (a staging ground which became Nairobi) three years later. By 1901, the railway reached Kisumu on Lake Victoria.

The building of the railway put the British into conflict with African societies which resisted the encroachment and attempted to disrupt the operations of the railway. In the first nine years of the protectorate, a third of the administration's budget was spent on military operations (Lonsdale and Berman 1979: 496). The most concerted attempt at obstruction was pursued by the Nandi, who engaged in seven years of resistance until finally being subdued. Conversely, some groups initially benefited from the British influx, such as the southern Kikuyu who sold food and other provisions to the British garrisons, and the Maasai who became military allies in the early years (Rogers 1979; Waller 1976). By 1905, superior military technology had enabled the British to put down most African resistance.

The railway and the British military presence opened the interior of Kenya to substantial foreign influence. Asian traders who had previously operated along the coast expanded inland and set up shops along the railline and in the new towns. Except in several exceptional cases, Asian traders had not previously moved inland for fear of their personal security and loss of property. With the British presence, they had the advantages of both security (which they would not provide for themselves) and the markets created by the influx of British government and settler investment. In addition, waves of new Asian immigrants sought their fortunes in the colony. Barred from access to agricultural land, they took to trading, artisanal work and manufacturing, as well as urban professions and administrative positions in the colonial bureaucracy. Throughout the colonial period, they maintained a 3:1 advantage in population over the British. In 1948, for example, there were almost 98,000 Asians in Kenya, compared to just under 30,000 Europeans (see Tab. 3.1).

Europeans came as military personnel, as colonial administrators and increasingly as settlers intent on farming and ranching in the fertile areas of the White Highlands. The British established the formal institutions of the colonial state, including an Executive Council and a Legislative Council. The latter operated on a reverse democratic principle (until 1952), in which the ethnic group with the smallest population (whites) was accorded the largest number of seats, while the group with the largest population (Africans) was accorded the smallest number of seats. The Asians held the middle ground, with both a population and an allocation of seats that was in between those of the whites and the Africans (Vandenberg 2002: 97). Control of the executive and legislative branches of the state allowed the whites to pass laws in their favor and thus to discriminate against

Table 3.1 Population by race, Kenya 1911-1989

Year	Africans	Asians	Europeans
1911	--	12,000	3,175
1921	3,700,000	23,000	9,650
1926	--	41,140	12,529
1931	4,100,000	57,135	16,812
1939	4,800,000	--	--
1948	5,700,000	97,528	29,660
1962	8,800,000	176,613	55,759
1969	10,900,000	139,039	40,593
1979	15,100,000	78,600	39,901
1989	21,300,000	89,185	34,560

Source: van Zwanenberg and King, 1975: 12-14; Kenya Central Bureau of Statistics 1981, Vol. I, Tab. 2 and 1994: Vol. I, p. 6-2.

Africans and Asians on issues of land use, labor and the right to engage in specific sectors, as discussed below.

The colonial state barred Africans from possessing land in the White Highlands but they came as laborers and 'squatters' when demographic pressure in the African areas (or 'reserves') intensified. The world-wide depression of the 1930s forced many white settlers into bankruptcy and the abandonment of their farms, although renewed economic activity developed during and following the Second World War. The colonial government also began to remove constraints on African agriculture and actively supported its development. This included lifting restrictions on the types of cash crops they could produce which did allow for African surplus generation and accumulation before the end of the colonial period (Cowen 1981). The lifting of restrictions was prompted by changing attitudes toward Africans but more so by economic imperatives stemming from the sterling crisis and the consequent need to expand colonial exports.[1] Many Africans, notably the Kikuyu in the central region, took quickly to the growing of newly introduced cash crops, such as coffee and tea. Throughout the African areas, small traders set up stores whiles others specialized in the more lucrative trade of agricultural commodities (Kitching 1980, ch. 6).

The problems of African land scarcity, other colonial restrictions and rising discontent among the urban poor in Nairobi generated intense political conflict which eventually erupted in the Mau-Mau rebellion of the 1950s. It was forcibly put down by the British but broader movements toward independence for African colonies were by then moving apace. By 1960, Kenya's Africans received the right to vote and, after a long transitional period, official independence was granted in December 1963. British colonial control thus spanned approximately 70 years. From this general outline of the colonial period, we will seek the nature of changing property rights and transacting relations and their contribution to the economic progress of the various groups in the colony.

TRADING AND TRANSACTING: INFORMAL NETWORKS AND FORMAL RESTRICTIONS

Contracting labor to build the railway

The building of the railway was planned and supervised by British engineers but most of the manual, artisanal and technical labor was supplied by Indians (i.e. Asians). Historical accounts of the use of Asian labor are not clear, however, on why Asians were used instead of Africans. Hollingsworth (1960: 47) suggests only that it was "deemed impracticable to rely on African labor for most of the construction work." Likewise, Mangat (1969: 32) notes that the Railway Committee "arrived at the conclusion that it would be hopeless to expect that the railway could be constructed at any reasonable cost and speed unless they were allowed to recruit Indian labor freely." While this attitude might be ascribed to the racial tendencies of colonial administrators, an institutional analysis of labor contracting (involving principal-agent problems) likely provides a more satisfying answer. British administrators had had experience with Indian laborers in the building of infrastructure projects in India. Also, the practice of wage labor was at this time more established in India than East Africa. As an accepted practice, there was an understanding by the agent (laborer) of what was required by the principal (railway managers). It would have been more costly for British engineers to use African labor because they would have needed to develop the institution of wage labor. In fact, the transaction cost advantage of employing Indian (over African) labor would have had to have been substantial to outweigh the transportation cost disadvantage of transporting workers from the sub-continent.[2]

More generally, foreign labor is easier to control and retain than indigenous labor. The latter are familiar with the local environment and thus have an easier exit option should conditions become too onerous. It is more difficult for foreigners to return home because they may lack the funds to book return passage. In the Kenyan case, return passage was provided by the employer only at the end of the contract. In short, the loyalty of workers to employers, even under harsh conditions, might be difficult to break because the employer represented the means of support and the ticket home. It is also more difficult for foreign workers to obtain an alternative livelihood in the local (alien) culture and they are easily recognized by the authorities if they break their labor contracts. Infrastructure projects in other colonies also relied on foreign indentured labor—such as the trans-Canada railway which was built in the 1880s using Chinese workers on its treacherous western sections.

For the Ugandan railway, the British imported 32,000 'coolies' or indentured laborers from India even though there were as many as three million Africans in the 'Kenya' area. Africans did supplement Indian labor in building and later servicing the railway, but their numbers never totaled more than 2,600. To entice workers, the British offered three-year contracts to those from the poor agricultural areas of Gujarat and Punjab. This provided for their food and wages, passage to Mombassa and return fare on completion of their contracts. Given the hot, humid conditions near the coast and at Lake Victoria and unfamiliar diseases, such as malaria, most of the workers availed themselves of their right of return passage. Of the 32,000 men who worked on the railway, 16,312 returned home of their own volition at the termination of their contracts. An additional 6,454 were invalided home, due mostly to disease but also work-related injuries. A further 2,493 died in Kenya, mostly from disease, but some more dramatically from lion attacks at the Tsavo river crossing. Only the remaining 6,724 stayed on in Kenya and Uganda (Mangat 1969: 39). While the Asian population grew partly from these original railway workers, they were not the sole basis for the development of the Asian community under colonialism. In subsequent waves of immigration, many other Asians sought new opportunities under British protection in the new colony. Those who did stay often took up positions with the railway or ventured off to the towns to set up *dukas* and engage in trading. Meanwhile, it took longer for Africans to become accustomed to British colonial structures and practices and to gain opportunities provided through the new administration.

TRADING NETWORKS AND FORMAL CONSTRAINTS

Colonialism provided new opportunities for trading but also imposed constraints on the activities of Africans and, to a lesser extent, Asians. By the mid-1930s, Europeans restricted the trade of key agricultural crops to official, licensed traders who channeled produce through marketing boards.

This allowed Europeans, and some Asians, to earn most of the middleman profits from buying locally and selling on to urban or foreign markets. Outside of official channels, the Asian business community built strong informal networks which included the trade of locally produced commodities and urban goods and the importation of foreign products. While Africans did participate in commodity trade, their activities remained more local. The potential development of an enhanced African trading elite, with the capacity for large scale accumulation, was thus constrained by the institutions developed at two levels: official British channels and the Asian trading network.

i) European trade and marketing restrictions

The increased organization of white producer interests in the 1930s resulted in greater settler control over the trade and marketing of agricultural produce. While the Kenya Farmers Association (KFA) already controlled the marketing of produce from European areas, it also came to control trade in the African reserves. Ironically, this was prompted in part by an African lobby of the state to restrict the activities of Asian traders who were squeezing out the activities of African traders (Berman 1990: 236). At the same time, the settler community (through the KFA) sought to reap the gains from buying African produce and selling at higher prices into urban and export markets. To do so, they needed to bypass and thereby undermine the local market centers run by Asians and to a lesser extent, by Africans. A secondary purpose involved the standardization of quality; settlers were concerned that the price offered for their produce was held down by the lower quality of African produce because buyers could not readily distinguish between the two. As institutional analysis indicates, when quality is not standardized, it may be costly for individual traders to assess. This will either raise the costs of transacting (if assessment is made) or push prices down to lower levels of quality. Finally, colonial officials were also interested in controlling prices against fluctuations.

To meet these various objectives, the colonial administration passed the Marketing of Native Produce Ordinance (1935) to restrict the sale of African-grown maize to licensed traders at official trading centers. It also restricted competition in the marketing of wattle, rice, cashew nuts and tobacco (Berman 1990: 236).[3] All produce had to be inspected and graded, and controls were placed on the prices paid to producers. This effectively allowed the KFA, and established Asians who obtained licenses, to gain control over the buying of commodities from the reserves. In response, considerable informal trade by Africans and Asians continued even after the restrictions were imposed (Anderson and Throup 1985).

From an institutional perspective, this example represents the dual and contradictory nature of institutional development. On the one hand, the marketing restrictions may be seen as an attempt to reduce transaction costs by setting prices, designating buyers and ensuring product quality. In fact, there has been no research on whether, for example, the quality requirements actually helped the colony to achieve a recognized higher standard (and therefore higher prices) for its agricultural exports. At the same time, however, the discriminatory aspects of the institution are evident in the effort to exclude Africans and many Asians from this expanding trade.

Several sources, notably the East Africa Royal Commission, suggest that the trading restrictions and marketing boards held back commercial development. While it felt that trading remained relatively competitive, it "would be even more so if it could be released from many of the restrictions to which it has been subjected" (EARC 1961: 72.). As for the marketing system, the Commission was rather emphatic in declaring that it was having a "deleterious effect" on the proper functioning of commercial distribution and was "a retarding factor in the economic development of East Africa" (*ibid.*). The Commission was even at pains to point out that while there might be a theoretical justification for quality controls (as noted) it felt that private traders had been doing an adequate job in accounting for variances in produce quality. The Commission suggested that the controls would only tend to hurt the less well-off producers, in this case the poorer Africans (*ibid.*).

Furthermore, the restrictions may have limited African advancement in the formal trading sector. The Commission argued that the system restricted the ability of Africans to "fulfill their commercial aspirations" (EARC 1961: 70), while Mangat (1969: 167) has suggested that the system may have "prevented the rise of an African commercial class" to rival the Asians during the colonial period. Similarly, Cowen (1981) suggests that while Africans began a serious process of accumulation in the late colonial period the marketing restrictions were an important constraint on their advance. The "[g]eneralized controls over household production eliminated the position of private merchant capital in the circulation of commodities" and "intervened against a spontaneous course of accumulation which had been started by an indigenous [African] class of capital" (Cowen 1981: 127). These restrictions reduced the African opportunities for accumulation and thus limited their subsequent, post-colonial, development.

ii) Asian trading networks

There is ample historical evidence of the economic importance of Asians traders and other businessmen during the colonial period. This is not well-recorded, however, in many of the detailed histories of colonialism because historians have tended to concentrate on agricultural production and on the tensions between white settlers and Africans over land rights and labor requirements. Mangat's (1969) history of the Asians in East Africa fills the gap by providing considerable detail on the success and expansion of Asian enterprise. Likewise, Himbara (1994) has helped to provide a broader view of Kenya's economic history by focusing on the Asian contribution, while Manji (1995) and Murray (1978) have also provided contributions. These histories have been able to draw upon colonial era documents which note the importance of Asian economic activity. An excerpt from the report of the East African Royal Commission provides one such example:

> the remarkable tenacity and courage of the Indian trader has been mainly responsible for stimulating the want of the indigenous peoples, even in the remotest areas, by opening to them a shop-window on the modern world and for collecting for sale elsewhere whatever small surpluses are available for disposal. The non-African trading system as it exists in East Africa is one of the most important assets which the economy possesses (EARC 1961: 65).

Instead of focusing here on the importance of the Asian role in the colony's development, this section considers what was required for that success. The accounts noted above tend to stress the hard-working, tight-saving, entrepreneurial nature of the Asians, along with their "economic resilience," "abundance of fortitude," and "perseverance" (Mangat 1969: 137). While this was likely the case for many Asians, many Africans undoubtedly had similar characteristics. An institutional perspective suggests instead that formal and informal institutions supported more advanced trade and investment by members of the Asian community.

At the formal level, Asians found it easier to adapt to the institutions established by the British because of greater familiarity with them. The protectorate adopted the rupee as its currency due to its use by Asians along the coast. It was retained until increased European influence resulted in a switch to a British-linked currency in 1920. The system of law in the Protectorate was predominantly the Indian Civil Law (civil law used by the British in Indian) until 1905 and many of the laws persisted much later into the colonial period. The Asians had established a presence at Mombassa and had become familiar with the operation of British institutions there. They were less adverse to working with them and less likely to contest the decisions which flowed from them. Asians accepted—indeed needed—the British military presence and administration because, like the British, they were foreigners in East Africa. The colonial project was, in many ways, a shared one between Asians and the British. The Asians needed the British to provide security and increase the demand for trade, while the British relied upon Asians to facilitate commerce because the white settlers were less interested in trade and because Africans had less developed trading networks with coastal and foreign markets. This shared project, despite the tensions between Asian business and white settlers in the first three decades of British rule, helped to forge the relations which allowed Asians to contract more effectively with the British. Conversely, Africans found it difficult to accept the legitimacy of British control and were not necessarily inclined to work within its structures. They viewed these institutions as alien. While many Africans did adapt to British institutions, it was less critical for them to conform because they had their own rural activities and community institutions.

We have already noted that the British relied on Indian labor to build the railway. There were other instances where British administrators and Asian merchants worked closely together. The initial recruitment of laborers to build the railway was contracted to two Asian merchants, A.M. Jeevanjee and Hussein Bux,[4] because of their commercial connections with India. In addition, Jeevanjee obtained the contract in 1899 to supply food for the 15,000 Indians working on the railway (Mangat 1969: 54). Jeevanjee also played a key role in the building of railway stations and the various municipal, commercial and residential buildings in Nairobi.

Only a limited number of Asian businessmen obtained such lucrative contracts, however, while, others began more modest enterprises. These benefited from membership of the Asian community in other ways. Unlike the British, Asians were denied rights to the White Highlands and thus needed to secure their livelihoods in urban areas, notably in commerce, business and the professions. Their greatest commercial assets were their links to each other; if they damaged those links by not honoring their contracts, their chances of commercial success and indeed survival in the colony were much reduced. Honoring contracts meant ensuring that goods were supplied on time and met the agreed quality standards, and that payment terms were met. In the case of distribution, wholesalers often provided goods to distributors on the basis of 50% down, with the remaining 50% paid by the end of the week (Manji 1995: 36). For those who could obtain these terms, it gave them a strong advantage over those who could not. Africans were often denied access to Asian trading networks in the first instance and thus did not gain the advantages of the trade credit which it provided. The inability to access such credit from Asian wholesalers was a "long-time handicap" for African traders, according to Kitching (1980, p. 185–6), and one which inhibited their growth and development throughout the colonial period.

Research conducted in the 1950s noted that "the attitude of Indian merchants to small-scale African retailers makes it very difficult for them to enter into trade at all, and certainly deprives them of the normal facilities of trade credit" (Newlyn and Rowan 1954: 222). Indeed, a number of Asian wholesalers indicated that they "certainly would not supply African retailers" (*ibid.* n. 1). The researchers labeled this a "strong prejudice" on the part of the Indian wholesalers but it is unclear whether it was meant in a pejorative sense. The attitude might be based on a specific intent to exclude Africans from this expanding trade but it is more likely that the reasons were based on the greater difficulty of enforcing contracts with traders who were not part of the Asian network. Africans might not be as familiar with Asian norms regarding payment and, more importantly, Asians would find it difficult to screen African traders, monitor their activities and use community reputation and social censure as a powerful deterrent against non-payment. In this regard, the ability to enforce contracts under a bilateral (African-Asian) punishment system would have been much less effective than under a multilateral system (cf. Greif 1993; see previous chapter). In this context, trade tended to expand within the Asian community rather than beyond it, even though Asians needed to interact (on a cash basis) with African commodity producers, sellers and consumers.

CREDIT INSTITUTIONS

The development of credit under colonialism provides another interesting example of how formal rules and informal mechanisms both aided transacting in some cases and constrained it in others. The issue of credit is complex because the indigenous system of credit and the new formal system did not blend well together, thus discouraging credit provision across the African/non-African divide.

i) The purpose of formal restrictions

At the formal level, the possibility for inter-racial credit transacting was constrained by the Credit Trade with Natives Ordinance of 1926, which limited the size of loans which Africans could obtain from non-Africans to £10. This was done not through a formal ban but by a provision in the ordinance in which suits brought before the courts which were above this amount would not normally be heard.[5] The regulation was later replaced by the Credit to Africans Control Ordinance (1948) which allowed Africans with a business license to be exempt from the restriction. Because most rural producers did not hold such a license, the changes did little to support the provision of credit to Africans. These ordinances effectively undermined the purpose of the formal enforcement mechanism regarding Africans. If the purpose of formal legal structures is to expand contracting through a broad impersonal system of enforcement, then that purpose is undermined by restricting its access to only certain groups. In other words, the British and Asian business communities obtained the benefit of formal contract enforcement while Africans did not. Any advantages in business held by the former were thus further reinforced through these discriminatory ordinances.

But were the ordinances designed specifically to discriminate against and thereby hold back the economic activities of Africans? The answer is both yes and no, for colonial officials were concerned with the two separate problems of African indebtedness and economic change. One of the primary motivations behind the ordinances was an effort to avoid the indebtedness of small African farmers. This concern arose not from the actual growth of indebtedness in Kenya but from the situation in India where, by 1945, total peasant indebtedness had reached £625 m. and was resulting in landlessness and social unrest (Throup 1987: 73). Colonial officials in Kenya were worried that a similar process would develop whereby subsistence farmers would borrow money intended for farm improvement but use it for consumption. These farmers were generating only a marginal surplus and it would be difficult for them to make repayment. In addition, officials were concerned that Africans misunderstood the nature of formal lending organizations. These officials felt that "in the minds of many Africans, banks are regarded as institutions which give money out in contrast to government which is regarded as an institution which takes money away" (EARC 1961: 98). The ordinances, therefore, were designed to avoid the potential problem of indebtedness by restricting credit in the first instance. If they were correct, it can be argued that in some ways colonial officers made a positive contribution to the lower strata of the African peasantry by restricting access to formal credit institutions which were different from indigenous institutions and not well understood by many Africans.

At the same time, the ordinances were enacted as part of a general policy to contain the economic progress of Africans. This was not done simply to contain African progress or to reduce competition with Europeans but was designed specifically to reduce the threat of social unrest. Based again on the British experience in India, where 25m. people were landless shortly before the end of British rule, Kenyan officials were concerned with upsetting the indigenous communal order by supporting a small elite of farmers and traders and thereby increasing the level of economic differentiation within African society. While such differentiation was likely to be a natural part of economic development, officials were concerned that it would eventually result in increasing tensions between wealthier Africans, with control over larger areas of land, and a growing stratum of poorer, landless people. To contain these developments, officials sought both to limit credit access (so that the elite farmers would not expand too rapidly) and to limit the establishment of individual rights in land. The ban on individual tenure was important because it would reduce the transferability of land, thereby restricting the use of land as collateral for credit. It would also limit the transfer of land from poor, indebted farmers to more successful farmers as a result of foreclosure or the need for repayment (Throup 1987: 72–73).

In fact, the effort to limit the extension of credit to Africans was likely to have been restricted more by the lack of individual title to land than by the two specific credit ordinances noted above. This was due to the fact that the transacting problems of screening, monitoring and enforcement had to be overcome even if no formal restrictions on credit contracting were in place. Without the possibility of using their basic asset as collateral, the basis for credit transacting was limited, especially between races where other community based information or sanctioning mechanisms were weak. The East African Royal Commission was rather clear in arguing that "borrowing depends upon the existence of a negotiable security" and that much of the land held by Africans did not meet the criterion of negotiability because there was no willingness to abandon control of land in the event that the loan could not be repaid (EARC 1961: 97). Without security, the burden of supporting the transaction lay in the prior screening for creditworthiness. However, because Africans and non-Africans had limited business dealings with each other and less information about each other, it was difficult to screen based on information or past experience. Outside credit would also not have been supplied to many rural Africans because of the high costs of administering such loans; or in the words of the Royal Commission, "heavy overhead costs [would be] involved in providing local lending facilities among scattered communities [and] in maintaining the accounts of small borrowers" (*ibid.*, p. 97).

While colonial officials were worried about economic disparities within the African community, they were also interested in increasing African production and knew that this might be effected through credit provision to some farmers. This notion arose after the war when colonial officials were more intent upon increasing exports by augmenting settler output with African produce. It coincided with a growing demand by progressive African farmers for credit to finance land improvements. Without the use of land as collateral, colonial officials considered methods based on personal security which might be possible if information about the creditworthiness (and business acumen) of Africans was available to non-African lenders. A program was implemented in which £10,000 was provided in the annual estimates of the colony and an additional £10,000 was made available to the African district councils. Loans made from these funds were extended to Africans based on the "personal knowledge which responsible government officers had of the character and past record of the potential borrower" (EARC 1961: 101). At the field level it was monitored by the African Land Development Board and "[n]o great difficulty [was] experienced in securing the payment of interest and the repayment of the loans" (*ibid*). However, the plan could not be expanded because of limited information; that is, there were only a limited number of colonial officers at the field-level with the 'personal knowledge' necessary to determine which African farmers were creditworthy. Later, there was some expansion of the program to provide credit to African traders (*ibid.*).

ii) Land title and European-Asian collateral

Unfamiliarity with the formal financial system and the lack of collateral were not felt in any similar fashion by European settlers or Asians merchants. Rights toward land that were developed by Europeans (and used by Asians) did involve individual freehold titles, which could be used as collateral for loans. Thus, the foreign system of securing credit with collateral coincided with the settlers' and Asians' approach to land rights. As immigrants, these communities had no customary rights to land which might have restricted transferability. In particular, the Asian community was denied access to most agricultural land and was limited to business in the cities, towns and at the railway stations. Because these were mapped out under colonial administration, urban plots were given formal titles. Almost all of the urban land was held by Europeans or Asians, while Africans were largely excluded:

> The land in the towns may be held by members of all races but only holders of land in private title or of leases or licenses have a secure tenure and these are nearly all non-Africans (EARC 1961: 216).

Foreclosure and repossession in the event of default were possible by private commercial banks, as well as the Land Bank which was set up by the colonial government to support investment in agriculture. Oddly, however, default and foreclosure on European settlers were largely avoided by the intervention of the government during the 1930s when the foreign demand for Kenyan commodities slumped. Many settlers could not meet their mortgage payments to commercial banks and the Land Bank stepped in to extend additional credit to settlers who faced foreclosure.[6] Indeed the financial situation of settlers was so precarious, and likely to undermine the future of the colony, that in 1936 an ordinance was passed which prohibited banks and other private lenders from foreclosing on settlers (Berman 1990: 167).

The importance of Asian commerce was also noted in the banking system. The first bank in the protectorate was the National Bank of India which set up in Mombassa in 1898 and was a subsidiary of a bank operating in India although controlled through London. Asians (and not Africans) were involved as managers and clerks in these banks and ethnic links connected the formal banking system with the Asian business community.

iii) Asian credit networks

Along with greater formal credit access, Asians also relied heavily on their own informal networks to gain profitable returns and to sustain each other's business ventures. These arrangements were based on reputation, trust and friendship and relied critically upon the information and sanctions provided by social, personal and business networks. One of the few detailed accounts of how these networks operated is provided in the business autobiography of Madatally Manji (1995), who specialized in processed food manufacturing (biscuits, breads, pastas, sweets) during the colonial and post-colonial periods.

At two critical junctures in his business career, Manji relied on informal contacts to provide the funds needed to either buy a new business or expand production. The first situation occurred in 1941 and involved Manji's attempt to buy his first bakery. He made an agreement with the owner, a Goan, who wished to sell for sh 10,000. A friend of Manji's father had agreed to provide the financial support but then backed out when Manji was unwilling to put up his house as collateral. Taking a stroll in Nairobi to sort out his problems, Manji met an Asian friend, Mr. Shariff, who was chairman of the Aga Khan Education Board. He asked Manji to come for tea to discuss his plans for expanding Asian education in the city. It soon became apparent, however, that Manji had other pressing matters on his mind. When prodded by Shariff, Manji revealed his predicament but suggested that he needed only sh 5,000.

> When I told him how much I needed, he told me to call on him at this office on the following Monday morning. He said he would have the amount ready for me then. Shariff was a generous man and his offer to

give me the money on Monday simply stunned me into silence (Manji 1995: 41).

To obtain the other sh 5,000, Manji realized that he could sell to a wholesaler the provisions which were part of the business (it was both a bakery and a provisions store). On the proposed day of the sale, he gave the Goan sh 5,000 (from Mr. Shariff) and made an agreement to pay the rest shortly. Having acquired access to the stores, he then sold the provisions to obtain the other sh 5,000 and soon paid the seller the remaining amount.

The business proved very successful and a larger, modern factory (under the name 'Whitehouse') was built on the basis of retained earnings and the funds provided by partners. The partnership eventually proved unworkable and Manji and his brothers pulled out in 1953 to found the current House of Manji factory in the city's industrial area. To secure the required equipment, Manji made an extended trip to the UK to meet with machinery manufacturers and close a deal. He was discouraged by the prices, however: "the total cost of the cheapest among the many plants was still higher than I could afford unless I received credit" (Manji 1995: 93). He then had another chance meeting, this time with an Asian businessman from Nairobi who happened to be an agent for the established confirming house, Davis Sopper. After a meeting with a senior company official, it was agreed that Davis Sopper would confirm all Manji's orders with machinery manufacturers and make the payments in London. In addition, Manji was granted 90 days credit on the payments, that is, Davis Sopper would make the payments to the manufacturer as they fell due and Manji would have 90 days to reimburse the confirming house. For Manji, this "was a more generous deal than I had ever seen or imagined" (*ibid.*, p. 94). More importantly, the backing of the confirming house made it easy for Manji to obtain generous credit terms from his chosen manufacturer. The company (T & T Vicars) agreed to 10% down, 10% on the receipt of shipping documents and the remaining 80% spread out over 24 monthly installments at no interest (*ibid.*, p. 94–95).

These arrangements allowed Manji to have a modern food processing plant in operation by 1954 but he continued to experience "serious cash-flow difficulties" (*ibid.*, p. 100) despite access to an overdraft facility at his bank. How he overcame this re-occurring problem provides additional insights into the informal financial operations of Kenya's Asian business community. Manji frequently borrowed from other Asian friends who were in business. He used his reputation to secure the funds, without putting forward any collateral. As he explained:

> The greatest asset I had at this point was my reputation as a straightforward and trustworthy man. I decided to put it to use by borrowing money from friends without collateral. It was a risk I had to take. Fortunately, there was no dearth of friends who were willing to and even eager to come to my assistance in my hour of need. When I asked them, many of them chipped in money against 90-day bills of credit without security (Manji 1995: 100).

Asian commercial enterprise was built, in part, on familiarity with the formal systems of collateral and banking but also on the informal networks which were developed to support the urban business community. Africans too developed trading activities during colonialism but not on the same scale as the Asians (and the Europeans). Kitching (1980, pp. 186–7) has suggested that African traders constituted only a 'nascent form' of merchant capital in the colonial period, which was 'firmly subordinated to Asian and European trading activity. The two latter groups dominated the wholesale trade in manufactured goods and the import-export trade, respectively.

FORMAL CONTRACTING AND ENFORCEMENT: THE LEGAL SYSTEM

Along with political institutions, the British also introduced a legal system to secure property and enforce exchange agreements. For matters between Europeans, a Supreme Court and related subordinate courts were established to adjudicate on civil and criminal laws developed on a European basis in the colony. For Africans, the situation was much more diverse as the British attempted both to ensure colonial control of African justice while also allowing Africans some freedom to decide local disputes on their own. The British decided that all civil matters and many of the less serious criminal matters involving incidents between Africans would be dealt with under African traditional law. The more serious criminal offences (such as homicide) would be tried under colonial law, in colonial courts.

African legal matters were managed in a relatively haphazard manner until 1930 when the colony passed the Native Tribunals Ordinance.[7] The ordinance empowered the colony's district officials to establish tribunals with African judges and 141 such tribunals were in operation by 1955. Appeal of the tribunals' decisions could be made to district officers and provincial commissioners, although officials in the field had little training in African legal procedures and limited understanding of traditional law. Furthermore, British officials implemented "radical change" in the functioning of the tribunals every two or three years (Ghai and McAuslan 1970:

150). These changes affected their "composition, procedure, [and] relations with indigenous institutions or the local native authority" (*ibid.* p. 158). A detailed government investigation into the tribunals in the mid-1940s found no real understanding of African law among British officials and called for a serious effort to gain such understanding so that the tribunals could be properly managed (Phillips 1945). It is no surprise then that the tribunals had little legitimacy in the community and instead were seen as part of the overall structure of colonial control (Berman 1990: 216). Compounding the problem was the fact that they were open to manipulation and corruption. The Phillips report hinted that this corruption was fairly well known and might be seen as sufficient to support a case for eliminating the tribunal system altogether. Phillips rejected that idea, arguing:

> The native tribunals in general cannot be said to be *so* corrupt or incompetent that the government is not justified at the present stage in giving them its support and employing them as agents in the administration of justice (Phillips 1945: 319, emphasis added).

In addition, there were serious problems with the administration of justice when Africans were called before British courts. They had difficulty obtaining a fair trial against white juries which were reluctant to convict a European for an offence committed against an African. Furthermore, justice was hampered by more mundane barriers such as language and procedure, which often left African defendants with little understanding of the proceedings against them (Ghai and McAuslan 1970: 173).

In summary, while the British might have thought that they were making a contribution to African society by introducing a British approach to the administration of justice, the actual benefits were questionable. The tribunals and British courts, along with discriminatory laws, did little to instill in Africans a respect for the fairness of British justice. If anything, the opposite was likely true: that the British legal system was seen as a means of enforcing discriminatory rights between groups in a multi-racial society.

CHANGING PROPERTY RIGHTS

As with trade and credit transacting, property rights under colonialism developed through a combination of discriminatory formal rights and evolving informal rights (due to increased land pressure). Because Europeans came as settlers intent on farming, while Africans also based their livelihoods on agriculture, land was a major source of conflict between them. Property rights did undergo serious change and evolution during

Table 3.2: Landholding by race, 1903-1960 (miles^2)

Year	European*	African reserves
1903	8	-
1905	1,240	-
1910	4,484	-
1915	8,244	-
1920	-	-
1925**	8,978	46,837
1930	10,699	48,295
1935	10,294	48,345
1940	12,746	n/a
1940-60	no significant change	Rose to 52,000

Sources: Sorrenson 1968: App. 1. & 1967: ch. 2; Colonial Report, Kenya, various years

Notes: Kenya's total land area was approx. 225,000 square miles, much of which is unsuitable for surplus production in herding or cultivation. The figures here represent the allocation of more valuable areas in the south-west quadrant of the colony.

* Figures include only lands held by European settlers ("alienated") and thus exclude Crown lands set aside by the colonial government for later sale or other uses such as forest reserves or national parks. The exception is 1940 which includes both "alienated" land and a small portion of land held by the Crown and available for white settlement.

** African reserve boundaries were officially established in 1926, which this figure reflects.

colonialism but because of the discontinuous nature of colonial intrusion, they evolved only partly in the manner suggested by the evolutionary theory of property rights.[8]

European settlers took possession of land under the protection and with the support of the colony's political and military apparatus. Instead of integrating with existing farmers and land use patterns, they used state power to gain and enforce exclusive communal rights to certain areas (notably the White Highlands) and private rights within those areas. This gave them some advantages over African farmers (lack of competition for land) which allowed them to generate a surplus and ensure their differentiation from the subsistence activities of Africans. The small number of white farmers, who held large tracts of land, necessitated the employment of African labor under a *squatter* system of land rights in which Africans worked on the white farms but were allowed to grow their own produce and keep livestock on plots provided for them on these same farms. In addition, some of the poorer white farmers rented out unused land to African farmers under a system of rights called *kaffir* farming. The exclusive European zone limited the natural (extensive) expansion of Africans through the traditional process of pioneering and bringing new land under cultivation. With increasing demographic pressure in the African areas (called 'reserves') and the potential for accumulation from selling surpluses in new markets, wealthier African farmers sought to expand land holdings. To secure their holdings against further encroachment by the British as well as against demands from within their own communities, these Africans lobbied for individual rights to be secured by the colonial state. State officials, worried that private rights within the reserves would cause differentiation and social tension between the wealthy and the subsistence producers/landless (as in India), denied Africans individual property rights for most of the colonial period. Only towards the end of the period, when the need to expand African production became important, was a framework of private land rights for Africans put in place. Meanwhile, Asians were denied access to agricultural land and thus concentrated their activities on trade and manufacturing in the towns and cities. The sections which follow set out the details of these various developments.

DEVELOPMENTS ON THE EVE OF COLONIALISM

Understanding colonialism's impact on land use and property rights is difficult without reference to pre-colonial developments. In Kenya, the late 19th century was a period of dramatic demographic change, involving both expansion in certain communities and contraction in others. These dynamics affected the nature of land control by various African ethnic groups in different ecological zones. The Maasai had been able, due to effective military skills, to gain control over a vast section of the Rift Valley and use this grazing area to build up their human population and herd sizes. At the same time, cultivators at higher elevations were expanding down to lower elevations on the valley fringes. These expansions created tensions between groups and often required defensive border regions which were unsafe for habitation. Of the highland cultivators, the Kikuyu in particular were continuing a long expansion from the Mount Kenya area south and west into Kiambu and the land near the Rift Valley which was bringing them into conflict with the Maasai (cf. Sorrenson 1967, 1968).

These patterns were checked in the 1890s by profound biological and ecological shocks which temporarily reduced land pressure. In the early 1890s, a cattle plague spread south from Ethiopia and the north-east coast and killed 90 per cent of the cattle herds in sub-Saharan Africa (Iliffe 1995: 210). It devastated the economies of pastoralists such as the Maasai and of mixed pastoralists such as the Kamba. The problem was compounded by successive years of low rainfall which culminated in a major drought and the Great Famine of 1898–1900. Thus, after generations of expansion and settlement the effects of disease and drought caused a halt to African pioneering at the turn of the century.

The degree to which societies were able to recover from the shocks depended on the nature and carrying capacity of the land they controlled and the importance of livestock in their food producing repertoire. The famine temporarily pushed back Kikuyu expansion in Kiambu and in the pioneer areas of the Rift Valley. But they, like the Meru, Gusii and other cultivators, recovered relatively quickly and even added laborers to their family-work units. Members of devastated communities at lower elevations sought refuge with them. Conversely, the dominance of livestock in the food repertoire of the Maasai had more devastating effects. They did maintain a presence, however, in the well-watered areas near lakes Nakuru and Naivasha and attempted to build back their populations. It was at this point that European settlers arrived in search of land. For at least the first 15 years of the 20th century, the conflict over land (aside from that of the Maasai) was somewhat limited, although European settlers sought out those areas which Africans also desired: cleared and broken ground for cultivation and previously grazed pastures for livestock.

APPROPRIATION OF AFRICAN LAND

The colonial administration provided European settlers with a system of secure tenure in landed property. This did not arise in an evolutionary fashion from greater demographic pressure for the British took up large areas for their exclusive use, usually much more than many of them could farm. The communal rights to the White Highlands stemmed from fact that they were invaders. The private individual rights within the area were based on their previous experience with private rights in their home countries.

The major area of land appropriation was the Maasai areas of the Rift Valley. The British eliminated the Maasai threat by containing their revival after the natural shocks of the late 19th century. While the Maasai were initially the chief military ally of the British, who rewarded their support with raided livestock to rebuild herds (Waller 1976), the British quickly increased their own strength which reduced their need for Maasai support. After considerable debate within the British government in 1904–5, the Maasai were induced to sign a treaty which moved them to two reserves: Laikipia to the north-east and a southern reserve, below Ngong and the rail-line. The reserves comprised 4,770 and 4,350 square miles of land, respectively. Not content with the areas liberated for them in the Nakuru-Naivasha area, European settlers began to covet the Laikipia reserve, as well. Using threats, the British further pressured the Maasai to leave this northern reserve and relocate solely in an expanded southern reserve. This move was strongly opposed by the Maasai because the new areas had a very limited carrying capacity. Against British threats they had little option, however, and the forced evacuation was completed by 1913. In addition, about 60,000 acres (110 square miles) was taken by white settlers from 1903 to 1906 in the Limuru-Kiambu area, outside of the Rift Valley and near to present-day Nairobi. In total, by 1915 the British had appropriated over 8,000 square miles of land for European use, much of it Maasai land in the Rift Valley (Table 3.2).

The encroachment of European settlers on traditional land was, however, only part of the impact which colonialism had on access to land. While white settlement constricted African land access generally, in other ways the British opened up access for certain tribes. In and on the borders of the Rift Valley, the British tilted the balance of control against the Maasai in favor of cultivators advancing along the edges. The Gusii may have expanded their territory by 50 per cent as a result of British operations, mostly because defensive zones were no longer needed and could now be inhabited. The Kikuyu cut down the width of border forests because they were no longer needed as a first line of defense. On the coast, the Giriama also extended their cultivation and hunting areas as a result of the British security presence (Berman 1990: 58). The British ability to put a stop to raiding, a common practice among many ethnic groups in East Africa, may have "effected a profound and far-reaching revolution" on general security and the areas which could be cultivated by Africans (Low 1965: 33). Thus, the British increased the general security of property as they established their authority.

The extent of white expansion reached its limits in the mid-1920s by which time 2,000 European settlers controlled about 11,000 square miles (Throup 1987: 38–9). By contrast, the 1926 boundaries allocated 46,000 square miles to various African tribes in the central region and along the coast. There were later additions to these areas but they often included more marginal land (such as 16,000 square miles in the Maasai reserves). The total figure of African reserve land reached no higher than 52,000 square miles by the late colonial period (see Tab. 3.2). These areas were home to about 3 million Africans. Thus the establishment of formal colonial property rights, including individual tenure, reserved about one-third of the relatively good agricultural land for use by a small number of white foreigners.

These rights were required, however, to entice settlers to take up farming and make investments in their land. Sensitive to African claims, protectorate officials initially resisted the demands of European settlers for freehold tenancies and long leases. Under the Land Regulations of 1897, white settlers were only allowed certificates of occupation for a duration of 21 years. Instead, the settlers proposed leases of at least 99—if not 999—years. After considerable disagreement between officials in Kenya and London, the settlers' lobby and the desire of some officials to induce greater European settlement led to the enactment of the Crown Lands Ordinance of 1902. It declared that unoccupied land was British Crown land and would be sold to settlers in parcels of up to 1,000 acres or leased for 99 years in unlimited sizes. Many common homesteaders purchased parcels of 160 acres with the proviso that if one-third was cultivated after three years, the settler could obtain an additional 480 acres.[9] Only with these property rights could settlers be enticed to invest in farming operations in the protectorate.

INSTITUTION OF SQUATTING

While the establishment of settler property rights and the demarcation of African reserves was in no way evolutionary, it generated factor scarcities which prompted the development of squatting as an institution. This evolved in the first two decades of the century because of the opposite and complementary needs of European settlers and many surrounding African communities, notably those of the Kikuyu. Europeans had access to large tracts of land but possessed neither the labor to work the land nor the finances to hire labor. African areas were increasingly abundant in labor but lacked adequate land. As a result, Africans were allowed onto settlements in the White Highlands under a new system of land use rights known as squatting. By the 1930s approximately 110,000 Kikuyu or 20 per cent of their population were working outside of the reserves, mostly as squatters (Berman 1990: 229). Africans were required to provide a portion of their labor to the European farmer in return for the right to cultivate their own plot and raise some livestock. Squatting thus captures the dual institutional aspects of discrimination and evolution. Discrimination led to an imbalance in land/labor scarcities which promoted the evolution of an institution to compensate for that imbalance.

Squatting did not, however, relieve the underlying discrimination which was the basis for the institution and, as a result, created problems for the principal-agent relationship it entailed. It did not work well for the principals (Europeans) because the agents (Africans) were not interested in providing their required labor payments or did so only to earn the cash necessary to pay the hut and poll taxes imposed by the British. Instead of working for the European, squatters were keen to invest their energy in their own crops and livestock. As noted, the Kikuyu had been slowly moving into the valley before the British conquest and felt that the land should accrue to them. The principal-agent relationship was thus undermined by the lack of consensus on the legitimacy of the arrangement. In an effort to make squatter families provide more labor, the British administration passed the Resident Native Laborers Ordinance of 1918. It required 180 days per year of labor and in exchange the African squatter was given a minimal wage and the right to live on and use European-held land for cultivating his own crops and grazing his stock.[10] The ordinance did not halt the problems, however, and with the collapse of global demand during the 1930s, many Europeans abandoned their farms which allowed Africans to become more entrenched in their own herding and cultivation activities in European-held territory. To re-take the initiative, the colonial government passed a new Resident Native Laborers Ordinance in 1937 which allowed Europeans to impose a more onerous labor requirement on the squatters of between 240 and 270 days per year. It also restricted the number of livestock which could be grazed and the acreage which could be cultivated.

The new RNLO and the question of squatter labor itself provide examples, detailed below, of how institutions change as a result of underlying economic interests. Provisions in the new RNLO also devolved powers on squatter issues to the settler-controlled District Councils. This was prompted by two pressures; one was the increasing involvement of settlers in the administration of the colony and their desire to exercise greater political control without the interference of British officials. The other pressure was based on a more fundamental economic difference within the European settler community which generated differing attitudes towards the institution of squatting.

The differences developed between beef and dairy producers, on the one hand, and cereal and plantation (coffee, tea and pyrethrum) cultivators, on the other. In livestock areas, settlers had imported high-grade cattle and were concerned that their herds might contact diseases from local breeds. At the same time, they had little need for squatter labor on their farms. European cultivators, on the other hand, were not concerned with livestock diseases but did need African labor to work their fields and harvest crops.

While most stock owners wanted to eliminate squatters and their livestock from the Highlands, cultivators wanted to retain them. In 1945, the District Councils, pressed by influential livestock interests, moved against the squatters and drew up rules for the elimination of small stock, along with reductions in cultivation rights (Throup 1987: 94). These rights were critical to Africans because the wages they received from the Europeans were far from adequate for sustaining their households. Indeed, official estimates made at the time suggest that only 22 per cent of squatter income was derived from wages, with the rest provided through the squatter's own crops and livestock (Throup 1987: 104).

Because the districts in the White Highlands had different proportions of livestock owners and cultivators, the various District Councils approached the squatter issue differently. For example, the Naivasha Council led the campaign to reduce squatter stock and developed a strict policy backed by the wishes of dairy and beef interests who had made heavy investments in foreign breeds. The council in Trans Nzoia, by contrast, included a much larger group of plantation owners who initially accepted a rapid de-stocking plan but later forced through a delay in its implementation and then decided on a more gradual approach which allowed them to avoid heavy African protest (Throup 1987: 95–100).

The example of squatting illustrates two important points. First, even institutions founded on discrimination have an economic rationale but the discrimination can undermine the functioning of the institution. Second, when economic interests evolve or there are uneven effects on the ability of beneficiaries to accumulate, the institution will likely become a focus of tension and change.

PRESSURE WITHIN AFRICAN RESERVES

Inside the African reserves, the development of land rights did, in part, precede along the lines suggested by the evolutionary theory of property rights. The expansion of land under cultivation was constrained by reserve boundaries which blocked the traditional process of land pioneering. At the same time, the development of urban and foreign markets increased the incentive for *mbari* (extended family units) to hold on to and increase their control and use of traditional land. As suggested by standard institutional analysis, this results in a demand for more specific rights to land, enforced by an evolving political-legal system. What the theory does not provide is some direction in understanding how these changes will take place. Silence on the matter suggests that it assumes that rights will be granted across the board to all current holders or users of land. However, given that informal rights tend to involve a variety of use and ownership rights for members of the community, and furthermore, given the nature of economic and social competition, it is more likely that a uniform strengthening of rights will not occur and that some will gain at the expense of others. This is likely to occur through the natural evolution of land rights but is also heightened in a colonial situation in which officials are concerned about the process of differentiation and about securing or maintaining the support of economic and political elites within the community.

This is what appears to have taken place in the Kenyan situation. One result of increased land pressure in the reserves was that the large and expanding *mbari* no longer wished to maintain the *ahoi* (landless) and other types of land users as tenants. Instead, they were eager to use the land for their own expanding families and/or for more intensive cultivation to supply the cash crop market in Nairobi. Tenants thus were moved off the land by the large African landholders. Those who lost their rights in the reserves migrated to the White Highlands to become squatters (although, as noted, the absorptive capacity of the Highlands declined after the war). Others moved to Nairobi in search of wage employment and often ended up being unemployed. These dispossessed Africans later provided support for the militant activities against colonial rule, culminating in the Mau Mau rebellion of the early 1950s (Berman 1990: 229).

At the same time, colonial administrators were ambivalent about the granting of individual rights to African landholders. As noted in early sections, this was due to their concern that providing more exclusive rights to land would create a growing differentiation vis-à-vis subsistence farmers/the landless and create social tension. Following the war, the colonial administration did grant some rights to those larger farmers who were deemed more 'progressive' (meaning that they were collaborators with the colonial authorities) (Berman 1990: 280). Landholders were eager to secure their plots through legal, written title—which was respected by the British—as a safeguard against further colonial expropriation.

ASIAN ACCESS TO THE WHITE HIGHLANDS

In addition to African demands, the Asian community was also keenly interested in access to agricultural land in the White Highlands. Indeed, much of the political debate in the first three decades of the century involved tensions between Europeans and Asians, with land as one of several key issues. As the East Africa Royal Commission later noted, "a 'White Highlands' policy was at the outset due rather to a fear of Indian settlement than to considerations of being swamped by the African"

(EARC 1961: 19). While Asians did hold small plots of land, mostly around Nairobi, they wanted the same rights as Europeans to buy or lease large agricultural tracts (Sorrenson 1967: 162). European settlers feared Asian competition and lobbied colonial officials to restrict their access. In 1903 and 1906, statements from the Secretary of State in London provided such a restriction by ruling in favor of the Europeans (Sorrenson 1967: 162–7). Nonetheless Asians continued to press this issue, along with two other key demands (representation in the legislature and unrestricted immigration). In 1923, these issues were decided in a British policy paper known as the Devonshire Declaration which guided policy on the Asian community for most of the rest of the colonial period (Hollingsworth 1960: ch. 8). Asians were allowed access to key residential areas in the towns (they had previously been segregated from Europeans) but were refused access to the White Highlands. Asian leaders protested by boycotting the Legislative Council and by organising the withholding taxes in the late 1920s. By the early 1930s, however, they admitted defeat and gave up the boycott. The preservation of the Highlands as a white settler area was subsequently given final sanction with the Highlands Order-in-Council of the British Government in 1938.

Such differentiated property rights to land were not altered during the colonial regime and had important repercussions for Asian business development. The bar on agricultural landholding likely prevented a greater number of Asians from settling in Kenya. Those who did stay built their businesses in the urban areas in trade, transport, craft industries and, increasingly, manufacturing. The concentration of Asian business in these sectors in the urban areas continued into the independence period and much of the manufacturing in Nairobi and Mombassa is still held by Asians, along with foreign firms. Moreover the situation in Kenya contrasts with that of the Asian community in Uganda. Some of the major business families there, notably the Mehta and Madhvani groups, were able to acquire derelict plantations in the early colonial period to grow sugar and cotton. The Mehta family began in the cotton industry and then branched out into sugar by buying 5,000 acres of old plantation land from the government in the 1920s. It also acquired sisal estates, along with cotton-ginning interests, in Tanganyika which had been owned by Germans but were sold as ex-enemy property by the British after the First World War. Similarly, the Madhvani and related families were able to acquire an overgrown sugar plantation in Uganda and establish sugar factories from which their business operations expanded to include other industries and other countries in East Africa (Mangat 1969: 139).

CONCLUSION

It is not possible to understand the nature of economic activity under colonialism without reference to the discrimination exacted through colonial policy. In terms of land policy, credit restrictions and rights to engage in more lucrative activities, regulations were clearly biased against Africans and also, but to a lesser extent, against Asians. This is not surprising, for the nature of colonialism is that it discriminates in favor of the colonizer. Formal institutions set up by the colonizer are designed to support this process of discrimination and thereby to increase the capacity of settlers to reap economic gains. This process maintains and increases the level of differentiation between the colonizer and the colonized. Institution formation from this perspective is not the result of a natural evolution arising out of increasing factor scarcities, nor does it involve the provision of a equitable legal framework which guarantees a universal defense of property rights.

At the same time, the analysis of colonialism is incomplete if it dwells merely on the issue of discrimination and how it is imbedded in colonial institutions and relationships. Economic activity is also supported by informal institutional networks which facilitate the process of trade, credit provision and rights to property. These informal mechanisms help to explain the success of the Asian community in Kenya during colonialism. Inherent in these informal institutional developments, however, is a similar process in which those who have access to the institutions reap benefits and have a greater capacity to accumulate than those who are excluded.

The processes of inclusion and exclusion were part of both the informal and formal institutional processes operating under colonialism. Furthermore, they help to explain the relative economic positions of the European, Asian and African communities which emerged in the independence era. Although formal institutions now favored Africans, they could not easily overcome the variation between groups in their levels of accumulation and they could not undo the informal networks which had developed. The story of how the colonial era affected the independence era is the subject of the next chapter.

Chapter Four

Land, Agriculture and Urban Business following Independence

The transition to African rule at independence resulted in a redistribution of land in the former White Highlands. This involved a political shift in the *right* to own property and a *de facto* shift accomplished through a government supported buyout of white settlers and the acquisition of this land by Africans. At the same time, another type of property rights change was taking place in African areas in which the tenure system was changed from informal to formally titled rights. This latter change, initiated under colonialism and carried forward in the independence period, was motivated by economic concerns and the effort to increase agricultural output. It involved a change in the institutional environment in which the claims on land use and ownership shifted from the informal structures of the community to formal structures involving written deeds, registries and courts for the settlement of disputes. These two institutional changes in property rights provided the framework for agricultural activity in the independence period. They are discussed in the first part of the chapter.

Changes in the rural sector supported the creation of a wealthy landed African economic class, notably among the Kikuyu of the central highlands. Members of this group, and their partners who controlled the state, wanted Africans to expand into urban-based activities (real estate, trade and manufacturing). This intended urban advance was supported by the state in the form of legal changes and investment finance. Whether the desired transition was successful or not has been a central question of both the first and second Kenya debates, as discussed in the Introduction. The second part of this chapter explores this issue further and concludes that Africans have made little advance into formal manufacturing. Meanwhile, the Asian community has strengthened its position in manufacturing and maintained its considerable role in wholesale and retail trade.

LAND

At first, the issues of land redistribution and land titling might seem unrelated. However, the analysis which follows explains that they are intimately connected and self-reinforcing. The redistribution of land from Europeans to Africans involved the settlement of many farmers on smallholder plots but also resulted in the purchase of large white farms by more affluent Africans. Thus the redistribution reinforced and further encouraged economic differentiation in the rural sector among Africans. Meanwhile, the nature of the titling program was such that larger farms benefited from the titling program while there was a negligible impact on small farms. This also reinforced the differentiation in the rural sector and was a natural outcome of the existing differentiation that flowed from and had been reinforced by land distribution. As a result, the institutional changes involving land around the time of independence not only fulfilled their objectives of redistributing land and providing a formal framework for ownership, but they also created a rural sector differentiated by the size of landholdings.

This argument is pursued in the course of the chapter. The following section focuses on land redistribution from whites to blacks at the time of independence. The subsequent sections examine the nature of titling. A brief overview of the theory of titling is followed by a short summary of the historical implementation of the titling program. The analysis then focuses on the effects of titling in terms of four key issues: i) the development of a land market; ii) productivity; iii) the use of land as collateral for credit; and iv) the impact on ownership disputes. The analysis of titling relies on the main studies on the issue conducted to date (Okoth-Ogendo 1974; Coldham 1979; Haugerud 1989; Mackenzie 1989; Barrows and Roth 1990; Carter *et al.*, 1994; Shipton 1995).

BUYOUT OF RURAL LAND AND ITS IMPLICATIONS

The transition to independence took four years from the announcement in 1959 that Britain would relinquish colonial control to the granting of full sovereignty in December 1963. This period was used, in part, by British and African leaders to negotiate the rights of white farmers and the means by which many would vacate their farms (Leys 1975). The British sought to ensure that white farmers received fair compensation for any land that was transferred to Africans. Conversely, many African leaders advocated the uncompensated expropriation of such land. It had been a creed of the nationalist struggle that whites had unjustly taken African land and that it should be returned without compensation. How the issue was resolved—with British financial support and with an African eye to the future economic prospects of the country—provides an interesting example of the important link between property rights and investment.

The land transfer from whites to Africans was designed to reverse the property rights discrimination which had occurred under colonialism. The main objective was the transfer of European mixed farms in the White Highlands. Most of the smaller plots were transferred before or shortly after full independence while many of the larger farms were transferred by 1970. By that time Africans had gained control of formerly European held land as follows (Leys 1975):

1.6 m. acres in large farms
1.5 m. acres in small farm settlement schemes.

This left Europeans (and foreign companies) with control of:

0.75 m. acres in mixed farms
4.0 m. acres in ranches and plantations.

Those mixed farms still held by Europeans at the end of the 1960s were largely bought out by Africans over the next decade. This overall approach served a number of economic and political objectives and made for a relatively smooth transition. The foremost objective was the transfer of property to Africans to relieve the hardship and overcrowding in the former African 'reserves.' This reduced considerably the political pressure on the new leadership. In total, about 500,000 Africans took possession of land in the former White Highlands, mainly through the Million Acre and Squatter Settlement schemes. Meanwhile, the purchase, in tact, of some of the larger farms satisfied the desires of the more affluent and well-connected Kikuyu for access to large commercial properties (Leo 1984). All purchases were made on a willing seller/willing buyer basis and thus allowed those Europeans who were interested in staying to do so. Finally, by allowing Europeans to retain control of ranches and plantations, they could contribute to domestic and export production at a time when Africans were likely not in a position to buy out or otherwise manage these large estates.

To make the transition, the African leadership under Kenyatta agreed that compensation would be paid to the white farmers. The funds used by

Africans to make the purchases came from private and public sources. Estimates of these sources, based on research by Leys (1975), are as follows:

£ 12.2 m. in public loans from Kenyan government agencies
4.3 m. in grant money (from the U.K. government)
7.8 m. in savings for the purchase of large farms
5.0 m. in commercial credit obtained by the large farms
0.5 m. in savings and other credit by small farms
2.7 m. in other government sources.

Thus, in total,

£ 32.5 m. paid by Africans to Europeans for land purchase.

In addition to these funds, Africans secured development loans from government agencies for the purchase of loose assets, such as livestock and machinery, and for making investments in the newly acquired farms. The government loans made to Africans for both land purchase and development were, in turn, mostly borrowed by the Kenyan government from the UK and, in the case of development loans, from the World Bank and the West German government. By 1968, the Kenyan government had borrowed a total of approximately K£16 m. from abroad to settle Africans on land outside of the colonial 'reserves.'

This process of transition had three far-reaching consequences. At a first level, the abandonment of the exclusive property rights regime of colonialism increased the capacity for Africans to support themselves through farm production. The land redistribution, notably the settlement schemes, greatly increased the number of smallholder plots and reduced overcrowding in dense former African reserves. These smallholder plots made an increasing contribution to the country's agricultural output in the independence era. By 1967, smallholders were already contributing 49% of all marketed agricultural production and by 1995 their contribution had risen to 68.4% (Haugerud 1989: 65; KES 1996: Tab. 8.5).

At a second level, the allocation of larger land parcels to more affluent or better connected farmers confirmed and accentuated the level of rural differentiation among Africans. It allowed for the transfer of large farms from one group of owners (whites) to another (Africans) and it gave those Africans the assets necessary for greater surplus production.

At a third level, the experience of the government-assisted land buy-out had a profound impact on the view taken by the African leadership towards urban trade and manufacturing. Conscious of the need to avoid accumulating more debt and aware that Africans had limited experience in managing such enterprise, the government took a cautious approach, and one which tended to maintain the structure of accumulation and ownership between the rural and urban sectors. This resulted in the maintenance of the ethnic cleavage between Asians and foreigners in the urban sector and Africans in the rural sector. The government did implement some measures to Africanize the urban sector but these proved largely unsuccessful. The details of that experience are provided in the second part of this chapter.

CONNECTION BETWEEN REDISTRIBUTION AND LAND TITLING

Along with the redistribution of rural land following independence, another important property rights change was taking place in the form of a move from informal to formal titling of land. While redistribution and titling might appear to be two very distinct aspects of the land issue, they are in fact closely related. They are related as a result of the second point above, that redistribution accentuated rural differentiation. Such differentiation is important in understanding the impact of titling on output because titling affects large and small farms differently. Large farms tend to benefit from titling while the impact on small farms is negligible. Thus the differentiation which occurred as a result of redistribution was deepened as a result of the move to formal titling. The different affects of titling on small and large farms is not evident from most of the research done on titling but is revealed in a close examination of the evidence to date. The purpose of the following analysis is to critically examine that evidence and to highlight the impact of titling on farm activity. We do so from an institutional perspective with an emphasis on transaction costs. Our underlying idea is that more complex institutions will be more cost effective for larger productive units because the costs of transacting can be absorbed by the increased output induced by the new institutions. This relates directly to the idea that formal institutions are costly to operate and thus tend to be most beneficial to those economic units for whom these costs are supportable by the increased benefit they obtain. Smaller units, with less to gain from formal institutions, are not in a position to pay the costs of supporting them.

THEORY OF LAND TITLING

The theory of land titling suggests that pressure from commercialization, population growth and technological improvements will induce an evolution in land tenure arrangements from common to communal property and then to individual property (cf. Platteau 1996). This latter stage is commonly associated with the use of formal legal structures to recognize and enforce ownership rights. The move to formal individual tenure aids agricultural development in two main ways: i) it increases security thus reducing uncertainty, reducing the extent of disputes and prompting an increase in long term investment in the land; and ii) it increases the transferability of land which in turn both allows for the development of a land market (facilitating the allocation of land to the most efficient producers), and enables land to be used as collateral so as to increase the flow of credit and thus spur investment.

The costs of securing and transacting in land are borne both by those who own (or are acquiring) land and by the state, which provides the formal institutions to enforce ownership and its transfer. The transition to and use of formal title will be affected by these costs and by the extent to which they are borne by the government or by private landowners (Platteau 1996). If the state lacks resources or is not otherwise prepared to provide sufficient support to titling, more of the costs of the system will be borne by landowners. If the latter are required to bear a significant portion of the costs, they will do so if the expected benefits outweigh the costs. Those in a better position to gain from land titling will likely be the larger, more progressive farmers who will be able to access credit and are aware of what new investments or improvements in technology might be undertaken. Smaller, less wealthy farmers will be less inclined to take up such activities. If smallholders are obliged to obtain title and the costs are reasonable, then many may obtain title as a defense mechanism against possible disputes and to remain within the law. In these cases, titling may have limited impact on their agricultural output. Thus, the benefits of titling on output do not arise unambiguously from titling but from the support which titling provides to those who are in a position to increase investment as a result.

HISTORICAL BACKGROUND OF THE TITLING PROGRAM

Kenya's rural economy was affected by the pressures of demography, commercialization and technological advancement during the colonial period. Informal land sales were increasing and land was becoming a "scarce marketable commodity" (Barrows and Roth 1990, 270). This evolutionary process was not taking place uniformly throughout the country, however, but was "geographically concentrated" (*ibid.*) in the more densely populated areas of the Central Highlands. These areas were feeling the full effects of crowding due to White Highland boundaries and were increasingly supplying urban demands for produce. This unevenness, nationally, is important to remember because the theory of land tenure suggests that formal titling is beneficial at a certain stage of development when informal rights are no longer adequate. The benefits of a national program of titling will vary according to the level of development of specific regions.

The colonial government's desire to increase African output and colonial exports, reduce land disputes and contain political alienation prompted the move to formal titling. The program, based on the Swynnerton Plan, was begun during the Mau Mau Rebellion in the mid-1950s and involved the determination of existing rights to land, the setting of boundaries, the consolidation of fragmented holdings and the issuing of individual titles which could be enforced by the legal system. The African 'reserves' in the Central Highlands were the first areas to be titled given their level of development and the extent of overcrowding. The program was mostly completed in this area by the end of the 1950s and was continued in less densely populated provinces by African-led governments after independence. Land in Nyanza and Western provinces was mostly titled by the mid-1970s while efforts in the Eastern, Rift and Coast provinces began somewhat later. In total, over 6 million hectares of land was titled by the end of 1981, covering virtually all of the country's 4 million hectares of arable land[1] (Barrows and Roth, 1990; WDI 2000). The costs of these efforts have been substantial; total expenditure from 1956 to 1974 was about £9.7 million and the government expected to spend a similar amount by 1978 (Okoth-Ogendo 1976, 170–1).

Kenya implemented one of the most comprehensive land titling programs in Africa and as a result it has been the "most extensive and widely studied of any country" in the region (Barrows and Roth 1990, 209). Because of the scale of the operation and its explicit implementation, it provides a test case for the contribution of formal rights to economic development. The results of existing studies highlight the difficulties which have occurred as a result of imposing a formal, individualized system of rights over an existing informal system. The country brief at the world's foremost research institution on titling, the Land Tenure Centre, suggests that the objectives of land titling have "met with limited success" in Kenya (Knox 1998, 176). The sections which follow provide a clearer picture of the successes and the limitations. Before discussing these issues, a brief overview of the rural sector is provided.

Kenya's agriculture sector is an important component of its economy, directly providing 16% of GDP.[2] This figure has declined steadily from 40% at independence, and that decline has been made up almost entirely by an increase in services (mostly tourism), with little change in manufacturing or other industrial sectors. Food is an important source of foreign exchange earnings, representing 43% of total merchandise exports by value. The main exports are coffee, tea and horticultural products (table vegetables and flowers, mainly sold in Europe). The sector has steadily increased its use of modern inputs. For example, the number of tractors has grown from 5,783 at independence to 12,844 in 2002, the latter figure representing an average of one tractor per 358 hectares of arable land. Fertilizer use has also increased steadily from 5.5 kg per hectare at independence to 31 kg in 2002. The intensification of farming has produced an increase in the value added per hectare of agricultural land from US$167 at independence to US$394 in 2002.[3] Largely due to high population growth in the rural areas, value added per worker in agriculture has increased only slightly since independence.

DEVELOPMENT OF A LAND MARKET

Evidence regarding the impact of titling on creating a more fluid land market is sketchy. The general consensus is summarized by Barrows and Roth (1990, 276) who argue that "a well-functioning land market has not been created in Kenya as a result of individualized tenure and land registration." They note, however, that a "fairly robust market" had developed in more commercialized areas prior to land titling and that the number of land purchases increased considerably just prior to—i.e. in anticipation of—the titling program. The "gradually increasing trend" which began prior to titling continued thereafter. From this analysis, it is difficult to draw a specific conclusion regarding titling's impact on the land market: it may be the case either that titling has facilitated the continuation of the trend or that the trend would have continued in the absence of a move to formal titling. If institutions need to change in an evolutionary manner, then the continuation of a trend may suggest that formal titling was neither premature nor overdue.

There are aspects of rural land holding in Kenya, however, which mitigate against an active land market, either in the event of titling or not. A number of these characteristics relate more to poorer households than they do to larger farms. Poor families often have small plots and little off-farm income which means that land is the basis for subsistence and that selling land means selling the chief asset which generates food and income. Even families with access to excess land will be reluctant to sell because their land is being held in trust for the next generation. As Haugerud (1989, 67) notes, "family retention of land for partible inheritance and for subsistence purposes limits the land market in densely settled zones." Land also provides community membership, social status and political influence. When families do sell land it is often because they are forced by circumstances in which they need to pay debt or secure resources. The sale of land often forces a greater dependence on wage labor as the main income source. Hardship sales may also arise from the death of the male head; a widow sells land because she may not be able to continue to farm it (Barrows and Roth, 1990, 277).

The land market has also been constrained by the actions of Land Control Boards, which from 1982 onwards[4] were instructed to use their powers to prevent the sale of land without the consent of all family members. The Boards require that all family members be consulted on the sale of land to ensure that one or more unscrupulous family members were not agreeing to sales without the consent of the others. The enhanced powers were also designed to reduce those forced sales which would render families destitute. As a result of these activities, it has been argued that the government has not allowed the market in land to fully develop (Barrows and Roth 1990; 276; Haugerud 1989).

While sales did take place prior to the introduction of titling, the evidence suggests that the large majority of sales which took place afterwards were based on the new formal system. Coldham (1979) found that most sales involved the formal registration of new owners, an indication that buyers wanted to have both *de facto* and *de jure* control of the land. Some 70% of land sales in East Kadianga (Nyanza) and 85% in Gathinja (Central Province) were registered, according to the study. These transactions took place in the 1960s and 1970s when the system was still fairly new and they occurred despite the costs, time and complications involved in registering the sales transactions. The study in Embu, on the north-east side of Mount Kenya, also found that sales through formal titles were taking place.

The problem with analyzing the influence of titling on the development of a land market is that there are no counterfactuals against which comparisons might be made. Land transfers were being made during colonialism and would likely have continued without formal titling. Land Control Boards and the needs for, and attachments to, traditional landholdings have constrained the full development of a land market but these factors are not specifically related to formal titling. If anything, the increased use of LCBs may suggest that the market was developing too rapidly and was being constrained to preserve an element of social stability in some rural areas.

The more important question is whether the land sales which did occur resulted in an expansion of output due either to a shift to owners who have brought previously unused land into production or a shift to producers who are more efficient than the previous owners. The studies on titling in Kenya have provided little statistical evidence to compare land use before and after sale. Several authors have suggested that land purchases have often not been used for cultivation. Haugerud (1989, 77) notes that in the early 1980s in Embu "more than half" of land purchasers were cultivating "less than two thirds" of their total land. These approximations are not very meaningful, however, unless we know how much of the purchased land was in cultivation prior to sale. If all of it was, then its sale resulted in a decrease in production, whereas if none of it was, then its sale would have resulted in an increase in production. A study based in Kisii found that 45% of purchasers were full-time farmers, suggesting that new land would be used to expand production (quoted in Barrows and Roth 1990, 277). The remainder were traders (41%) or government employees who would be less likely to farm the land but they could rent it out. Here again it is unclear whether the land was previously in productive use. The study noted that sale by widows "was a typical case," suggesting that land might not have been maintained in production. The Kisii study noted that "many" land purchasers had not put the new land into production even ten years after acquisition and "in a few cases, holdings were never cleared." If holdings were not cleared, then it was likely that they were not in use prior to purchase.

Barrows and Roth (1990, 277) argue that the reasons for land purchase are often not related to immediate production. The main motivations behind purchase are: inheritance for children; allocation of a parcel to a wife in a polygamous marriage; speculation; and "least important, to acquire a source of revenue." It might be noted that purchases of land for inheritance or new wives do constitute the expansion of family output, even if, in the former case, production may be undertaken some time in the future. The sale by recent widows is also a case in which the sale of the land allows for production to be maintained. This leaves speculation as the major source by which land might be taken out of production. This would only be the case, however, if the land had been in cultivation and was being taken out. Speculation does not preclude production, which can be undertaken through rental.

To conclude the evidence from existing studies is too general, lacks the necessary supporting data and is methodologically too simple to assess whether titling has channeled land to more efficient producers or brought land into production. While it is clear that there are features of the smallholder sector which would tend to limit the extent of land sales, there is no evidence that larger producers have not been using titling to expand production. The only major concern is that land is being held temporarily fallow for inheritance or for speculative purposes.

PRODUCTIVITY

An equally important question is whether titling has increased agricultural output by supporting greater investment. Except for one detailed study, there has been little analysis of investment/productivity issues. The study of Embu concluded that there is "no striking differences in farming techniques among larger and small farmers" (Haugerud 1989: 76). Larger farms are assumed here to have been created through purchase, which was facilitated by titling. The study does not provide a measure of productivity but suggests that larger farmers are more apt to use animal traction (as opposed to no traction), although smallholders tend to use slightly more fertilizer. It notes that for Kenya, "there is no conclusive data concerning the relationship between farm size and land and labor productivity" (*ibid.*). The issue of productivity is not addressed by Coldham (1979), Mackenzie (1989) or Okoth-Ogendo (1976). The literature review by Green (1987) does not deal with the issue directly but does highlight the problem of distinguishing titling effects from other efforts to develop agriculture in the independence period:

> The issue is particularly difficult because it is hard to determine to what extent increases in productivity over a certain period have been due to land registration and to what extent they have been due to other causes. In Kenya, the many new programs and opportunities which accompanied independence have made this distinction especially difficult (p. 20).

The only way to overcome this problem is to obtain data which distinguishes between titled and untitled land and then to control for other possible factors.

This method is used in the detailed, econometric study conducted by Carter *et al.* (1994). It is based on a data survey of 109 farms in the Njoro area of the Rift Valley, formerly of the White Highlands. The mean size of farms is 9.5 acres but they range from very small units of under one acre to larger ones of up to 80 acres. A division of the sample into titled and untitled farms indicates that maize yields were found to be 23% higher on titled farms (1125 kg/acre) as against untitled ones (912 kg/acre) (*ibid.*, p. 145). Not only was land productivity found to be higher but profit per acre was also higher for titled land regardless of whether family labor (high on untitled plots) was costed at shadow prices or not costed at all. These figures provide evidence that titling is correlated with—and therefore might cause—higher productivity. The researchers argued, however, that this initial statistical analysis is "naïve" because other factors, notably market access as proxied by farm size, were not taken into account. When the sample was divided into size categories, descriptive statistics revealed that farms of 3–5 acres produced an average of 782.5 kg/acre compared with farms of 20 acres or more which reaped 1,756 kg/acre. As a result, the titled/untitled distinction and small/larger distinction could both explain differences in productivity. Greater efficiency may occur *on* titled land, but this does not necessarily support the argument that it is occurring *because of* titling, especially when we know that titled farms are also larger.

Regression analysis was used to determine the relative significance of the size and title variables and the results show the title variable as insignificant while size was significant against dependent variables of output, family income and profit per acre (*ibid*, p. 167). The results suggest that it may not be title *per se* but the impact that it has on size which allows for higher output. Why might size affect per unit output? The researchers suggest that it is related to 'market access,' which is defined as the "terms on which a farm unit can gain access to capital and participate in other commercial relationships" (*ibid.*, p. 151). Larger farms are better able to access factor suppliers (who charge less) and commodity buyers (who pay more) than is the case with the smaller farms. It is not clearly stated why this should be but, because it involves 'commercial relationships,' it does point to the costs of transacting. The larger farms are better able to provide collateral, may purchase and sell larger quantities and might have more frequent dealings, over a longer time period, with input suppliers and commodity buyers. These factors decrease the per unit costs of transacting. Because of such market access, titling may be more beneficial to larger farms because new land can be purchased and the costs of titling for the farmer can be supported from the increased output because overall costs are lower due to increased market access. (No figures are provided on the per unit costs of inputs or the prices paid for commodities, however.)

The factors affecting productivity may be more complicated than merely market access, however. The researchers note that larger farms plant more lucrative crops. All farmers tend to allocate their first 4–5 acres to inter-cropping maize and beans (mainly for household food supply), while excess land is put into pasture and fodder crops (to support dairy). Any land in excess of 15 acres is used for high-earning cash crops (*ibid.*, p. 157). Large farms, with more titled properties, allocate a larger percentage of land to wheat, which is not grown by smaller untitled farms because of the lack of excess land.

To conclude, the existing literature is rather mute on the issue of whether titling leads to increased productivity. The one study which addresses the issue in a direct and methodologically sound manner suggests that titling may support increased productivity by allowing good farms to increase in size, which in turn increases both market access and the capacity to plant a greater proportion of more highly profitable cash crops. What is only briefly noted is that titling itself is related to market access because the use of land as collateral increases access to external finance. It is to this aspect of titling that we now turn.

COLLATERAL FOR CREDIT

Credit is another area in which it is important to distinguish between the size of farms. Most studies reveal that the majority of smallholders have not used their titled land as collateral to obtain credit. The minority of farms which are using title for credit are larger farms. This represents not so much an inherent problem of titling *per se*, but a problem of establishing formal institutions in a rural environment which is not sufficiently developed to make it worthwhile.

The study in Embu found that 15% of titleholders (225 out of 1545) had taken out loans against their land (Haugerud 1989: 78). Such loans ranged in size from a few hundred to several thousand shillings and were contracted from government agencies and commercial banks. Among the cotton growing farms, some 62% (31 of 50) of the loans which were secured were obtained by those who had purchased the land subsequent to the initial registration of titles. A study among the Luo in South Nyanza, found that by 1981, four years after titling had been completed, 6% of land titles (77 of 1,242) had been used to obtain agricultural credit (Shipton 1995, 171). A review of the loan portfolio of the Agricultural Finance Corporation (AFC), the government's chief creditor to the rural sector, revealed that in most districts less than 2% of titleholders were receiving loans in any one year (Okoth-Ogendo 1976, 175).

One of the main reasons for not using titled land as collateral is that smallholders do not want to take the risk of default and the loss of land because, as noted, it constitutes their main productive asset, source of standing in the community and the place where their ancestors are buried. In addition, the importance of land in rural communities often results in community efforts to resist foreclosure by banks, making the latter even less likely to offer credit. Shipton notes that,

> [s]ince men live with relatives and ancestral spirits all around their homes and farms (and some have dependent . . . land clients too as potential supporters), it is practically impossible for financial institutions to take

> away their lands when they default. . . . Farmers have become reluctant to seek the loans [and] financiers to grant them (Shipton 1995: 171–2).

In the 1970s and early 1980s, efforts to auction off land obtained as a result of loan default sparked community riots. On several occasions President Moi was forced to impose long moratoria on such auctions to maintain social stability (*ibid.,* p. 172). By the mid-1970s, the AFC was increasingly resorting to threats as the only means to attempt to secure repayment (Okoth-Ogendo 1976, 195). It was also during this time that the Land Control Boards were strengthened to ensure that unscrupulous family members were not selling land without the consent of other members or that land would not be seized in the case of default if it left family members with inadequate land to maintain subsistence.

The use of land as collateral works better with larger landholders because they have more separately titled plots and the loss of any one plot will not jeopardize the family's survival. Furthermore, pledging titled land as security is often only a necessary not a sufficient condition for obtaining credit. Off-farm income, notably from an urban salary, and social standing are also important considerations for lending agencies (Okoth-Ogendo 1976, 175). In addition, banks often decline to provide credit to smallholders because the loan size is too small for lending income to cover the transactions cost. This latter is part of the general problem of lending to small productive units, be they in agriculture or other sectors. When lending institutions have limited personnel, they will tend to concentrate their lending on high growth areas, such as, in the case of Kenya, the Central Highlands (*ibid.*).

The study by Carter *et al.* (1994) specifically tested for whether higher investment, leading to greater productivity, on titled land were due to security effects or credit effects. Security effects arise when a farmer feels more secure about his landholding and thus more willing to make longer-term investments in the land. Credit effects are related to the use of land as collateral, as discussed. The results indicated that the "the provision of legal title has little effects on the farmers' perceptions of the security with which they hold land" and that the increased investment on titled land is due to credit effects (*ibid.*, p. 165). Because this survey is more detailed and contains a greater range of farm sizes, it suggests, over the evidence from the other studies reviewed, that land may be useful as collateral for larger farms.

REDUCTION IN DISPUTES

The evidence suggests that the disputes over land have not decreased as a result of titling and may, in fact, have increased. Here again we encounter the problem of counterfactuals. From the mid-1950s to the 1980s (the time covered by many of the studies), Kenya was experiencing a population growth rate of nearly 4%, among the highest in the world, and was making important advances in increasing agricultural output. The number of disputes would be expected to rise under these circumstances regardless of whether a program of formal titling was implemented or not. The extent to which the titling program may have reduced the rise in disputes, or added to it, is almost impossible to gauge and no figures of this nature are found in the literature.

Haugerud's study in Embu suggests that the level of disputation has increased rather than declined as a result of the overlap of the two systems, formal and informal. She concluded that "growing conflict over access to and disposition of land titles divides families and strains resources of all levels of the Kenyan legal system, from local elders and assistant chiefs to government courts" (Haugerud 1989: 80). The usefulness of titles in reducing disputes is based in good measure on keeping the registry up-to-date. Here the formal system has failed in making its procedures understood, easy to use and economically accessible so as to ensure a reliable, on-going record for disputants and the authorities. The difficulty of keeping the registry current occurs when land changes hands, which is done either through sale or inheritance. Coldham (1979) found that inheritors were particularly negligent in registering new titles: only 3.4% of inheritances in Kadianga (Nyanza) and 21.4% in Gathinja (Central Province) were registered by the early 1970s. As a result, "the register fails to reflect what is happening on the ground" (*ibid.*, p. 618). He suggested that low registration of inheritance transfers may be the result of the "complex procedures" set out in the 1963 law governing such transfers. He concluded that, "given the bureaucratic hurdles which have to be overcome, the fees that are payable at each stage of the process, and the likelihood that several years will pass before matters are finalized, it is not surprising that so few successions are registered" (Coldham 1979: 619).

The registration of sales was much higher (70–85%), although any non-registration tends to make the entire system less reliable. Coldham suggests that for the formal system to be effective, it "would require the establishment of enforcement machinery on a scale that would be impractical in present day Kenya" (*ibid.* p. 626). This suggests, again, that the costs of establishing and maintaining the institutions must be weighed against the benefits. If smallholders find formal institutions of little help in increasing investment and output, then it is unlikely that they will go through the expense of ensuring their titles are properly registered. Large farms, which do benefit, are more likely to take the time and make the effort.

SUMMARY

We set out to determine, using the available research, whether Kenya's program of rural land titling has had an important impact on rural economic performance. The existing evidence on which to conclude such an inquiry is limited. It does appear, however, that titling has been important for larger farms, which can use land titles to facilitate the purchase of land and can use land as collateral to obtain credit and make investments. These effects have not been shared by smallholders, however, who find it much more difficult to secure capital for land purchase or investment and are not predisposed to use land as collateral. Where they are willing to put up land as collateral, their small size makes it costly for banks to transact with them. We need to rely on the detailed statistical analysis of one important study, that by Carter *et al.* (1994), to conclude that titling supports the activity of large farms. On many issues, it is difficult for researchers to provide counterfactuals: what would have happened in Kenya's rural areas, especially its more populous ones, if titling had not been introduced. The theory of property rights suggests that a formal system is beneficial at a particular stage in the development of a rural economy. This occurs when the existing informal structure of land tenure is inadequate to deal with disputes and with the need for land transfer. It does appear that some producers have reached this stage.

The titling process has reinforced the economic differentiation which was set down at the time of independence. The redistribution of land from whites to blacks involved the parceling of land into smallholder and into larger farm plots, thus solidifying a process of differentiation which had been developing in the colonial period. Thus the two major property rights changes which took place around the time of independence (redistribution and titling) reinforced rural differentiation and supported the development of a wealthy landed African economic class. This class and its partners in government were behind a number of changes to *urban* institutions designed to support an African advance into trading and manufacturing. The particular nature of that process, involving Asians as well as Africans, is analyzed in the sections that follow.

URBAN SECTOR FOLLOWING INDEPENDENCE

Independence gave Africans control of the state and allowed them to alter those aspects of the formal institutional environment which had curtailed their activities during colonialism. As noted, they used the state to gain control of the White Highlands. They also altered the institutional environment in the urban sector in an attempt to *Africanize* trade and manufacturing. Unlike the rural sector, however, Africans had limited experience in urban business, had established few formal sector firms and had no developed networks either amongst themselves or with non-African business. These other firms had obtained a large head start and it was unclear how helpful the state might be in overcoming the disadvantages facing Africans.

These two issues, changes in the control of formal institutions and the resilience of informal (notably Asian) business networks, form the basis for the analysis in the sections that follow. It is argued that the changes in the control of formal institutions had relatively little impact on African involvement in formal sector business, notably in manufacturing. Thirty-five years after independence, Africans are still largely excluded from this sector. We begin the discussion with an examination of the impact which the buyout of rural land had on the views and actions of the African leadership regarding urban business.

IMPLICATIONS OF THE RURAL LAND BUYOUT

The experience of the government-assisted land buyout had a profound impact on the view taken by the African leadership towards urban trade and manufacturing. Rural land passed from European to African hands as a result of a compensated buyout. This created a public sector debt burden which inhibited the government from embarking upon a similar program to Africanize urban business. The public debt incurred from the land buyout represented nearly one-fifth (19%) of all new foreign debt contracted by the government between 1961 and 1968. It was expected that by 1970, the government would be paying K£1.4 m. in debt service for these settlement schemes. As a result, the new African government voiced serious misgivings about the value gained from saddling the country with a foreign debt, which would "pose a heavy burden on the rest of the country and hold up the development of other sectors" (Kenya 1965b: 151). The main economic policy framework at the time spelt out in simple terms the regret that was being felt in government circles regarding the land program: "It is unlikely that Kenya, in accepting the debt burden [for land settlement] has obtained economic benefits of anywhere near the amount of the debt incurred" (Kenya 1965a: 37).

Learning from the experience, the African leadership decided not to embark upon a similar process of buying out non-African commercial and industrial establishments. At the same time, it ruled out an uncompensated buyout for fear that it would hamper future investment (and aid).

It could undertake a different strategy from the farm buy-out, in part, because there was far less political pressure for the government to redistribute urban assets.

The government justified its position by arguing that its primary objective was growth and that "if Africanization was undertaken at the expense of growth, our reward will be a falling standard of living." Nationalization of industry and commerce would fail the 'growth test' on three accounts: it would lead to a loss of financial resources, a loss of skilled personnel and a loss of inward investment. As the report noted:

> The money paid for nationalized resources and the people who managed them before nationalization would most likely leave the country increasing our foreign exchange and skilled manpower problems. There is also the firm likelihood that nationalization would discourage additional private investment thus reducing further the rate of growth of the economy (Kenya, 1965a: 26).

The report specifically stated that inexperienced managers would likely lead nationalized firms into bankruptcy, resulting in Africanization being a "temporary rather than a lasting phenomenon" (*ibid.* 28). To further reassure expatriates, the government passed the Foreign Investment Protection Act, 1964, only one year after formal independence.

EFFORTS AND OUTCOMES OF AFRICANIZATION

The government did maintain the objective of promoting a greater African presence in the urban economy, however. This it did by buying equity stakes in foreign subsidiaries, by supporting state enterprise and by providing finance to new private African firms. In addition and by far the most controversial measure was the enactment of the Trade Licensing Act in 1967.

The TLA restricted the sale of specific goods in specified areas to Africans. It required that non-citizens (often interpreted to mean non-Africans) could not trade outside of core business areas in the cities and towns in a list of (mostly basic) commodities. In consequence a large number of Asian-owned businesses had to be vacated with the express intent that they would be taken over by Africans. The focus was on retail trade although it was directly linked to the wholesale trade, much of it controlled by Asians. In 1974, the act was amended to include the manufacture of some basic commodities but this was repealed two years later.

One of the chief problems with the implementation of the act was the lack of an adequate number of Africans willing to take over Asian shops. By 1971, the Minister for Commerce and Industry was telling parliament that many firms owned by non-Africans were being closed but that few Africans were coming forward to take them over. He noted that in Nairobi and Mombassa 262 shops had been required to cease operations (given 'quit notices') but that only 63 Africans had made application to take them over. Thus, the institutional environment was supportive of African entry but Africans themselves were not taking up these opportunities (Ikiara 1988).

A similar problem occurred regarding industrial development. The Kenya Industrial Estates (KIE), a government agency, established industrial areas with worksheds in the major cities and towns to support African entry into small-scale manufacturing. In a review of the program in the mid-1980s, it was found that while the sheds in Nairobi were occupied, only 8 of the 22 sheds in Mombassa were filled some ten years after they had been established. A similar government program in the 1970s involved the establishment of Rural Industrial Development Centers but it too met with limited success as the centers were largely unoccupied by the mid-1980s (Ikiara, 1988: 233).

The government also established or carried over from the colonial era a variety of financial institutions and credit programs to support Africanization. Major ones included the Development Finance Company of Kenya (DFCK), the Industrial and Commercial Development Corporation (ICDC), the Industrial Development Bank (IDB) and the loans program of the KIE. The government also nationalized (with compensation) two foreign banks and merged them to create the Kenya Commercial Bank. It also established a wholly new bank, the National Bank of Kenya. An important part of the mandate of these development and commercial banks was to support the Africanization of private commerce and manufacturing by supplying finance to African businessmen.[5] These banks soon found however that "most indigenous entrepreneurs did not have adequate resources for such large undertakings" and that there was little for the banks to support (Ikiara 1988, 228). For example, neither DFCK nor the IDB would provide loans below a minimum of Ksh 400,000 and the IDB would not invest in any project which had a value of less than Ksh 1 million. Because Africans had not built up large enterprises, they were denied access to these loan programs. By the early 1970s program administrators realized that they needed to redesign their programs to suit the small-scale nature of the new African entrepreneurs.

These new schemes did not generate the success envisaged however. The ICDC divided its loans program into two categories, one involving medium and large loans which went to companies in which the ICDC itself held some equity, and the other, a small loans scheme, for firms in which ICDC had no equity. Loans under the first category were extended mostly to non-African firms and were considered highly recoverable, with the equivalent of 9.6% of the outstanding loan value set aside for bad or doubtful debts. The situation with the small loans scheme was much different, however. The ICDC's annual report for 1994, not an untypical year, indicated that a full 55% of its total portfolio (K£910.5) was considered by the corporation to be bad or doubtful (ICDC 1994). The KIE experienced similar problems with its lending and industrial estates programs for small African businesses. The entire program collapsed in the early 1980s because it was able to recover only a very small portion of its loans. The organization was only later revived in a scaled down version (minus the estates) with the help of the German aid agency, GTZ.[6] Even when these various credit programs reduced the size of the loans available to small firms, they were also still too large for African entrepreneurs. A review of the lending activities of the Rural Industrial Development Program in the mid-1970s revealed that the average loan size was Ksh 27,000 whereas the mean value of machinery and other equipment owned by the firms who came to the RIDP for assistance was only Ksh 3,000. The loans were channeled to a few select businesses, with over half of the loan portfolio used to purchase generators, instead of small tools and equipment (Livingstone 1976, 500).

This evidence from specific government programs is in line with the more general conclusions which were being voiced in the early 1990s regarding the outcome of Kenya's attempts to Africanize industry. In a review of the 'Kenya debate,' Colin Leys noted in the early 1990s that "Africans (as opposed to Kenyan Asians) were still virtually unrepresented in manufacturing" (Leys 1994: 235). Himbara's survey (1994) of 100 large manufacturing firms in the late 1980s showed that over 80% were owned by Kenyan Asians and that many of the remainder were owned by the state or foreign firms. My own survey, detailed in the following chapters, also revealed that Africans are under-represented in small-scale manufacturing and dominate only micro and informal sector activities. Thus, one of the main conclusions from the first Kenya debate also holds for the second debate: Africans have made little advance into the formal manufacturing sector. This is despite the fact that they have made advances in capital accumulation beginning in the late colonial period (Cowen 1981; Swainson 1980; Leys 1982A).

EXPLAINING AFRICAN BEHAVIOR

The lack of a significant African presence in the urban formal sector, despite the government's promotion efforts, suggests that the development of an effective urban entrepreneurial class from an indigenous people involve much more than providing support programs. The development of such a class will be inhibited by a number of barriers inherent in the group and the development process, and not readily overcome through government support.

First, few Africans had had exposure to urban business and thus lacked knowledge of their operations and familiarity with related markets. The Asian community began to build its activities and knowledge from the 1920s and as first movers set up in areas where there was little existing competition.

Entrepreneurial Africans also had strong incentives to focus on activities such as agriculture in which they were successful instead of diverting their energies into activities in which they lacked experience and expertise. Indeed, research by Cowen (1981; 1982) on the colonial period has indicated that surplus accumulation for Africans took place primarily in the agricultural sector. If a surplus was generated in agriculture, it was logical that it would be re-invested in that sector instead of being channeled into risky ventures in manufacturing, for instance. In the independence period the Kenyan government had, at least initially, maintained policies which allowed farmers to take advantage of high international prices for primary commodities such as coffee and tea. Entrepreneurial African farmers were accumulating capital in agriculture and were re-investing in agriculture. It is erroneous to equate 'entrepreneurial' with urban or non-farm activities because farming is also a productive activity in which the factor inputs need to be marshaled in an efficient manner and the output properly marketed to generate a return. If a large number of Africans did not come forward to buy Asian firms or take up places in government industrial parks, it does not follow logically that there was/is a lack of African entrepreneurs. Instead, African entrepreneurs in the rural sector have decided not to leave their activities.

A proper comparison of the business success of Asians and Africans would need to involve a comparison of the sectors in which each group is dominant. While Africans appear not to have penetrated formal manufacturing to an significant extent, it is also true that the high growth period in the first two decades of independence was based on agriculture, notably coffee and tea exports. As Chege has recently argued,

> In assessing the country's outstanding performance from 1964 to the mid-1980s, the engine of growth by all professional accounts lay not in immigrant groups but in African-run smallholder agriculture (Chege 1998, 220).

He notes that output per hectare of coffee in Central Province compares favorable with other producing countries such as Columbia, India and Indonesia. Detailed research suggests that there were considerable efficiency gains from investments in capital and reductions in operating costs in tea production through much of the independence period (*Ibid.*, pp. 220–1). This needs to be taken seriously as agriculture has accounted for between 30–40% of GDP for most of the independence period, while manufacturing has accounted for only 10–12%. (If there is a transition taking place in the Kenyan economy it represents a movement from agriculture to services, notably tourism).[7] The focus on manufacturing, both in the original Kenya debate and in the work by Himbara, may represent an older tradition of analysis which equates economic progress with industrialization and implicitly may equate economic development with the leading business group engaged in manufacturing. There is no logical reason to make this connection, notably for economies in which the development of agriculture has not reached its full expansion and potential.

Africans were also capitalizing on new opportunities to invest in land, which were provided by the end of colonialism. We have noted the large investments by Africans in obtaining parcels in the former White Highlands during the 1960s and into the 1970s. Land purchase is not only useful for expanding production, but it represents a good store of value and provides non-economic value in African communities, even if not put to productive use. As Leys noted in the early 1990s, "land is still the most reliable source of capital accumulation by the Kenyan African bourgeoisie, as well as a source of security, social status and political influence" (Leys 1994, 232). In those areas of traditional habitation such as the former African reserves where the availability of land for sale declined in the independence period, farmers with a surplus made investments in urban land. Such surplus generation and re-investment will be missed in surveys focusing solely on manufacturing.

Along with land, Africans have tended to enter non-agricultural sectors which are less risky than manufacturing. These activities include real estate development, construction and transport. In these areas, assets tend to retain their value, there is limited investment in machinery/technology and there are limited requirements in terms of training and knowledge of techniques. Swainson's (1980: 185) detailed study of ownership during the transition to independence concluded that "the primary source of accumulation of capital in the post-colonial period has been real estate, farming, transportation and commerce." It might be added that that statement also contains a fairly accurate ordering of importance of those activities. Heyer has also noted that the agricultural surplus has been channeled into 'trade, transport and other non-agricultural businesses in the rural areas' (quoted in Sharpley 1981, p. 317). This is not a specifically Kenyan phenomenon, as the local population in other African countries and other parts of the developing world has tended not to move directly from farming into urban manufacturing. Instead a process of learning and capital accumulation is first conducted through these other activities (see Forrest, 1994, on Nigeria). A specific focus on manufacturing will fail to highlight these other areas of African investment.

Evidence drawn from unsuccessful government support programs must also not be treated uncritically. It may provide evidence of either unsuccessful attempts by Africans to enter urban business or the moral hazards created by the Africanization program itself. The strong political pressure to achieve Africanization may have encouraged program administrators and loan officers to extent loans without stringent scrutiny of investment proposals, effective monitoring of loan use or adequate efforts to ensure repayment. This may have encouraged people to come forward who were not fully committed to their new ventures but realized that funds were available and repayment could be avoided. According to interviews conducted by Ikiara (1988 233–4), senior credit managers at KIE felt that African entrepreneurs showed a "lack of commitment," acted as absentee entrepreneurs while focusing on other activities and often hired inexperienced managers to run their new enterprises. This is not evidence of a lack of entrepreneurship *per se*, but a preoccupation with other economic activities, possibly combined with a willingness to source easy government credit.

There may also have been important entry barriers for Africans wishing either to take over Asian firms under the TLA, or otherwise establish themselves in sectors and urban locations dominated by Asians. What has not been adequately discussed in the literature on the TLA is whether the Asian community used its economic position to covertly undermine African entry. Many Asians did leave the country in the 1970s as a result of the TLA[8] but others adopted Kenyan citizenship to remain within the legal requirements and they, along with those who retained British citizenship, may have employed other tactics to guard their business positions. The report of a government committee on Africanization in the early 1970s did suggest that non-Africans were using whatever means they could to prevent African entry into urban business. It noted that "serious loopholes . . . have been exploited by the immigrant communities to their best advantage" to overcome the requirements of the TLA. One method was the refusal to rent business premises to Africans or to rent them out only at inflated rates (quoted in Swainson 1980: 192). Given the heavy Asian presence in urban land ownership, this may have constituted an important barrier.

It is also possible that Africans were deterred from entry by the presence of informal networks which were dominated by Asians (and Europeans). This could have been used by Asians if they felt a general antipathy towards Africans because of the TLA, but there are also economic-institutional reasons why, for example, trade credit might not have been extended or information about markets, technologies or factor inputs may not have reached the new entrants. Indeed, from the institutional perspective business is not just about possessing capital, being able to hire workers and having some entrepreneurial talent. It also involves access to low-costs networks with suppliers and customers which channel information and provide a means to enforce agreements. New entrants would be excluded from these agreements because they had not yet developed their reputations with suppliers and customers. They would have lacked an established reputation with the result that they would be at a disadvantage relative to established firms. At least in the first decade and a half of independence, Kenya's Asians and Africans were in opposite positions. Asians lacked government support but were established in urban business in both trade and manufacturing and were supported by informal networks. Africans had access to government support but lacked the experience, established presence and network connections.

The network argument can only go so far in explaining the difference in the ethnic presence in urban activities, however. It needs to be assessed against the possibility of Africans forming their own networks. In previous chapters, we have noted the development of African informal institutions in rural areas. There would need to be specific reasons why they could not be developed in the urban sector. There were connections among the emerging Kikuyu business interests following independence. There might be barriers to entry because many of the suppliers were non-African. If we say that ethnic cohesion is useful in the business community, then it is unclear why it would not apply to all ethnic groups, instead of just Asians. It would take some time for these to be established, however.

Those Africans who did enter urban manufacturing might have felt the influence of being outside of informal networks because of their small size and lack of formal status, not simply because they were African. The African manufacturing sector which has developed has been comprised of poor migrants. Kenya did not lack entrepreneurs; it lacked entrepreneurs with sufficient capital to make a go of it in the formal, urban sector. The term 'informal sector' came into widespread use in development circles following an ILO study on Kenya in the late 1960s and early 1970s which analyzed the possible importance of this sector for labor absorption (ILO 1972). A study by SIDA at about the same time estimated that there were up to 25,000 informal sector 'industrialists' operating in the country, employing as many as 70,000 people (quoted in Livingstone 1976, 497). Because these entrepreneurs were often urban migrants, they had limited funds with which to invest in technology, build factor inventories and utilize either formal sector business premises or those rented out on government industrial estates. They entered the sector not as a diversification strategy to expand a family's rural activities but as a means of survival if they had no land or their (expanding) family had little prospect to expand agricultural activities. Following migration, they faced high urban unemployment in the formal sector and so took to the informal sector to earn an income. By 1994, the number of people engaged in the informal sector throughout the country surpassed that of the formal sector for the first time (1.79 m to 1.51 m; KES 1996, Tab 4.1). The government's annual economic report noted that "it is possible that its growth merely reflects a shift from open-unemployment to that of underemployment in the informal sector" (KES 1996, 62). Their efforts to generate a surplus are not only affected by the lack of resources but also the competition of similar migrants. The country's high population growth rate and the limited possibilities for land expansion in many areas have spawned an informal manufacturing and petty trade sector which comes as close to the textbook case of perfect competition as one is likely to encounter. The call on their resources from family commitments in the rural sector also inhibits the accumulation of surplus for re-investment.

The nature of these firms makes it difficult for them to develop supporting networks with more established formal sector firms or with other informal African firms. Because of their large numbers, the high levels of entry and exit and the lack of formal business premises among informal sector firms, Asians firms find it difficult to distinguish among them and to develop long-term relationships. These same factors, notably the high failure rate, make it difficult for them to establish networks with other African firms, although the more established ones are able to do so. Government efforts, notably in the first two decades, focused on larger scale firms and even the small-scale loan schemes were out of reach for micro-entrepreneurs, as noted. Indeed, sometimes these small enterprises were the subject of specific discriminations particularly when located on vacant public land which had to be cleared for redevelopment. Major clearances took place in Nairobi in the late 1980s and early 1990s for redevelopment. King (1996, 32) notes that since the 1950s one of the major factors affecting the development and permanence of informal sector areas has been "slum and shanty town" clearance activities of the municipal and sometimes national governments.

In summary, the explanation for the limited entry of Africans into urban manufacturing likely falls on the coincidence of a strong Asian presence and associated networks and the traditional strengths of Africans in agriculture and related activities. There has been a limited tendency for the more successful farmers to enter urban business because they have lacked experience in that area and instead they have focused on re-investment in more familiar activities. Those Africans who have entered urban manufacturing and trade have little capital and have often been forced into these activities by the lack of opportunities to take up formal sector employment. One segment of the African community with the businessmen had the resources but not the willingness to invest in manufacturing, while another segment focused on the sector but had little resources to build strong businesses.

CONCLUSION

This chapter provides an overview of ownership and economic activity in the rural and urban sectors following independence. Emphasize was placed on the efforts of the Kenyan government to support the buyout of white settlers and the Africanization of urban business, notably in manufacturing and trade. The two sectors are closely related because wealthier African landowners formed the class which the government sought to move into urban business. Moreover, the government's efforts in the urban sector were conditioned by the political settlement involving the take-over of European held farms in the White Highlands. By agreeing to a compensated buy-out, the new government was forced to borrow money from abroad for on-lending to Africans to make farm purchases. It decided against a similar strategy for the Africanization of urban business but did establish credit programs, bought limited equity stakes and provided industrial estates to encourage African entry. Most notably, it passed the Trade Licensing Act to reduce competition from Asian traders outside of core urban areas and provide opportunities for Africans to take over these activities. Even with this support, Africans were often reluctant to come forward to take up new ventures. The chapter has sought to provide an explanation both for the limited uptake of some of the opportunities and more generally for the relatively limited presence of Africans in the manufacturing sector even thirty years after independence.

The explanation is multi-faceted but begins with a recognition that the emerging African economic elite was firmly rooted in agriculture and related rural-based activities. They had gained considerable knowledge of that sector and the move to urban-based activities involved considerable risk, notably when the sector was already inhabited by Asian and foreign firms. Instead, the surplus developed in agriculture has tended to be reinvested in either agriculture itself, in rural and urban land purchase or in activities such as transport and construction. Furthermore, limited entry into urban business may also have been affected by the strong informal networks which were developed by the Asian population. New African entrants find it difficult to become part of these networks.

Those Africans who did enter manufacturing and trading tended to start out with very limited resources, as they were often poor migrants to the city in need of an income but finding limited opportunities for formal sector wage employment. Their limited resources have made it difficult for their firms to grow. Three subsequent chapters deal with the nature of these micro-enterprise activities and provide a comparison with small Asian-owned firms in the formal sector.

Chapter Five

Metal Manufacturing: Location and Technology

The three preceding chapters provide an historical account of the Asian-African divide and more specifically of the Asian predominance in urban manufacturing. No detailed evidence has been provided, however, to confirm that the divide exists currently. This chapter and the two which follow do provide such evidence and are based on a survey of over 120 micro, small and medium sized manufacturing firms in Nairobi's metal sector. Not all of the larger firms are owned by Asians and not all of the smaller firms are run by Africans. Nonetheless, there is a clear divide between the larger, more formally established Asian firms and the many smaller, more informal African ones.

This size/ethnicity divide is also marked by a geographic or locational divide. Larger firms are located in three main industrial areas or estates of the city while the smaller firms are located in other areas. The current chapter is structured on the basis of location and attempts to provide a feel for the nature of these different groups of enterprises in terms of their investment, technology, product quality and other features. Chapter 6 then provides a more detailed analysis of different legal and financial institutions and the extent to which enterprises of different size and ethnicity can access them. Chapter 7 provides an analysis of the extent to which there is an informal institutional network operating among Asian enterprises that gives them advantages over African firms. In addition, we explore the idea that the current divide is based on a past process of capital accumulation. As we shall see, Asian firms start out larger than African firms, which suggests that their owners may have access to capital derived from previous accumulation. Throughout these chapters the focus is three elements: differences, notably in size, between African and Asian firms; access to legal and financial institutions, both formal and informal; and finally, the effects of an historical process of capital accumulation.

The current chapter is the most general of the three and provides the most qualitative data. The presentation is structured on the basis of the main locations where metal manufacturing is conducted. The qualitative analysis includes comments from proprietors, brief business histories and workshop observations. This is supplemented with descriptive statistics presented in Tables 5.1 to 5.4. A final section uses the Mann-Whitney statistical technique to determine whether the apparent differences between firms in the six locations are statistically significant. The evidence is provided in Tables 5.5 to 5.7. The main conclusion is that there are important differences between firms in the formal areas relative to firms in the less formal areas. These differences relate to firm size, number of employees, access to finance, level of starting capital and the use of technology. There are only minor differences *amongst* firms in the formal areas and *amongst* firms in the less formal ones. Gikomba does appear, however, to exhibit characteristics which places it in an in-between, or semi-formal, position.

SURVEY AND SAMPLE

The survey employed a structured questionnaire which was administered in person with the owners (and in some cases a senior manager) of firms at the lower end of the overall size distribution. To focus on firms in similar sectoral activities, the survey concentrated on manufacturing in the metalwork sector. This includes a variety of activities in which goods are produced by changing the shape of steel or other metal inputs. The focus on manufacturing allowed for the exclusion of many firms involved only in trading (retail or wholesale) for which the entrance requirements in terms of capital, technology and technical skills are lower. In all, 116 useable questionnaires were generated with responses to 64 questions for each business. The questions and responses relate to size, credit activities, inputs, products, technology and investment. If divided into the standard size categories for surveys of this kind (micro: 0–9 employees, small: 10–49 employees, medium: 50–99 employees), the distribution of firms is 65 micro, 45 small and 6 medium. Micro enterprises are under-represented (relative to the overall population of firms) because household-based production was excluded. This was done deliberately.

The only previous detailed survey of the small end of the distribution (Parker and Torres 1994) was based on a survey of household production and avoided commercial and industrial areas. At the same time, the survey conducted by the World Bank under the Regional Program for Enterprise

Development (RPED) focused on established firms. The survey conducted for this study complements those other two and provides a unique composition of less formalized and more formalized firms. The small number of medium-sized firms makes it difficult to draw inferences from that size category. There was no known bias in the surveying which would have resulted in this outcome. Instead, it may represent an important characteristic of the private sector; the *missing middle* of the enterprise and production structure of African countries. Firms with more than 100 workers were excluded from the survey. For several reasons, a pure random sample was not developed and used. The use of an official list would have biased the survey in favor of those firms listed with the Register of Companies and would have excluded many micro firms. Furthermore, even if the register was used it is unlikely that it would have provided a real random sample as the actual sample (responses obtained) would be determined by the willingness of owners to complete the questionnaire.[1]

Instead, sampling was determined in the following manner. Several business directories were used to develop a list of firms in the metal sector, and phone calls were made to determine (and then exclude) those that were engaged only in trading.[2] The addresses of the remaining firms were used to locate the formal business areas of the city where metal manufacturing firms were operating. The author then spent considerable time walking these areas and speaking with the proprietors of firms on the list and with other firms nearby. The informal areas were sampled using the 'walk, locate and talk' approach. Based on preliminary discussions, a questionnaire was drawn up, pre-tested and finalized. It was then administered to firms in six major industrial and light-industrial areas. An effort was made to survey as many firms in each area as possible, except for Kamukunji where there was easy access to a large number of very small firms. Only eight firms were surveyed in Kariobangi and thus conclusions drawn from data obtained in that area should be treated with caution. In all other areas at least a dozen firms were surveyed. Respondents were asked to indicate their ethnicity. A useful breakdown was achieved with 71 African-owned firms, 42 Asian ones and three others which had joint ethnic ownership or did not otherwise fall into the two main categories.

LOCATION

In the process of surveying, it became apparent that firms were concentrated in specific locations and it appeared that firms in a given location exhibited similar characteristics in terms of size, formality, African/Asian ownership, product lines, use of technology and other issues. Thus, a division based on location was considered useful in understanding the nature of SME operations. In this regard, two issues stand out: one, there may be important differences between the formal and informal areas. The second issue is whether these different locations are in fact part of an inter-related and graduated process of firm development. That is, it may be true that firms grow to a certain size in one area and then move or 'graduate' to another area. These issues are considered in the analysis below. First, however, a brief overview of the different locations is provided.

The chief location for all types of manufacturing is the aptly named Industrial Area, located to the south of the city centre. The largest firms concentrate there because it provides the space for large-scale operations

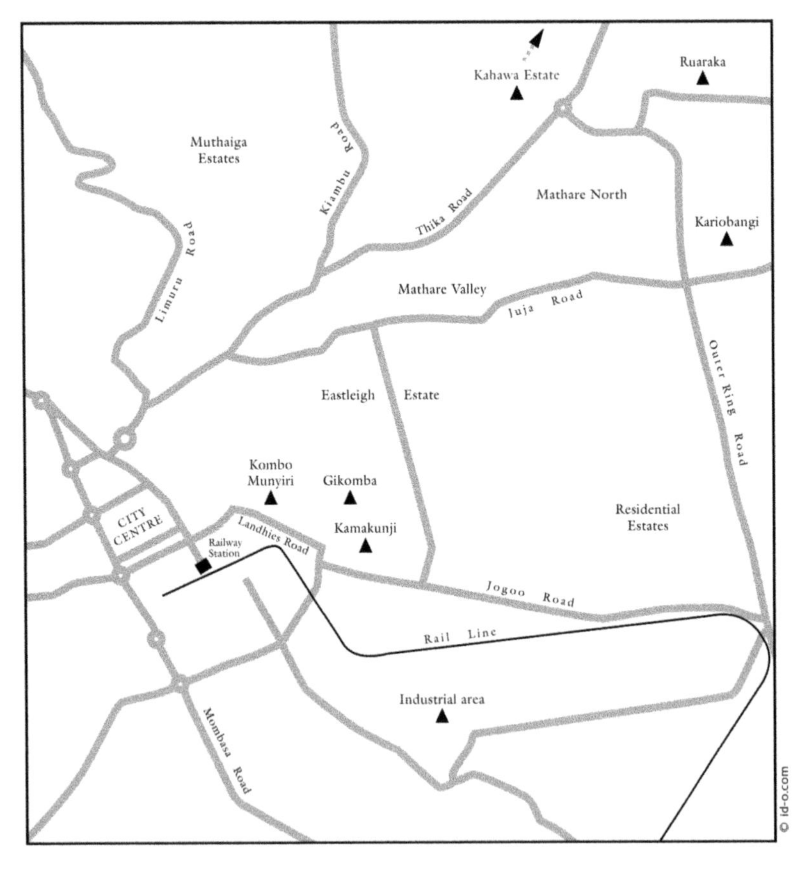

Map 2 : Nairobi, with metal-working areas surveyed (▲)

and because they supply or purchase from other large firms. Firms producing household or consumer products do not need to be close to consumers because they distribute through wholesalers or through retailers located in more strategic areas of the city and the country. For the smaller firms the opposite tends to hold: they need less space for production and their firms are a base for both production and retail sales. In all, the firms were divided into six locations, some of which were geographically close to each other but seemed to represent distinct levels of business activity. Furthermore, making a six-way locational distinction allowed for more detailed analysis (than a three-way comparison based on firm size or a two-way comparison based on ethnicity). Too much generalization can obscure important nuances in the data. The six areas, in ascending order based on firm size, are:

Estates: the Kahawa residential estates at the north-east corner of the city, which had its own small-scale market and production areas, 12 firms surveyed.

Kamukunji: a concentrated metal-working site, near a main road between the city centre and other areas, 24 firms surveyed.

Kariobangi: a light industrial area in the west, located on a main road but next to a large, insecure shantytown, 8 firms surveyed.

Gikomba: close to Kamukunji but with more formalized buildings, usually rented and sometimes containing lathe equipment, 16 firms surveyed.

Kombo Munyiri: a road near Gikomba with a concentration of metal-working firms, involved in the auto trade or other activities and using quality lathes and cutting and grinding equipment, 13 firms surveyed.

Industrial Area: the city's main industrial area + several firms from the Baba Dogo/Ruaraka area which also possesses formal firms, 42 firms surveyed.

The last two areas are more formalized and developed with larger firms, more established business premises and a much greater use of machinery. What is also fairly apparent is the ethnic segmentation in the city: the first four areas contained only African businesses, while the last two areas included a diversity of ownership but were dominated by Asian firms. The descriptions and analysis in the next section focus on four of the six areas. The two areas in which only a small amount of surveying was conducted (Kahawa Estates and Kariobangi) are discussed in Appendix 1 at the end of the book. Dollar figures are provided for those unfamiliar with the value of the Kenyan currency. At the time of surveying, 59 Kenyan shillings (Ksh.) equaled US $1.

KAMUKUNJI

The Kamukunji metal-working site is where Nairobi's micro-enterprise sector is at its most visible and vibrant. The open-air displays of goods, the sales being transacted along the outer perimeter and the constant sound of metal being hammered into shape give a sense of activity and production. Probing deeper into activities in this location provides a glimpse of both how the business community works and what constraints it faces.

The site is shaped as a rectangle of about 50,000 square meters, an area equal to about two-and-a-half football pitches. There are about 75 businesses here with a total of 350 people, both owners and laborers. It is bounded by public roads on three sides, including the heavily traveled Landes Road, a major artery that connects the city center with residential areas to the east and the Industrial Area to the south. The two other sides are bounded by a side-road, Sakwa, onto which cars and light trucks turn from Landes. The sites along these roads are highly prized because they provide direct access to customers. The other workshops do not have road access and are only accessible along walkways running into the rectangle.

Each business has some type of enclosed structure that is made of wood and topped with corrugated steel sheeting. It normally contains a lockable area where tools, supplies and finished products can be stored overnight. It normally covers only a portion of the site, however, and is usually too small to provide an area for working. In many cases the roof of the enclosed structure is extended to provide an unenclosed work area which is free from rain. Work is done under these roofs or in open spaces, including the walkways and the roadsides. Micro-enterprise manufacturing in Kenya is often referred to as the *jua kali* sector, which literally means, 'hot sun' in Swahili and denotes the fact that the work is done without protection from the sun. In 1986, President Moi unexpectedly stopped his motorcade to view the metalwork activity of Kamukunji and made a promise to provide workers with protection from the sun. The promise was kept with the construction of a number of 'nyayo sheds'; large roofs suspended on wooden pillars high above the workers. These sheds are still in existence but now cover only a portion of the Kamukunji site.

The combination of location along a major artery, proximity to the country bus station and the production of consumer goods means that Kamukunji is both a production site and a metal goods market. Finished goods are displayed in the open; most prominent are metal boxes (or trunks), stacked eight high in some places, painted blue or green, decorated with stenciled, white decals. These are used for household storage to keep clothes and other valuables dry and clean in both urban and rural dwellings.

Other goods include: metal buckets, ladles, wok-like cooking pans (called surafias) and grills (barbecues), all of which can be used by households or small restaurants. Some producers specialize in *jikos*, small stoves with a clay interior (for the charcoal) and an outer metal frame, on which a pot or surafias is placed for cooking. All producers here work with metal; there are no carpenters, tailors or produce sellers. Some suppliers which service the metal trade are incorporated into the rectangle: a used-metal dealer, a supplier of rivets and new steel, and a paint retailer, who buys in large cans and sub-divides into smaller ones.

Businesses share and rent tools, while laborers with metal-working skills seek employment, much of it on a casual or piece-work basis, from the businesses which have immediate orders to fill or need to replenish finished goods inventories. Some of the businesses have been in operations here for many years and appear relatively prosperous. The question of them 'graduating' from Kamukunji—moving up by moving out—involves not only the issues of size and success but also of markets. This is a recognized site of metal goods production (including custom production) and of sales of low-cost consumer goods on a retail basis or to wholesalers. Moving out involves finding a similar combination of characteristics, which might be difficult. Moving up to more permanent business premises, on a more established road, would likely result in the loss of access to customers and certain established patterns of business interaction.

The site is densely populated and there is a high demand for plots by laborers who want to become entrepreneurs. The land here is not owned by the entrepreneurs; instead they possess private use rights on common property. To manage the allocation, the enterprises have organized a business association which assigns the plots to new operators, usually based on the recommendations of other plot holders and/or direct familiarity with them. One new plot holder had been working previously for his brother and secured a plot of his own based on his brother's recommendation. The decision to give up a plot to a new entrant may involve a cash transaction. One proprietor said he paid Ksh 55,000 ($930) to acquire a plot with a small structure that had a good location with access to the road. An additional Ksh 20,000 ($340) was required to get the business started, which suggests that in some cases there might be a substantial investment to obtain and put into operation a new plot.

While property rights are recognized within the community, they are not sanctioned from the outside. These plots cannot be used as collateral and it might be useful to establish recognized legal title to the land. While this might be an important step in the area's development, it is not certain that these small plots would have collateral value with the banks. Even if they did, the

Table 5.1 Firm characteristics - Kamukunji

		Median	Mean	Min.	Max.
Size					
Asset value	Ksh	110,000	249,208	10,000	1,000,000
Labourforce (workers)	no.	4.0	5.0	1.0	10.0
Starting capital	Ksh	13,630	47,692	147	590,551
Age of firm	years	6.0	7.1	0.5	15.0
Part-time operation	years	0.0	1.1	0.0	12.0
Owners' previous experience	years	0.0	0.9	0.0	7.0
Education					
Total	years	11.0	10.7	7.0	15.0
Total higher	years	0.0	0.4	0.0	3.0
Technical college	years	0.0	0.4	0.0	3.0
University	years	0.0	0.1	0.0	2.0
		no.	**total**	**%**	
Registered	no. of firms	7	24	29%	
Access to bank loan	no. of firms	1	24	4%	
Access to trade credit	no. of firms	0	24	0%	
Finance for last machine purchase	no. of firms	**no.**	**total**	**%**	
Savings		8	24	33%	
Bank loan		0	24	0%	
Installments		0	24	0%	
Informal loan		0	24	0%	
NGO		0	24	0%	

Source: author's survey, US$ 1 = 59 Ksh (Kenyan shillings)

banks might still find that the small size of the loan requests would make it uneconomical to transact. Like the titling of farm land as discussed in Chapter 4, there is no certainty that titling these urban plots will allow for increased investment. The same problems may apply: plot-holders may be unwilling to use their plots as collateral, the banks may be unwilling to lead, and the added investment may not lead to additional business.

The characteristics of enterprises in Kamukunji are further revealed by the descriptions statistics provided in Table 5.1. Of the 24 firms surveyed, the median firm used just under Ksh 13,600 ($230) to start the business. This low level stems in part from the fact that proprietors spent rather limited time as laborers in the sector before beginning their own operations. In Kamukunji, the average proprietor spent less than one year as a laborer in the metal sector before opening his own operation. Of all of the areas surveyed, Kamukunji had the lowest level of educational attainment. Entrepreneurs had an average of less than 11 years of schooling, which is mostly accounted for by primary and secondary education. The median owner has no training at a technical college and no university training.

These firms have also been in business for a shorter period of time compared with those in more formalized areas. The median firm has been in operation for just over six years, slightly more than in Kahawa (3.5) but less than in Gikomba (8) and the Industrial Area (15). What this actually means is uncertain. While some of the more established firms may have built sufficient capital to move to better quarters, it is also possible that there is a high rate of firm deaths and thus firms leave and new ones replace them. Some enterprises may feel that the returns are too low and so they try their luck elsewhere. Business permanence varies considerably in this area: the oldest firm had been operating for 15 years, and a further seven had been in operation for 10 years or more, representing a full one-third of the sample.

The lack of adequate start-up capital limits the level of technology purchased and therefore the type and quality of goods that can be produced. Many businesses own only hand tools (hammer, tin-snips), with which they are rather adept at fashioning articles such as pails and, with a borrowed welder, boxes. Many of these firms were interested in buying grinders, to smooth the rough surface of welds for a more finished product. A limited electrical supply was available to run the welders, which could be easily purchased in city shops.

The burden of personal and family expenses makes it difficult for these firms to develop to a higher level. In addition, because there are many operators starting in at a low level, this segment of the market tends to be highly competitive with limited opportunities to generate a surplus. Indeed, the trick that appears to be needed to keep ahead of competitors is to move into more advanced goods at higher levels of technology. Without proper security and proper infrastructure, such as an adequate electrical supply, it is unlikely that significant advances in technology (for example lathe equipment) can be envisioned.

Only one of the 24 firms surveyed here had ever borrowed from a bank (Tab. 5.1). Asked how they had financed their last machine purchase, many did not answer the question because they had no real 'machinery.' Of the eight which did respond, all indicated that they had financed the purchase from savings; none had used informal loans or installments. Thus the area remains cut off from external financing. They may have difficulty obtaining informal finance as well because their extended families and those with whom they associate may have little or no money to lend. A group of firms are involved in a Grameen-type peer monitored credit scheme organized by Kenya Rural Enterprise Program (KREP). The group has received loans in yearly installments since 1995. It began with 10 members and added eight others, although four have been excluded from the group for not honoring their obligations. The four firms from my survey which were involved in the group were older and more established. According to several Kamukunji proprietors who were not involved in the scheme, the interest rate is too high (about 25%).

The median value of the firms surveyed in this area is Ksh 110,000 ($1,860), which is about the same as the Kahawa area but just over half of the value of firms in Gikomba, the next step up (Tab. 5.1). The smallest firm was valued at Ksh 10,000, while there were seven firms with a value of Ksh 50,000 or less. At the upper end, the two largest firms valued their businesses at Ksh 1 million ($17,000), and another two firms were valued at Ksh 500,000 or more.

As noted, the workers are usually not permanent but hired on a casual basis when orders are secured or inventories need to be replenished. They are usually paid by the piece, instead of by the hour or the week. One worker had four years of experience in the sector. It takes him about 45 minutes to make a medium-sized metal box, which is the size of a large Western suitcase, and he is paid Ksh 50. A larger box takes an hour to make and he collects Ksh 80 in pay. He can make 10–12 medium boxes in a very full day. He receives an additional Ksh 10 for painting, which takes little time. Steel for a medium-sized box costs about Ksh 300 and the paint it about Ksh 50. When the cost of labor is added (Ksh 60), the total cost is Ksh 410 and it sells for Ksh 500 ($8.50). While these figures are rough estimates, they do suggest that margins are thin.

The survey contains inadequate data to estimate surplus generation at the firm level, but it is unlikely to be great. The example of a young progressive firm might shed some light on the issue, however. The firm was one of the few firms in Kamukunji solely engaged in producing wheelbarrows. The proprietor, a young man, had a truck and used it to market the product in Kisumu, Nakuru and Eldoret, as well as in Nairobi. He worked eight hours per day now in the slow season but in the peak times he starts at 6 a.m. (sunrise) and leaves to return home in the suburban estates after dark (7:30 p.m.). The busy months are during the main harvest season from January to March when people have money from the sale of farm produce. The slowest months are from April to August, when the crops are growing in the fields.

In a peak month, this proprietor can earn Ksh 15,000 and over a whole year he takes home about Ksh 50,000 ($850). He estimates that this is about Ksh 2,000 to 5,000 more than he could make as a laborer in a factory. "That's why we like to work here," he said, "it's better than the industrial area." He has a rather makeshift structure which stands on a plot on the fringe of Kamukunji. He would like to move to a better site in the rectangle but there are currently no vacancies. He is a relative newcomer here, having only operated his firm for four years and he is not well known to the members of the *jua kali* association who decide the allocation of plots.

GIKOMBA

Within a 10-minute walk from Kamukunji is another African metalworking area called Gikomba. Despite the short distance, the contrasts are great, the most notable being the size and permanence of buildings in which the firms operate. These structures are solid, made of concrete blocks, with proper foundations, watertight wood and metal roofs and doors behind which tools, machinery, supplies and finished goods can be locked out of sight and out of reach. The entire area is made up of three long streets, connected with a few short ones. The streets are potholed, and susceptible to water pooling after it rains but they are negotiable at all times by cars and light trucks. While some work is done under the sun in front of shops, much more of it is done indoors especially where machinery is not readily moveable. Large doors at the front of the shops are usually left open, to provide light and to ease the interaction with neighboring firms or with suppliers or potential customers. Peering into the shops, they appear cavernous not only because of the height of the ceiling and the depth of the shop but because in many cases the space is more than ample to house the equipment and materials. This is not true of all shops but there does often appear to be a mismatch between the space available and its use. It seems as if the buildings were intended for much larger operations. In some instances the size of the product (grain grinding mills or trailers) requires a large space.

The nature of what is produced and the machinery used to produce it clearly is an advance from Kamukunji. Here there are several imported metal lathes of reasonably high quality that are used for producing or machining replacement parts for other machines. Larger mounted (but nonmotorized) metal cutting and bending machines are also in evidence. This is not an area for consumer goods production but for light industrial goods. Some producers make band saws, table saws and wood lathes, mounted with electrical motors, for the small-scale furniture industry which is located on adjoining streets. A few firms make posho mills of various sizes which are bought by small cooperatives up-country. These are used for the grinding of maize to make maize meal, the country's staple food. Another producer makes hand-drawn goods trailers using axles and pneumonic tires salvaged from old cars. To this he fashions a metal frame that supports a wooden platform on to which goods can be loaded. Some of these can be seen in operation in the markets on adjoining streets. Thus another important difference is that this area, because it services other businesses, is closer and more integrated with them and not secluded like Kamukunji. There are established suppliers of metal and wood products that feed local manufacturers. There are, however, a number of smaller producers, little different from those in Kamukunji, whose places of work are more secluded and open onto side alleys. Some occupy workshops together with other independent artisans. It is a thriving community of constant activity.

One business is engaged in making small balances (scales) and weights, which are sold to the Kenya Post and Telecommunications Corporation (KPTC), for weighing mail in the country's post offices. The base of the balance, the largest part, is created with molten metal in a small foundry. The foundry was located in Gikomba but had to be moved to Kariobangi because of problems with fumes in the building. The bases are brought here, assembled with the use of additional components and painted silver. The weights are cut here but not in the laborious manner of a worker with a hacksaw but in a mechanized, unmanned setup with an electric metal saw. It operates automatically to slowly cut three-inch sections from a long metal rod, which has a diameter of about two inches. A hose is suspended next to the saw blade to provide a sprinkle of water, which keeps the blade from overheating. These three-inch sections are then machined on a lathe at the front of the shop to provide a rounded knob at the top so that they weight can be lifted easily on and off the balance.

Table 5.2 Firm characteristics - Gikomba

		Median	Mean	Min.	Max.
Size					
Asset value	Ksh	200,000	453,125	60,000	2,000,000
Labour force (workers)	no.	5.5	6.2	1.0	20.0
Starting capital	Ksh	44,154	88,709	2,950	578,035
Age of firm	years	8.0	9.9	3.0	32.0
Part-time operation	years	0.3	1.8	0.0	11.0
Owners' previous experience	years	2.0	5.2	0.0	23.0
Education					
Total	years	14.0	12.9	8.0	16.0
Total higher	years	1.5	1.7	0.0	4.0
Technical college	years	1.5	1.7	0.0	4.0
University	years	0.0	0.0	0.0	0.0
		no.	**total**	%	
Registered	no. of firms	8	16	50%	
Access to bank loan	no. of firms	0	16	0%	
Access to trade credit	no. of firms	1	13	8%	
Finance for last machine purchase	no. of firms	**no.**	**total**	%	
Savings		10	16	63%	
Bank loan		0	16	0%	
Installments		4	16	25%	
Informal loan		0	16	0%	
NGO		1	16	6%	

Source: author's survey, US$ 1 = 59 Ksh (Kenyan shillings)

Once machined, the weights are then taken to the rear of the shop where they are placed on a master scale for exact measurement. If the weight is too heavy, metal is bored from the bottom; if it is too light, lead is added. One can see that there is some sophistication of technique here, some investment in technology, and some effort to mass-produce while minimizing labor costs.

Conversations with proprietors in this area suggested that the premises were mostly rented, not owned. Still, the extent of machinery use meant that the value of these firms was noticeably higher on average that the firms in the less developed metal-working areas. A total of 16 firms were surveyed from this area, including small artisans and more substantial industrial goods producers. Descriptive statistics of firms surveyed in this area are provided in Table 5.2. The median firm value here is almost double that of Kamukunji at Ksh 200,000 ($3,400), and the capital used to start these business represents more than a tripling from the other area to just over Ksh 44,000. The median number of employees per firm is only slightly higher (5.5 compared to 4) reflecting a common finding from the survey; namely that 'larger' firms are represented by much greater capital intensity, not a much higher number of workers.

This suggests that it is important in quantitative analysis that firm size be gauged by both asset value and the size of the workforce. This is especially true in areas where labor is abundant and therefore inexpensive. The difference in value may be partly attributed to differences in the age of firms, the median here is 8 years, compared to 6 years for firms in the other area.

The financing characteristics of these firms are slightly different from firms in the other African areas (Tab. 5.2). None of the 16 firms surveyed had ever borrowed from a bank. Asked about the purchase of their last machine, all firms provided a response, indicating that, unlike Kamukunji, they had made recent purchases of true machinery. While there was an emphasis on the use of savings (10 of 15 firms suggested it was the sole source of financing), three indicated that the machinery was financed through installments. This is significant because it suggests that these firms were purchasing larger machines, which sellers would not expect to be paid for in a single transaction). More importantly, the firms could agree to such installment provisions with machinery sellers because they had established places of businesses. This not only invites general confidence on the part of the sellers but it also allows for the repossession of machines in the case of non-payment. Because the lathes and other items were not highly specialized, repossession can lead more easily to re-sale.

KOMBO MUNYIRI ROAD

From the side streets that make up Gikomba, one has only to take a short walk down the New Pumwani Road to reach the more established industrial and commercial area along Kombo Munyiri Road. Although heavily potholed, the road is wide and suitable for the two-way traffic of heavy supply trucks. There are no makeshift buildings here and none of the work is conducted in the streets or in front of workshops. The buildings are made of brick and are of much greater size. If several of the more sophisticated shops in Gikomba contained a lathe machine, here there are shops with four, five and, in one case, a dozen lathes. If Gikomba is a noticeable step up from the operations in Kamukunji, Kombo Munyiri is an even greater step up the industrial chain from Gikomba.

More sophisticated technology is used for more complex work. At the far end of the road, the firms concentrate on the re-engineering of motor vehicle parts, notably crankshafts and cylinder blocks. While garages which provide vehicle repair were not included in the survey (considered a service), a number of metal machining establishments, which work on vehicles parts, were included because of the high technology and the industrial nature of the activity. The work focuses on crankshafts and cylinder blocks. The crankshaft is the central moveable component of a vehicle engine and transfers power from the pistons to the axle. Over time the place at which the piston is attached to the shaft becomes worn, takes on an oval shape and causes a reduction in mechanical efficiency. To regain efficiency, it is necessary to grind the oval to make it round and then refit the piston with a larger bearing. This involves turning the shaft on a high quality lathe. While removing, grinding and replacing the crankshaft is an elaborate process it can result in considerable cost savings for the vehicle owner. The shaft can be worth one-third of the value of the entire engine and its refurbishment is a low-cost alternative to replacing it with a new shaft or obtaining an entirely new engine. The cylinder block is a heavy metal component through which the pistons are driven to generate the engine's power. If the engine overheats from a lack of coolant in the radiator or some other break down in the cooling system, the block may warp and create an uneven fit between the block and the cylinder head. Grinding involves smoothing the surface of the block so that the head can be properly fitted. This activity involves modern grinding equipment which, like the metal lathes, is imported from advanced industrial countries or India. The large size differential between firms in this area and those is Gikomba and Kamukunji relates not so much to the size of buildings or the workforce. It relates to the amount of capital invested

Table 5.3 Firm characteristics – Kombo Munyiri

		Median	Mean	Min.	Max.
Size					
Asset value	Ksh	9,000,000	14,200,000	300,000	40,000,000
Labour force (workers)	no.	18.0	17.2	6.0	30.0
Starting capital	Ksh	698,616	1,294,681	3,226	4,504,505
Age of firm	years	18.0	19.1	1.5	38.0
Part-time operation	years	0.0	0.0	0.0	0.0
Owners' previous experience	years	2.0	4.3	0.0	20.0
Education					
Total	years	11.0	11.7	7.0	15.0
Total higher	years	0.0	1.0	0.0	3.0
Technical college	years	0.0	1.0	0.0	3.0
University	years	0.0	0.0	0.0	0.0
		no.	total	%	
Registered	no. of firms	13	13	100%	
Access to bank loan	no. of firms	6	13	46%	
Access to trade credit	no. of firms	3	12	25%	
Finance for last machine purchase	no. of firms	no.	total	%	
Savings		4	13	31%	
Bank loan		3	13	23%	
Installments		3	13	23%	
Informal loan		1	13	8%	
NGO		0	13	0%	

Source: author's survey, US$ 1 = 59 Ksh (Kenyan shillings)

in the technology which allows these firms to undertake specialized, high value-added work in the vehicle industry.

The data collected by the survey and presented in Table 5.3 indicate large differences in the scale of operation in this area compared with Gikomba.

While the median level of starting capital in Gikomba is Ksh 44,000, here it is Ksh 700,000 ($11,860) and similarly the median current value of firms in the two areas are Ksh 200,000 and Ksh 9 million ($152,500), respectively. The *current value* of the median Gikomba firm is, therefore, more than one-third of the *starting capital* of the median Kombo firm. The Kombo firms also employed more workers, 18, compared with 5.5 for Gikomba. Differences in the size of the workforce in the two areas are much smaller than differences in capital value, indicating that capital per worker is much higher in Kombo. Gikomba firms employ about 1/3 the number of workers as those in Kombo, but the value of firms is 1/45 of those in Kombo. The Kombo firms were in operation longer as well, 18 years compared to 8.

The firms in this area have greater access to formal finance and a more diverse range of financing sources (Tab. 5.3). Six of the 13 firms have access to bank credit while three firms (of 11 responding) used a bank loan to finance the last machine purchase. Other sources of finance for machine purchase include: savings (4), installments (3), and informal loans (1). In other respects, however, Kombo firms showed only minor differences from their Gikomba counterparts. Their owners had the same length of experience working in other metal manufacturing businesses (2 years) and on average had negligible experience operating their firms on a part-time basis. The level of education among Kombo proprietors was slightly below that of those in Gikomba, the Estates and Kariobangi. This may be due to the fact that Kombo proprietors set up their firms earlier, when obtaining a secondary education was less common.

The other noticeable difference between Gikomba and Kombo Munyiri is the ethnic make-up of ownership. This is predominantly an Asian area, with 10 of the 13 firms owned by members of that ethnic group. This figure even under-represents the ethnic distribution because all African firms encountered were enticed to participate in the survey while a portion of the Asian firms did not complete the questionnaire. Moreover, Kombo is both a fabrication/machining area as well as a trading location where metal and non-metal supplies are sold, mostly as supply inputs. The trading firms are also overwhelmingly owned by Asians. The most successful African proprietor in this area noted that it was difficult to become established in an Asian area and to undertake types of metal work (machining and car parts refurbishing) that are normally associated with the Asians. He explained the situation in this way:

> It was only a few years ago that the African started doing this type of work, with the lathe and these [engineering] machines. In the beginning, it was hard to convince people that I could do it. They would

> always go to the Asian because they think that they get better quality. It was hard to convince them that an African can do just as well . . . But then I got some customers and I do good work so they came back.

To purchase machinery, he convinced his bank to provide a loan by demonstrating his understanding of running a business and providing the requisite collateral, in his case land. "For loans, I explained what I wanted to do, gave them cash flow projections and provided collateral," he said. The fact that he possessed land that was recognized by the bank suggests that he was a man of some means.

Discussions with Asian businessmen revealed that their families had been in the metal-work sector for decades and that they therefore gained from the capital and knowledge accumulated from that experience. The brief histories of two such businesses highlight the difference with the African just noted.

One business in this area was begun in 1965 by an Asian man and subsequently passed on to his son (the current owner), whose own son now works in the firm and will inherit it. While still relatively small, this firm has been built up over 32 years. It is located in the vehicle works area and its main activity is making auto springs, u-bolts and center bolts for axles. Like many other businesses in this area, it also takes on a variety of general engineering work, such as the provision of grills and gates for security. The workshop contains a variety of machines, including several cutting and bending machines made by the owner himself. One of the particular characteristics of the metal sector is that machines are made from the same material as the products and therefore it is not uncommon for proprietors to generate their own simple machinery. This suggests that technological upgrading may involve not only the purchase of new machinery but also the ability to develop technology suitable for the tasks. The important question is, however, to what extent can self-made machines guarantee the quality and precision needed for highly skilled work? The higher precision lathe equipment, for example, is imported, even though there are some businesses producing metal lathes in Kenya.

Much further along the road is a boiler maker who custom builds water tanks and then fits heating elements to them. The family has had a long history in the metal sector in Kenya. The current owner's grandfather came from the Indian sub-continent near the time of the building of the Mombassa-Uganda railway and worked as a bellows boy for a blacksmith in Machakos. This initial work involved manning the bellows; pumping oxygen into the coal furnaces used to heat metal.

His son was also a blacksmith in Machakos, who made the outer iron strapping for the wheels of animal-drawn carts. These were made by heating and hammering metal, without the use of the blow torches and welding equipment currently used in the fabrication of boilers. The son of the current owner keeps track of income and expenses by doing the accounting. The owner was interviewed after he had written on the questionnaire, "I don't believe in credit." In a sparse office overlooking the shop floor, he explained his adherence to the Muslim prohibition against earning interest and said that almost all of his business was conducted on a cash basis. He was proud of his family's 90-year tradition in the Kenya metal sector and of his own business. "I don't make a lot of money," he said, "but I make a living and you can see that I employ about 20 workers." He also has been able to participate twice in the haji and a picture of the holy mosque in Mecca is almost the sole decoration on his office walls. He represented the common, small family-run Asian workshop that had been built up over several generations. Understanding this family background, it may be more appropriate to compare the newer African businessmen, not with this Asian, but with his father or his grandfather.

While much has been made of Asian business success, failures also occur. One businessman interviewed was closing up and hoping to sell off the building and machinery. The business, which was a partnership, had concentrated on the repair of equipment used to dry and process coffee beans. It had contracted mainly with coffee cooperatives. It was one of about 25 such firms in Kenya, of which about 15 were more established, like this one. He blamed the problems of his business on the lack of (reasonably) prompt payment from the coffee cooperatives. Previously, payments were received in 6–7 months but more recently that had slid to 15–18 months. "You know that they are going to pay but it takes a longer time," said one of the partners. Deregulation in the coffee processing sector had increased the number and reduced the size of co-operatives and this was affecting their ability to accumulate the funds necessary to make prompt payments. While previously each cooperative operated 10–15 factories, they now operated only 2–3. This development has been going on for three years and was affecting both the coffee industry itself and those firms which serviced it, he said. The purpose of creating smaller co-operatives was to reduce corruption, but he argued, "whether small or large, the corruption is still there." The problem of receiving payment, along with the high interest rate on loans and overdrafts, had created severe cash flow problems for his firm.

He felt that interest rates would stay high or even increase until the political situation was resolved. He and his partners had considered converting the workshop to another line of business but that would have required new machinery and would be difficult to finance given the high interest rates. Some of the partners were near retirement and, with British passports, were considering a move to the UK. He himself was not yet ready to retire and was developing a pharmaceuticals wholesaling business with a friend, who was a chemist.

Asked more generally about the business success of Asians in Kenya, he said that they took a longer-term perspective towards business than did Africans. "We keep plowing back in whatever we make . . . to make sure the company is on a strong footing," he said. "We work long hours without expecting anything." He had less hospitable things to say about African entrepreneurs and suggested that they possessed the opposite characteristics (they expected quick returns, they did not commit themselves to the long term, they did not re-invest, etc.). His views on the differences between Asians and Africans mirrored those of several other Asian businessmen interviewed in the Industrial Area. Such opinions likely have some impact on the nature of business and credit relations between Asian and African businessmen, although it would be very difficult to gauge. If trust is an important element in relations between contracting parties, as some analysts suggest (North 1990; Platteau 1995), it would be difficult to build such trust between ethnic communities when such negative attitudes exist.

INDUSTRIAL AREA

The large sprawling Industrial Area, to the south of the city, is where the bulk of Nairobi's, and indeed Kenya's, manufacturing is carried out. Large trucks rumble up and down the main arteries and turn along the small connecting roadways delivering supplies and carrying away goods from factories. In some cases, these factories employ hundreds of workers. There is a noticeable difference between this area and the five other locations in this study; it is the sheer size of operations. And yet, in amongst the large factories there are plenty of smaller operations, some with as few has five workers toiling away in workshops not much different from those in Kombo Munyiri. The survey focused on this smaller element, screening out any firms with 100 employees or more, and even then only six medium-sized firms (more than 50 employees) were included. The sample statistics provided thus represent the smaller end of the size distribution of firms in the Industrial Area (Tab. 5.4).

Table 5.4 Firm characteristics – Industrial area

		Median	Mean	Min.	Max.
Size					
Asset value	Ksh	13,000,000	26,500,000	200,000	250,000,000
Labour force (workers)	no.	20.0	27.5	1.0	85.0
Starting capital	Ksh	522,480	3,556,818	33,921	59,100,000
Age of firm	years	15.0	17.2	1.0	55.0
Part-time operation	years	0.0	0.3	0.0	4.0
Owners' previous experience	years	2.0	6.3	0.0	30.0
Education					
Total	years	14.0	13.4	6.0	17.5
Total higher	years	3.0	2.3	0.0	5.5
Technical college	years	1.5	1.5	0.0	5.5
University	years	0.0	1.0	0.0	6.0
		no.	total	%	
Registered	no. of firms	41	42	98%	
Access to bank loan	no. of firms	20	42	48%	
Access to trade credit	no. of firms	30	40	75%	
Finance for last machine purchase	no. of firms	no.	total	%	
Savings		20	42	48%	
Bank loan		5	42	12%	
Installments		7	42	17%	
Informal loan		4	42	10%	
NGO		0	42	0%	

Source: author's survey, US$ 1 = 59 Ksh (Kenyan shillings)

The range of products made in the metal sector here is broad. It includes: farm tools, agricultural trailers, water towers, tanks to store the fuel under petrol stations, overhead bay covers for those petrol stations; springs and mufflers for the auto market; metal chairs and beds for hospitals; and countertops with basins for kitchens and restaurants. There are foundries for casting manhole covers, lawn furniture, machinery parts and lawnmower bases. One firm is trying to service the niche market in gym equipment. There are several firms making molds for plastic items such as the small, thin boxes used for the burgeoning trade in market-ready vegetables destined for European supermarkets. Along with these items, there are many firms (including many of the firms covered in this survey) conducting engineering work, some of it similar to that found in Kombo: the repair and maintenance of machinery for other firms and the grinding of crankshafts and cylinder blocks. Supplying these firms are a dozen steel rolling mills, using ingots, mostly imported, and melted scrap.

The area is a mix of domestic and foreign firms; the latter maintain large operations but they are few in number. Recognizable names include SmithKline-Beecham, Glaxo-Wellcome and Brooke Bond, but the metal sector is almost totally devoid of foreigners, except for vehicle assembly. The survey included 43 firms in this area; 32 owned by Asians and eight by Africans (Tab. 5.4). The remaining three had either white Kenyan, British or joint African/Asian owners. Furthermore, these figures likely over-represent the African presence because every African owner encountered was surveyed but not all Asians were. Furthermore, the larger firms excluded from the sample were all Asian-owned. It is on this basis that we can confirm that manufacturing is dominated by Asians and that there has been only limited penetration by Africans.

Even with a concentration on the small end of the distribution, the differences in size appear in the descriptive statistics provided in Table 5.4. The median value of the 43 firms in this area is Ksh 13 million (substantially higher than the Ksh 9 million for Kombo). There is a large range here from the smallest firm with a value of Ksh 200,000 to the largest firm valued at Ksh 250 million ($424,000). The amount of money used to start a firm here is lower at about Ksh 522,500 million ($8,860), compared to about Ksh 700,000 in Kombo. The larger size is not mirrored in a corresponding difference in longevity. Indeed, the median age of firms here is just over 15 years (1982), compared to 18 years in Kombo. Nonetheless, some firms have been able to survive for decades. Five firms began operations during the colonial period. The oldest was founded during the Second World War and makes temporary metal sheds, used by construction companies at rural sites or by aid organizations for refugee camps. Another eight were begun before 1970 and 13 started operations during the 1970s. As a subset, the average African firm in the sample was begun in 1989 and while the oldest wholly owned African firm began in 1967, the second oldest started only in 1980.

Regarding finance, the range of sources is broader here than in any of the other areas, although it may appear somewhat surprising that many firms have not used bank loans to finance investments. As shown in Table 5.4, only 22 firms have ever borrowed from the bank and when asked how they financed their last machine purchase, 20 firms indicated that they had replied solely on savings. Of the remainder, five had used a bank loan, seven had used installment payments and four had relied on some type of informal loan from family or friends. In discussions with Asian businessmen in this location, it did become apparent that they had access to considerable sums of money if need be. One businessman suggested that he could easily borrow Ksh 100,000 ($1,700) informally and on a short-term basis to meet a cash flow bottleneck. Others also suggested that they could borrow from business colleagues in the event of short-term cash shortages. "But we pay it back," noted one of them.

It must not be assumed that credit is always and easily obtainable for Asians, however, as the case of one foundry owner well illustrates. The businessman had developed his own foundry where he cast large steel elements for use in machinery and for other purposes. His firm has been in operation at its current location for about eight years and in the previous year he built the foundry himself over a period of six months. It had a large foundry cylinder about 10 meters in height, with an adjacent platform from which high-grade scrap metal, such as engine blocks and wheel drums, could be deposited into the cylinder. Using coke (a solid fuel made from coal), the bottom of the cylinder is heated to a very high temperature to melt the scrap. The molten metal is then transported to a nearby sandy area where impressions are made in the sand to cast whatever is required. His product line includes iron lawn furniture, manhole covers, cast iron pipe joints, cement mixers and metal presses with large metal rollers. He also made metal lathes, casting the parts himself. He orders the coke from Germany but it needs to be paid in advance and takes several months for a shipment to arrive. He sometimes sells some of the coke to other small foundries. There are several in Kariobangi but they are much smaller and mainly dormant now, he said. His operation represents one aspect of a domestically oriented machine tool industry, which is still at the infant industry stage (see Matthews 1987).

One of the reasons for setting up the foundry was to eliminate the financial constraints and quality control problems of contracting out component fabrication to other foundries. Prior to building his own foundry, he had had a three-month line of credit with a quality foundry. At one point he obtained a large order which required the casting of machine components. The foundry would not extend more credit to him until he paid back the outstanding balance from previous work. He was not in a position to do so and decided to use another foundry which extended new credit. The work was of low quality, however, and his customer was not satisfied. Afterwards he decided to build his own foundry to ensure the supply and the quality he needed. Quality is an important consideration because components which are poorly casted will break under heat and pressure when used in heavy machinery. He is also now engaged in custom casting for others but because his operation is new, he has found it hard to convince would-be clients that he produces quality products. Once he obtains orders, he gets repeat business because the quality is evident, however. This example suggests that confidence is an Asian as well as an African problem. He has borrowed from his bank in the past but the terms are difficult with an interest rate of 30%. If he had borrowed to build the foundry, payments would have come due before the foundry was generating revenue.

Interviews with proprietors also turned up alternative explanations for the relative lack of an African presence in the industrial area. One such explanation is that along with Asian networks for trade and finance based on better information and community sanctions, the Asians also collude to keep Africans out of manufacturing or particular sub-sectors. The market for specialized products is small and therefore collusion or discrimination against new entrants is relatively easy to organize. It is very difficult to investigate collusion, but one African proprietor did explain how he was a victim of collusion between a supplier and a bank.

He had recent suffered serious business reversals but was still in business. He said he had been squeezed by the Asian business community after engaging in the production of products using specialized steel inputs. A problem arose because he was required to make a trade credit payment at the same time that a bank loan payment was due. He concluded that the supplier and the bank manager, both Asians, demanded payment at the same time knowing that he could not make both payments and would be forced to default. According to him, the supply bill had been due for some time but payment was not demanded until the bank loan also fell due. He suggested that the banker and supplier knew each other and forced the payments to undermine his business. "They don't present the bill," he said. "But then when they know that your balance is low, then they present it." He was taken to court and forced to give up collateral, which undermined his business. He also said that Asians sell cheaper to other Asians than they do to Africans and that they offer twice the cash discount.

He was bitter and his advice to other African businessmen was to not take credit or otherwise do business with Asians if it could be avoided. He suggested that Asians "want to put Africans out of business" and that they can only compete by colluding against Africans. He was working on re-establishing his firm by operating a supply chain free from Asians and ordering specialized steel inputs directly from the UK.

His situation contrasted with that of another African businessman in the industrial area who had built up, with his partners, a substantial business designing and building electrical switching panels for factories. He trained as an engineer and he imported some of his equipment from Europe and the Far East. He had a positive attitude towards Asians and did most of his business with them; indeed his shop, in the dense northern district of the Industrial Area, was surrounded by them. He said that business was business and there were no racial barriers. "People will come because of good service," he said. "Everyone can see whether the work done is shoddy or of high quality." Asked specifically about Asian customers, he opened a binder and leafed through payment receipts, showing that along with several orders from multinationals, the bulk of his work was done for Asian-owned companies. "We have a lot of Asian customers," he said. "We do not say that the Asian community is a hindrance; there is no discrimination."

The Asian grievances against Africans were directed at those in government. Generally, Asian businessmen felt that the government could do more to provide a stable economic framework with lower interest rates, much better infrastructure and a reduction in the constant requests for bribes. The latter two problems are highlighted here with specific examples.

The roads in the Industrial Area are in poor condition and are a constant reminder of the government's inability to maintain even the most basic infrastructure. The problem became so bad in Ruaraka that a number of firms banded together to initiate and finance the reconstruction of an important section of the main Baba Dogo Road. Even without knowledge of its financing arrangements, however, it is evident that this road is peculiar, for it is the only road in the city made from bricks. A kilometer-long section of the road, which is about 10 paces across, was built at a cost of Ksh 24 million ($407,000) and was entirely financed by 70 businesses located along the road or on adjoining sideroads. Bricks were used instead of paving because the latter holes too quickly. This is partly due to the rains and the condition of the underlying soil, but it is also because there were closed sewers along the road, which tend to clog and force water to run over the road. The new road has been built with open ditches and the water is channeled into a nearby section of the Mathare River. The road is expected to last 10 years. "We want to show the government that this is the way to build roads," said one businessman, who runs a construction company nearby, and who explained the operation. This private financing of infrastructure, notably road building, has been advocated more generally by the chairman of the Kenya Association of Manufacturers, an Asian, who has said that infrastructure cannot be left to the government.

A much more infuriating problem for businessmen is the requirement of providing bribe payments to ward off the incessant harassment of government officials. While the corruption of government funds and aid resources is well know, small-scale bribery is less well known but it reaches into the heart of Kenyan manufacturing. The problem arose in discussions with an older Asian businessman engaged in metal casting, extrusion and fabrication. Previously, his family was engaged in goldsmithing and the sale of jewelry from five shops in the city center. The shops were looted during the attempted coup in 1982. Everything was taken from the displays and much from storage too, but luckily a two-ton Chubb safe, which held some valuables, was shut as the intruders entered. The looting prompted the rest of the large family to immigrate to Europe (the UK mostly) and North America. He stayed behind—he doesn't like English weather—and diverted into metal fabrication.

He explained that as many as 20 government officials come to his business every month, demanding bribes and threatening fines for minor, usually unfounded, offences. They show government business cards, but he is unsure as to whether they are actually government employees or are only impersonating them. The officials say they will close him down for an infraction of some code if he does not pay a bribe. "Our water supply was cut because we gave no bribe," he said. Moreover, when he does need the government's assistance, the services provided are slow and inadequate. He was the victim of eight thefts in three months but the police were always slow to respond. He has been in Kenya all his life and remembers what it was like under the British: "then if you ring the police, they are here in 3–5 minutes; now they ask you to come and pick them up with your car!" He had nothing positive to say about the political and bureaucratic system and the safety it is supposed to provide. "From the bottom to the top, it is completely wrong," he said. "This is a bribe country."

He was not the only one who voiced concerns about bribery and government harassment, but it is rare that businessmen will discuss the matter without being prompted. After the above interview, another Asian businessman along the same street made similar comments. "There are

20 or 30 different ones [government officials], not everyday but very frequent," he said. In Kombo Munyiri one businessman was so fed up he was thinking of joining his brother who ran a similar business in England. The problem was not only confined to Nairobi. The manager of a stainless steel sink-stamping operation spoke of the packets of cash which he gave his truck drivers to get his shipments past the various (bogus) police inspections and roadblocks on the way to Uganda. The bribes cost as much as the tariffs, he said. Several other businessmen said that they do not bid for government contracts because the process requires kickbacks and other forms of corruption.

The issue of corruption was not part of the questionnaire because it was initially assumed that the constant talk of corruption in Kenya was confined to the waste of government revenue or aid funds. Furthermore, an attempt was made to steer clear of political issues. Most businessmen did not discuss the issue unless prompted. When I became aware of the problem and did ask about it, they (Asians) all confirmed that it took place. Many became extremely animated and angry. For this research, it is not easy to place the problem within the framework of institutional analysis because it is not clear how it affects contracting or property rights. It is an important element of the institutional environment in which businesses operate, however, and it affects them both directly, because they must pay these bribes, and indirectly because it spoils business-government relations. One example of the latter is the attempt by the engineering department of the University of Nairobi to establish a government-assisted internship program with firms in the metal sector. The firms will not cooperate because they are treated so badly by government.[3]

When the problem of harassment is widespread, it seems irrelevant to discuss the mechanisms by which the state might encourage technological upgrading, the move into export markets or similar activities pursued by developmental states in East Asia or elsewhere. The first step in providing government support to business is a simple one: eliminate this harassment. Similarly, the first simple step in infrastructure provision is to ensure that the road network is properly maintained.

STATISTICAL ANALYSIS: MANN-WHITNEY TESTS

To test for differences between the locations, a series of Mann-Whitney tests were conducted, each time using two of the locations and testing for a significant difference between them for a given variable. Mann-Whitney is a commonly used, non-parametric ranking test and was selected due to

Table 5.5 Differences in size and starting capital by business location in Nairobi. Results of Mann-Whitney U tests (two-tailed)

	Kahawa	Kamukunji	Kariobangi	Gikomba	Kombo Munyiri
Kamukunji					
Current value	0.893				
No. of workers	0.598				
Starting capital	0.054				
Kariobangi					
Current value	0.865	0.570			
No. of workers	0.784	0.809			
Starting capital	0.354	0.205			
Gikomba					
Current value	0.083	0.058	0.365		
No. of workers	0.512	0.945	0.687		
Starting capital	0.562	0.021*	0.444		
Kombo Munyiri					
Current value	0.000*	0.000*	0.001*	0.000*	
No. of workers	0.000*	0.000*	0.000*	0.000*	
Starting capital	0.002*	0.000*	0.005*	0.003*	
Industrial area					
Current value	0.000*	0.000*	0.000*	0.000*	0.528
No. of workers	0.000*	0.000*	0.000*	0.000*	0.189
Starting capital	0.000*	0.000*	0.000*	0.000*	0.918
	African				
Asian					
Current value	0.000*				
No. of workers	0.000*				
Starting capital	0.000*				

* significant at 5% level

the small number of observations in some locations and the non-normal distribution of many variables.[4] These data characteristics precluded the use of parametric ANOVA tests. The values of the variables are interval in nature (i.e. number of years, value in shillings, etc.). Significance was tested at the 5% level using the SPSS software program. The results are provided in the three tables.

Firm size (value): The results in Table 5.5 show significant differences between the size of firms (as measured by value) in the two more formalized areas (Kombo and the Industrial Area) as against the firms in all of the less formalized areas (Estates, Kamakunji, Kariobangi and Gikomba). Within the less formalized areas, there are no differences except between Gikomba and other areas. This is in line with observations made during sampling such that Gikomba was more developed than the other areas. The only other important result is the lack of a difference between Kombo and the Industrial Area, but this is likely explained by the fact that the smaller end of firms in the Industrial Area is included in the sample. Upon being asked informally, several firms in Kombo indicated that they saw no need to move to the Industrial Area and would only do so if they changed substantially their line of business and needed much larger premises.

Firm size (number of workers): Table 5.5 also provides results on firm size based on the number of workers. These results are almost exactly the same as those for size based on current value. The exception is the area of Gikomba which shows no difference from the other less formalized areas. This is in line with the observation that what distinguishes Gikomba is the level of machinery use. Again, there is also no difference between Kombo and the Industrial Area.

Starting capital: The pattern for size held also for the amount of starting capital (measured in real terms) needed to start the business (Tab. 5.5). A clear distinction was evident between the two more formalized areas and the four informal ones. Median starting capital in the informal areas reached no higher than Ksh 45,000 ($765), while in the two formalized areas, it was Ksh 522,500 and just under Ksh 700,000. There was no difference between the two formalized areas. Within the less formal areas, there was some difference between Kamukunji and two of the other areas, notably because starting capital in Kamukunji is very low.

Ethnicity, size and starting capital: Testing for differences based on ethnicity, instead of location, the analysis revealed a significant difference between African and Asian firms for starting capital and for both firm size variables, as shown by the results presented at the bottom of Table 5.5.

Longevity: Regarding longevity (the number of years the firm had been in operation), the test results again show a significant difference

Table 5.6 Differences in enterprise longevity, previous employment and part-time operation. Results of Mann-Whitney U tests (two-tailed)

	Kahawa	Kamu-kunji	Kario-bangi	Gikomba	Kombo Munyiri
Kamukunji					
Years of full-time operation	0.155				
Years of part-time operation	0.771				
Owner's previous experience	0.001*				
Kariobangi					
Years of full-time operation	0.665	0.348			
Years of part-time operation	0.710	0.523			
Owner's previous experience	0.754	0.014*			
Gikomba					
Years of full-time operation	0.025*	0.227	0.071		
Years of part-time operation	0.129	0.087	0.057		
Owner's previous experience	0.407	0.029*	0.660		
Kombo Munyiri					
Years of full-time operation	0.000*	0.000*	0.001*	0.010*	
Years of part-time operation	0.133	0.082*	0.202	0.004*	
Owner's previous experience	0.523	0.081*	0.794	0.927	

(continued)

Table 5.6 *(continued)*

	Kahawa	Kamu-kunji	Kario-bangi	Gikomba	Kombo Munyiri
Industrial area					
Years of full-time operation	0.000*	0.000*	0.001*	0.025*	0.316
Years of part-time operation	0.715	0.389	0.862	0.003*	0.159
Owner's previous experience	0.833	0.015*	0.957	0.915	0.601
	African				
Asian					
Years of full-time operation	0.000*				
Years of part-time operation	0.000*				
Owner's previous experience	0.000*				

* significant at 5% level

between the two formalized areas and the four less formalized ones (Tab. 5.6). Within the less formalized areas, Gikomba exhibited some differences relative to two of the other areas, again confirming its more intermediate status between the formal and non-formalized areas.

Part-time operation: The survey also asked about the number of years of part-time operation. This question was included in the survey when it became apparent that there was a difference in the level of starting capital between locations and ethnic groups. The hypothesis behind the test is whether the owners of larger firms had first operated their firms on a part-time basis so that they could accumulate capital from waged employment. Better educated and established residents of the city might find it easier to obtain such employment, relative to migrants or poorer urban residents. The tests results presented in Table 5.6 suggest that there is some difference, notably for Gikomba and Kombo relative to the other areas. The summary data indicate that these areas have, respectively, the lowest and the highest mean figures for part-time operation. Overall, the summary statistics for the six areas show little variation and it can be concluded with some certainty that this factor does not explain the great differences in firm size.

Previous experience of owner: Owners were also asked about their previous experience working in the metal sector. This would provide an opportunity to gain technical knowledge as well as to amass capital from wages. The idea arose from stories about immigrants from the Indian sub-continent who obtained good-paying jobs with Kenyan Asian businesses, worked for four to five years to amass capital and then started on their own.

The results presented in Table 5.6 show that there was little difference between the various locations regarding the length of time previously spent by an owner as a paid employee in another metalworking business. The exception in all cases was Kamukunji, which was significantly different in comparison to all other locations. The summary statistics reveal that the median Kamukunji owner did not spend any time working for other metal businesses before starting his own operation. In other cases, the median was 2 to 3.3 years. This may suggest that Kamukunji absorbs many Africans who start a business because of the difficulty of obtaining paid employment.

A comparison between Asian and African owners revealed no significant difference in terms of the length of pervious employment (Tab. 5.6). This is only relevant if the level of remuneration is somewhat similar. If not, then the stories noted above may still be relevant, as some commentators noted that Asian employees are paid more than Africans for doing similar work in Asian-owned businesses.

Human capital: The final area tested was human capital, as proxied by years of schooling of the owner. The results are provided in Table 5.7. The hypothesis is that a better-educated owner may have better basic skills (literacy, numeracy), better technical skills (technologist or engineering training) and possibly better organizational skills. In particular, technical skills would be more important for these production-related firms than for trading businesses. The questionnaire only asked about the schooling of the owner, however, not the firm's workforce. This is less of a concern than it may at first appear because in small firms the owner often trains workers and his knowledge of production techniques will have a significant impact on the efficiency of production. As well, the owner will often undertake or supervise most aspects of administration. Two additional caveats should also be made, namely: that the quantity not the quality of education is being measured; and that a key ingredient of business success, entrepreneurship, is not being measured.

It was expected that areas with more micro firms would have lower levels of technical and university training and possibly also lower levels of

Table 5.7 Differences in education, by business location. Results of Mann-Whitney U tests (two-tailed)

	Kahawa	Kamu-kunji	Kario-bangi	Gikomba	Kombo Munyiri
Kamukunji					
Total years of education	0.128				
Higher (college-university)	0.000*				
Technical college	0.000*				
University	0.604				
Kariobangi					
Total years of education	0.969	0.097*			
Higher (college-university)	0.868	0.000*			
Technical college	0.930	0.000*			
University	0.824	0.397			
Gikomba					
Total years of education	0.548	0.011*	0.781		
Higher (college-university)	0.218	0.012*	0.309		
Technical college	0.371	0.009*	0.572		
University	0.280	0.435	0.186		
Kombo Munyiri					
Total years of education	0.582	0.240	0.397	0.144	
Higher (college-university)	0.008*	0.119	0.013*	0.255	
Technical college	0.014*	0.101	0.025*	0.255	
University	0.298	0.452	0.202	1.000	

(continued)

Table 5.7 (*continued*)

	Kahawa	Kamu-kunji	Kario-bangi	Gikomba	Kombo Munyiri
Industrial area					
Total years of education	0.338	0.001*	0.457	0.484	0.035*
Higher (college-university)	0.673	0.000*	0.831	0.405	0.030*
Technical college	0.074	0.009*	0.149	0.605	0.439
University	0.260	0.029*	0.397	0.039*	0.046*
	African				
Asian					
Total years of education	0.522				
Higher (college-university)	0.814				
Technical college	0.499				
University	0.147				

* significant at 5% level

basic education (primary and secondary). The results in Table 5.7 provide no clear pattern, except that owners in Kamukunji have significantly lower levels of education than all other areas except Kombo. In terms of ethnicity, there is no significant difference between Africans and Asians. From this we might conclude that education levels appear to be fairly evenly distributed among owners in the various locations. Thus differences in business success can be accounted for by differences in years of education but might be related to the quality of education, entrepreneurship qualities or the family background of the owners.

CONCLUSION

In conducting a firm survey, one is struck by the diversity of products, techniques and machinery, even when dealing only with small firms engaged in metal fabrication. This chapter has sought to provide an understanding of that diversity through a qualitative and descriptive analysis of different metal manufacturing areas in Nairobi. At the same time, statistics collected in the course of quantitative surveying have provided data on which to make distinctions based on size, location and ethnicity. This reveals a large mass of micro and very small, informal sector firms and a group of larger and more technologically advanced firms in the formal sector. Within this broad characterization, five specific findings might be highlighted.

First, the Asian predominance in manufacturing which Himbara (1994) found among large-scale manufacturing firms (100+ workers) is replicated among smaller firms. The micro firms in the informal areas are owned by Africans, while in the formal areas, firms with permanent structures and considerable investment in machinery are predominantly owned by Asians. Thus, African ownership in manufacturing is not only limited at the upper end of the firm-size distribution but is also limited among small but formalized firms.

Second, there appears to be little in the way of a graduated structure of firm development at the small end of the size distribution. Firms in the four informal areas had similar characteristics and any apparent differences thrown-up by descriptive statistics did not, for the most part, prove to be significant when tested on the basis of Mann-Whitney analysis. There is some evidence, however, that firms in Gikomba exhibit characteristics (size, starting capital, longevity, machinery use, etc.), which place them somewhere between the micro firms of the informal areas and the small firms of the formal areas.

Third, the analysis revealed that the specific indicator used for firm size can effect the results of statistical tests. Using the number of workers as an indicator of size will tend to hide differences in investment level, notably investments in machinery. These investments will be better captured by an indicator of the firm's asset value or expected sale value. Our tests showed that firms in Gikomba were not significantly larger than those in other informal areas when the number of workers was used as the variable for size. However, when the value of the firm (owner's expected sale value) was used, then there was a difference within these less formalized areas. This difference may be relevant for understanding credit markets because providers of credit may be more likely to judge the size of a firm based on physical assets rather than the number of workers. Assets may provide better evidence of a past ability to accumulate capital, a current ability to provide collateral and a future capacity to generate revenue.

Fourth, the difference in firm size between formal and informal areas is strongly mirrored by a difference in the level of starting capital. This suggests that firms are larger because they start out larger and that African firms may be small because most of them start out that way. Initial investment and either growth or permanence may be related, however. Micro firms are unable to invest in the machinery needed to enter more lucrative market niches and instead get caught in a low-equilibrium technological trap in which they must compete with a multitude of similar firms, all of which have difficulty generating a surplus. Thus, the chief problem for micro firms may be their lack of starting capital, as distinct from their lack of capital during operation.

Fifth, there is little variation in the length of part-time operation, the previous experience of the owner or the level of his schooling across all the areas surveyed. Data on these factors were specifically sought and analyzed to determine if they might account for differences in starting capital. We hypothesized that if a firm operates longer on a part-time basis or if the owner has more previous experience and a better education, then he may have amassed more capital through paid employment. The lack of variation suggests that the ability to amass starting capital may be related instead to the wealth of the family and the ethnic community. We explore the issue of starting capital in greater detail in the following chapters.

Chapter Six

Legal and Financial Institutions for Enterprises

Small firms operate in an environment of legal and financial institutions, to which they have greater or lesser access. In this chapter we seek to map that environment and to explain the specific institutional mechanisms which are at work. In doing so, we address four specific research questions.[1]

First, can we confirm that the larger firms in our survey have better access to formal institutional arrangements such as trade and bank credit and use of the legal system to settle disputes? It is likely that larger firms appear more credible and trustworthy and have built up stronger relations with banks and other businesses. At the same time, because they are larger, they engage in filling larger orders, making larger payments and attempting to secure larger amounts of financing. The higher value of transactions reduces, relatively, the associated administrative costs; it becomes economical for banks and other businesses to provide credit to them and it is cost effective for them to engage the court system to settle disputes.

Second, if we can confirm the association between size and the use of formal institutions, then the follow-on question is how do firms achieve their size level? Here we draw on the existing literature which suggests that very small firms tend to stay small whereas larger firms start off larger. This suggests that size is not so much a function of growth but of initial investment. While the latter will be based on the personal wealth and connections of the new entrepreneur, we suggest that it will be also be based on the ownership structure he chooses. Whether he organizes his firm as a sole proprietorship or combines with others to form a partnership may have an important bearing on a firm's initial size and therefore on its access to formal institutions for finance or dispute resolution. This possibility is considered with a test for a correlation between size and ownership structure.

Third, we investigate the possibility that the basic positive correlation between firms size and access to (or use of) institutions may not hold for some institutional mechanisms developed by very small firms. The hypothesis here is that when very small firms are barred from access to regular financial institutions, they develop other mechanisms to alleviate their financing constraints. The correlation between size and use of these institutions would therefore be negative; they are more prevalent among smaller firms. Here we investigate the use of prepayment (i.e. downpayment on large orders) and the use of purchase orders as collateral for relieving working capital constraints. In addition, the use of joint purchase arrangements for reducing costs is also investigated.

Fourth, the analysis addresses the issue of whether ethnic-information networks operate to provide better credit access to Asian-owned firms. This issue is difficult to test statistically because African firms are smaller and Asian firms are larger and therefore it is often unclear whether size or ethnicity is affecting institutional access. The only way to do so is to compare the strength of association from two tests, one in which size is the independent variable determining access and the other in which ethnicity is independent. For each institution analyzed in this chapter, two such tests are conducted.

The answers to these questions can be summarized briefly at this stage. Our tests do confirm that larger firms have better access to trade and bank credit, are more likely to be registered and reveal a greater tendency to use the court system to resolve payment disputes. Second, we find that size is strongly associated with ownership structure such that partnerships are much more likely to govern larger firms than are sole proprietorships. Entrepreneurs who are able to organize with others into partnerships are more likely to achieve a size-threshold which facilitates their access to established financial institutions. Third, the smallest firms do overcome their lack of access to regular financing options by developing other mechanisms. The results suggest that they engage heavily in the use of prepayment and purchase-order collateral to gain access to trade credit. Larger firms also use prepayment extensively, however, although they make very little use of purchase-order collateral (likely because they already have access to regular trade credit). Finally, we cannot distinguish between ethnicity and size effects using techniques which involve nominal or ordinal variables, as was the case for this chapter. Stronger techniques are needed.

These issues and results are addressed in greater detail in the analysis which follows. Subsequent to a section on methodology, the chapter is organized on the basis of distinct institutions. These are, in order of appearance: firm registration, security of property, use of the legal system, access to trade and bank credit, ownership structure, joint purchase arrangements, prepayment, and purchase-order collateral. A concluding section summarizes the main findings.

METHODOLOGY

The analysis is based on qualitative information gained from discussions with proprietors and on data provided through a structured questionnaire. The latter included many questions on the institutional environment in which firms operate and the informal institutions which firms developed to govern relationships between themselves. Use and non-use of each institution is cross-tabulated against a quartile breakdown of firm size (based on its current asset value). In this way, we can search for a relationship between firm size and access to each institution. This is supported by the calculation of a Cramer's V statistic (discussed below) to measure the strength of association. Because this study suggests that access to particular institutions may be based on or supported by ethnic-information networks, we also test the strength of association between access to an institution and the ethnicity of the firm owner. This is measured also by Cramer's V.

Cramer's V takes a value between 0 (no association) and 1 (perfect association). Because there is only one independent variable, we would expect that values would be low and thus suggest a basic interpretation that an association of less than 0.2 is 'weak,' that 0.2 to 0.4 is 'medium' and that greater than 0.5 is 'strong.' A more detailed explanation of Cramer's V is provided in Appendix 2. The results of the data analysis for each institution (i.e. financial or legal mechanism) are provided in each section.

Frequent reference is made to the fact that African firms tend to be concentrated at the smaller end of the size distribution while Asian firms are clustered at the larger end. This is confirmed in a cross-tabulation of ethnicity with a quartile breakdown based on size. Some 77% of African firms fall within the two lowest quartiles, while only 4% are in the upper quartile. Conversely, only 8% of Asian firms are in the two lowest quartiles and these are all in the second quartile. A full 54% of Asian firms are located in the upper quartile. All firms (3) with combined ethnic ownership (partnerships) are located in the upper quartile.

FIRM REGISTRATION

One aspect of the formal institutional environment is the system of firm registration. There are two systems in Nairobi, one involves the registration by Nairobi City Council which is basically a permit to conduct business and is verifiable by local police and city authorities. The other is a listing with the Register of Companies which is required for more established firms and provides the official distinction between the formal and informal sectors. The city council requirement was used in the survey because it is a legal requirement and thus provides the criterion for determining which firms are operating fully outside of the law. Sampling for registration levels is a useful means of characterizing firms. It is doubtful, however, that registration is a causal factor regarding firm size or growth. Many firms register at the time of their establishment or, for the more micro operations, when they reach a certain (viable) stage in their development. It eases relations with authorities and is a requirement for any official dealings with many other private sector firms or with government agencies. The lack of registration in our sample appears to be a matter of size, not of any deliberate attempt by larger, profitable businesses to remain underground.

As showed in Table 6.1, some 33% of firms in the sample were not registered; most of these were the smallest firms. Three-quarters of firms in the lowest quartile were not registered, while all firms in upper quartile were. Along with figures from the middle quartiles, we find a distinct relationship between size and registration. This is confirmed by the Cramer's V statistic which shows a significant and strong correlation of 0.6 and indicates that larger firms are more likely to be registered. Regarding ethnicity, we find that all Asian firms are registered while only about half of African firms are. Not surprisingly, Cramer's V statistic is strong and significant at 0.5 indicating that Asian firms are more likely to be registered than African ones. The two results are related, of course, as smaller firms tend to be owned by Africans. Still, it is interesting to note that even the unregistered firms in the third quartile are African-owned. This is due to the fact that some larger African firms are located in 'informal' business areas. It is also true that a presidential decree removed registration obligations for firms in Kamukunji.[2] All but one of the unregistered firms were located outside of the two formal industrial areas.[3]

Generally there might be two broad explanations for non-registration: either firms are hoping to avoid government notice or they are too small for the cost to be covered by any benefit. Avoiding government notice is likely linked to the desire to avoid taxation or regulation. It is

Table 6.1: Firm registration

		Registered	Not registered
Size quartiles		%	%
1		25	75
2		63	37
3		82	18
4		100	0
Cramer's V		0.606	
significance		0.000	
Ethnicity of owners			
African	n = 71	47	53
Asian	n = 41	100	0
Combin.	n = 3	100	0
Cramer's V		0.553	
significance		0.000	

Source: author's survey; % figures refer to the total within the quartile or ethnic group

important to realize that if firms wish to avoid detection then it is unlikely that they would have agreed to participate in the survey or would have indicated their real reasons for remaining unregistered. Despite my best efforts (in Gikomba in particular), the underground operations suggested by King (1996) could not be located or accessed. As a result, only 8% of unregistered firms in the survey indicated they "did not want to be noticed by the government" (results not shown). The main reasons for non-registration were: cost (32%), perceived lack of benefit (24%), the feeling that procedures were too complicated (16%) or that it was not required (19%).[4]

SECURITY OF PROPERTY

The institutional literature suggests that property rights provide security for investment and collateral for credit.[5] Of the three aspect of property rights—state expropriation, disputes with neighbors and illegal entry (trespass and theft)—it is only the latter which is of particular concern in the formal areas of business activity. In these areas, formal property rights are recognized by the legal system and business owners can either own or rent premises with limited dispute about their right to the use or possession of that property (aside from those common to any established real estate market). Qualitative questioning indicated that businesses were mainly concerned with the level of public security regarding illegal entry and theft. Complaints were voiced about the slow response of the police to calls to investigate burglary and one interviewee recounted how he was asked to provide transport for officers investigating a break-in at his firm. Firms' best defense was to provide a high level of security themselves with the use of alarm systems, locks, security bars and gates. A USAID report on SMEs actually cited the rising incidence of crime as a factor which was likely to expand the market for customized metal work (Masinde 1994).

It is not clear whether the lack of security in Nairobi inhibited investment by domestic businessmen. One owner (of a large firm, excluded from the sample) told the story of being confronted in this office with half a dozen armed gunmen who shot out the office windows, assaulted him and took cash. He and his partners had plans to set up a much larger plant but the incident made them have second thoughts. The lawlessness which accompanies political activity tends to affect retail shops in the city's commercial centre more than formal industrial firms. Many of those fearful of their business security left the country after the rioting surrounding the failed coup attempt in 1982.

In the informal areas, the problems are different. Micro firms have set up on vacant land because they cannot afford to rent or purchase premises and thus have no right of ownership. These entrepreneurs often build lockable storage compartments out of wood or metal to keep their tools, in the absence of an enclosed business premise. In Kamukunji, the *jua kali* association has responded to concern about theft by hiring a night-watchman to patrol the area. More able businessmen, who can generate a surplus, have the possibility of moving to more formal, rented premises in relatively close proximity in Gikomba.

In Kamukunji, a system of private land rights has been developing under community control. The land was initially vacant and entrepreneurs set up shop. It has become well-recognized as a metalworking and sales location and there is now competition for work sites. A new entrant must pay an outgoing firm for the site and any structures, while the *jua kali* association, which keeps track of who occupies which site, screens new entrants who often need a reference from an existing firm. This does indicate that the agglomeration of small firms in this area is acting like a business community with norms and informal practices governed by community organization. Unfortunately, the survey questions focused on

Table 6.2a: Non-payment

		Has a customer ever not paid for an order?	
		Yes	**No**
Size quartiles		%	%
1		47	53
2		58	42
3		77	23
4		68	32
Cramer's V		0.238	
significance		0.113	
Ethnicity of owners			
African	n = 65	55	45
Asian	n = 41	74	26
Combin.	n = 3	100	0
Cramer's V		0.212	
significance		0.086	

Table 6.2b: Use of the courts

		Has your business used the courts to settle an unpaid order?	
		Yes	**No**
Size quartiles		%	%
1		0	100
2		6	94
3		46	54
4		37	63
Cramer's V		0.471	
significance		0.000	
Ethnicity of owners			
African	n = 47	9	91
Asian	n = 33	33	67
Combin.	n = 3	100	0
Cramer's V		0.469	
significance		0.000	

Source: author's survey; % figures refer to the total within the quartile or ethnic group

credit issues and therefore did not specifically gather data on the ownership of plots or work sites.

USE OF THE LEGAL SYSTEM

The legal system is the chief instrument of the formal institutional environment by which contracts are enforced. Its potential use can reduce the adverse selection of unreliable transacting parties and lower opportunistic behavior once an agreement has been reached. In addition, its actual use can enforce restitution. The use of the courts in the developing world, including Kenya, tends to be limited by administrative inefficiency (Vandenberg 1998). Meanwhile micro and small firms often find that the costs of using the system outweigh the benefits, notably because the value of funds in dispute may be rather small relative to court and lawyer's fees. Transacting with the use of the legal system tends only to be efficient for larger firms. Smaller firms tend to find other ways of screening or they side-step the problems by limiting the extent of inter-temporal transacting and resort more to spot cash transactions.

Firms were first asked whether they ever experienced non-payment by customers. The results are provided in Table 6.2a. Not surprisingly, 63% indicated that they had experienced non-payment problems. While firms of all sizes experienced this problem, it was slightly more pronounced in the two upper quartiles. This is likely due to the fact that larger firms may do more work on order. Nonetheless, the tested association using Cramer's V statistic was insignificant for both size and ethnicity, that is, neither size nor ethnicity has a significant bearing on whether firms experience non-payment problems. Those firms which had had payment problems were then asked whether they had ever used the courts to resolve such disputes. As indicated in Table 6.2b, only 22% had used the courts and, of those cases, almost all were from the two upper quartiles. This supports the general intuition that the smallest firms are not served by the formal legal system. The association between size and court use is strong and significant with a Cramer's V statistic of 0.5, meaning that larger firms are more likely to use the court system. Because larger firms are Asian-owned, there was a similar measured association between ethnicity and court use. The Cramer's V statistic indicated a strong degree of association (0.5), indicating that Asian firms are more likely than African firms to use the courts.

The problem of cost was addressed in a supplemental question which asked firms why they did not use the legal system. The main response was that it was too expensive (44%), while another 17% of firms took matters in their own hands (literally) by retrieving the goods from the offending

Table 6.3a: Trade credit access

		Buy steel inputs on credit	Do not buy steel inputs on credit
Size quartiles		%	%
1		4	96
2		9	91
3		43	57
4		73	27
Cramer's V		0.591	
significance		0.000	
Ethnicity of owners			
African	n = 62	10	90
Asian	n = 40	70	30
Combin.	n = 3	33	67
Cramer's V		0.591	
significance		0.000	

Table 6.3b: Bank credit access

		Have borrowed from bank	Have not borrowed from bank
Size quartiles		%	%
1		0	100
2		4	96
3		39	61
4		56	44
Cramer's V		0.542	
significance		0.000	
Ethnicity of owners			
African	n = 67	8	92
Asian	n = 42	52	48
Combin.	n = 3	33	67
Cramer's V		0.499	
significance		0.000	

Source: author's survey; % figures refer to the total within the quartile or ethnic group

customer.[6] One interviewee indicated that he actually had the assistance of a police officer in retrieving goods. A further 11.5% indicated that they do not trust the courts to be fair, while an additional 8% indicated that they did not possess sufficient understanding of the legal system. The remaining 20% indicated a combination of the four above factors (cost, self-retrieval, distrust, lack of understanding). We should be particularly carefully not to interpret too much from these percentage figures for the total number of firms involved in the response was 64 (half our sample) and thus individual responses are based on several firms in some cases. Nonetheless, the figures may indicate that if a low-cost and accessible means of dispute adjudication could be devised, it might help to raise the level of inter-temporal contracting.

TRADE AND BANK CREDIT

The survey also considered firms' access to bank loans and trade credit. It can be hypothesized that smaller firms have limited collateral with which to secure bank credit and that their lack of an established business presence makes it more difficult to secure trade credit. The results of the survey, provided in Tables 6.3a-b, indicate that bank borrowing was restricted almost entirely to firms in the two upper quartiles. What is interesting is that only slightly more than half of the firms in the upper quartile had ever borrowed from the bank. Similar results were revealed for trade credit although more (almost three-quarters) of upper quartile firms used trade credit. Not surprisingly, size was significantly and strongly associated with trade credit and bank credit access. Cramer's V statistics of 0.6 and 0.5, respectively, indicate that larger firms have greater access to these forms of credit. As well, credit access was significantly and strongly associated with the ethnicity of the firm's owner. Cramer's V statistics of 0.6 for trade credit and 0.5 for bank credit indicate that Asian firms have better access to these forms of credit than do African firms. To separate out these two effects and to assess whether there are strong ethnic-information networks at work in the credit market, a probit analysis is applied to the data in the following chapter. A more detailed discussion of access to credit is provided there.

OWNERSHIP STRUCTURE

At the firm level, Kenyan law provides for a variety of ownership/governance structures; notably sole proprietorship, partnership, limited private company and unlimited publicly-traded company. Because the

Table 6.4: Firm registration

		Sole proprietor	Two partners	Several partners	Limited company
Size quartiles		%	%	%	%
1		72	25	3	0
2		71	25	4	0
3		32	50	14	4
4		26	22	52	0
Cramer's V		0.353			
significance		0.000			
Ethnicity of owners					
African	n = 71	66	25	9	0
Asian	n = 42	17	38	31	2
Combin.	n = 3	0	33	68	0
Cramer's V		0.318			
significance		0.000			

Source: author's survey; % figures refer to the total within the quartile or ethnic group

survey focused on the small end of the size distribution, all the firms were organized either as sole proprietorships (51%) or partnerships (48%), with only one firm (1%) constituted as a limited private company.[7] These results and those which follow are presented in Table 6.4. The partnerships had either two partners (30% of all firms) or several (18%). Almost three-quarters of the firms in the first two quartiles were operated as sole proprietorships. Conversely, 64% of firms in the third quartile and 74% in the fourth quartile were operated as partnerships. The measured strength of association, using Cramer's V statistic, is significant and medium at 0.4, indicating larger firms are less likely to be sole proprietorships and are more likely to be partnerships. In this case, it is likely that size is the dependent variable, which is determined by the form of ownership structure. The advantage of a partnership over a sole proprietorship is that it allows for the pooling of resources, notably financial, which will be important for small manufacturing firm which require capital to purchase technology. The drawback is that the firm needs to be able to support two partners (and their families).

The extent of partnerships may be an indication of the degree of social capital in the community because the individual partners need to be able to trust each other in the business arrangement. If partnerships are based on (extended) family, they may represent an effort by such families to pool resources for business success. The importance of family in the Asian business community has been well documented (Zarwan 1977). In our survey, however, many of the small African firms are owned by rural-to-urban migrants and were either spatially detached from their families and/or working to provide money for them. The possibility of channeling resources into partnerships in manufacturing may be constrained by these arrangements; that is, the degree to which extended African families collectively join this sector may be limited. Summary statistics in Table 6.4 bear out the tendency for Asians to be more involved in partnerships: only 17% of Asian firms were constituted as sole proprietorships while 66% of African firms were organized under a single owner. The Cramer's V statistic shows a significant association of 0.3 indicating that Asian firms are more likely to be organized as partnerships than are African firms.

That said, examples of 'partnership-like' activities were observed among the micro African entrepreneurs which were categorized as sole proprietorships. The sharing and rental of tools are common in the micro areas where activity is often done side-by-side in open areas. The rental of welders is common in Kamukunji, for example. As well, micro firms which require the use of large cutting equipment often subcontract specific tasks to the owners of such equipment. Another, rather unusual, arrangement was found in Gikomba where a group of metal workers regularly sub-contracted each other whenever any member of the group obtained an order. They tended to make simple implements such as tools for digging. Orders were filled using a division of labor as might be found within a single firm. When specifically asked, however, they all stressed that they operated their own businesses and they ticked 'sole proprietorship' on the questionnaire. This may be another reason why it is important for micro manufacturing firms to be located near each other.

In dense areas of similar sub-sector activity, such as metalworking in Kamukunji or Gikomba, the ability of sole proprietors to pool the use of machinery may mitigate against the formation of partnerships. If there is a variety of firms which own different types of machinery, sub-contracting may develop as a common practice. The potential for sub-contracting may also enter into the decisions by some firms to invest in more advanced machinery, as the income to pay for new machines may flow both from own production and from sub-contracted work. These issues were not

Table 6.5: Joint purchase

		Does your business purchase steel in bulk with other firms?	
		Yes	**No**
Size quartiles		%	%
1		28	72
2		14	86
3		7	93
4		8	92
Cramer's V		0.240	
significance		0.114	
Ethnicity of owners			
African	n = 64	22	78
Asian	n = 40	5	95
Combin.	n = 3	33	67
Cramer's V			
significance		0.236	
		0.051	

Source: author's survey; % figures refer to the total within the quartile or ethnic group

specifically investigated through the questionnaire, however, but arose from observations in the course of sampling.

JOINT PURCHASE

One institution which might represent an effort by very small firms to reduce costs is joint purchase. It involves designating one buyer to purchase for several firms so as to meet the minimum purchase requirement set by a steel mill or a wholesaler. In particular, very small firms might be eager to obtain off-cuts from the steel mills (new steel in non-standard shapes and lengths) which are commonly sold by the tonne—too much for a small firm to purchase at one time. Among NGOs in Nairobi, joint purchase is seen as a means by which small firms might co-operate to lower their input costs and thus compete more effectively with slightly larger firms. Several firms also mentioned joint purchase during the course of pre-testing of the questionnaire.

The survey found that the number of firms participating in joint purchase was rather low, 17 firms, or 16% of the entire sample. As shown in

Table 6.5, this arrangement was used most by the smallest firms: 28% and 14% in the first two quartiles, respectively. Less than 10% of firms in the two upper quartiles were engaged in joint purchase. The Cramer's V statistic for joint purchase relative to firm size was 0.2, indicating a medium and significant association at just over the 10%-level. The result suggests that smaller enterprises are more likely than larger ones to engage in joint purchase arrangements. Regarding ethnicity, Cramer's V statistic was also 0.2 indicating a strength of association at the medium level but with a higher level of significance at just over 5%. This supports the argument that Africans are more likely to engage in joint purchase than Asian firms. One-quarter of all African firms are involved in joint purchase. This may be due in part to the location of their firms in informal areas, farther from suppliers. Larger firms in the formal sector are in a position to buy on their own from the mills or from traders.

The questionnaire assumed that joint purchase took place with steel mills but this was cross-checked with another question on the source of steel purchases, i.e. whether from a trader or from a mill. This revealed that all of the firms involved in joint purchase bought their steel from traders, an outcome not expected by the above reasoning, although there might be a number of possible explanations. It may be that traders are purchasing in bulk from the mills on order for a group of micro firms. It is more likely, however, that micro firms organize a bulk purchase from an established trader, be he engaged in new steel or scrap. It is not necessarily the case that this is being done to meet a minimum purchase requirement or bulk-purchase price discount. Many micro proprietors do not have their own vehicles and many of the steel traders are located outside of the informal metal-working areas. Micro firms may be organizing a joint purchase for transport reasons, with someone who has or can arrange for the use of a light truck. While this is a likely explanation, it would need to be supported by further evidence not available from the current survey.

Finally, because NGOs are keen to promote joint purchase as a way of supporting the small firm sector, the survey asked how these co-operative arrangements came to be established. Only two of the 17 firms indicated that it was 'arranged by a community group, business association or aid organization.' For the other firms, the arrangement developed through informal co-operation initiated by the firms themselves.

PREPAYMENT (DOWNPAYMENT)

Small manufacturers tend to be engaged heavily in customized, as opposed to mass, production. As a result, a large proportion of output is

Table 6.6: Prepayment (downpayment)

		Does your business ask for a downpayment on large orders?	
		Yes	**No**
Size quartiles		%	%
1		90	10
2		96	4
3		89	11
4		77	23
Ethnicity of owners			
African	n = 67	91	9
Asian	n = 41	83	17
Combin.	n = 3	67	33
Cramer's V		0.157	
significance		0.256	

Source: author's survey; % figures refer to the total within the quartile or ethnic group

likely to be produced on order. This is borne out in our survey in which 57% of firms produced three-quarters or more of their output on order while only 5.4% of firms did not produce on order. When producing on order, firms must reduce the opportunistic behavior of customers who might not return to collect and pay for the goods. This can be overcome through the requirement of a downpayment, which consists of whole or partial prepayment for the goods. In addition to shielding the producer from opportunism, it also serves the more practical purpose of providing smaller firms with the working capital necessary to buy the inputs needed to fill the order. As shown in Table 6.6, a full 87% of surveyed firms asked for a downpayment on large orders and this activity was common across firm size and ethnicity. As a result the association between downpayment and either size or ethnicity was insignificant, as shown by the Cramer's V results.

The importance of prepayment as an institutional device can best be illustrated by an interview with a retailer located in central Nairobi who, like most downtown merchants, is of Asian origin. Various African micro manufacturers come to his store once or twice a week with items to sell. The merchant buys what he needs mostly on a cash basis but

Table 6.7a: Purchase order collateral: bank credit

		Has your business used a customer order to obtain a bank loan?	
		Yes	**No**
Size quartiles		%	%
1		0	100
2		13	87
3		4	96
4		4	96
Cramer's V		0.213	
significance		0.179	
Ethnicity of owners			
African	n = 67	6	94
Asian	n = 42	0	100
Combin.	n = 3	33	67
Cramer's V		0.270	
significance		0.017	

Table 6.7b: Purchase order collateral: trade credit

		Has your business used a customer order to obtain trade credit?	
		Yes	**No**
Size quartiles		%	%
1		35	65
2		29	71
3		11	89
4		12	88
Cramer's V		0.259	
significance		0.066	
Ethnicity of owners			
African	n = 66	27	73
Asian	n = 40	12	88
Combin.	n = 3	0	100
Cramer's V		0.201	
significance		0.106	

Source: author's survey; % figures refer to the total within the quartile or ethnic group

sometimes he places larger orders, say for about 100 pails. He provides a prepayment for a portion of the whole order and provides subsequent payments as portions of the whole order are delivered. This ensures both that the product will be delivered and that the producer can finance the inputs. "They don't have money for materials, so I give them 100 shillings for 10 to 15 pails and when they come with the pails, I give them more [funds for the next batch]," he said. "They want the business so they come back." Opportunism is reduced by this simple means; it requires little reliance on trust or community sanctions and works across the ethnic divide.

PURCHASE ORDER AS COLLATERAL

The possibility that purchase orders were used as collateral was also investigated by the survey. For those firms with little physical collateral and a limited reputation among suppliers, a purchase order may signal to a supplier that the credit can be repaid through future revenue generated by the order. Given that small firms deal in orders of relatively small value, it may be hypothesized that this institution is more commonly used for trade credit than to secure a bank loan.

As shown in Table 6.7a, only 5% of firms had secured bank credit in this manner. All of these firms were African-owned, in addition to one firm of mixed ethnic ownership. The relationship between size and the use of purchase order collateral was insignificant, according to Cramer's V test of association. However, the relationship was significant for ethnicity with a V statistic of 0.2, indicating a medium strength of association.

The survey did find that purchase orders were used more readily to secure trade credit with 22% of all firms in the survey indicating such use. As shown in Table 6.7b, almost three-quarters of such firms were from the two smallest quartiles. The association between size and this type of purchase order collateral was significant at just over the 5% level, with a medium strength of association as indicated by a Cramer's V statistic of 0.3. The result indicates that smaller firms are more likely to use this type of credit mechanism than larger firms. The reason for its greater use among smaller firms is that larger firms have existing trade credit access and therefore are less in need of gaining such access through the presentation a purchase order. For small firms without regular trade credit access, however, it may be a useful means of easing working capital constraints. On a regular basis, only 6% of firms in the two lowest quartiles purchase their steel inputs on credit but a much higher portion of these small firms (32%) have used a purchase order to access trade credit on a one-off basis. This suggests that the financing constraints of the smallest firms may not be as great as indicated by figures on regular trade credit access.

CONCLUSION

This chapter has analyzed the legal and financial institutions used by micro and small firms in Nairobi's metal sector. The survey went beyond the standard questions regarding access to trade and bank credit to inquire into other financial arrangements, including the use of purchase orders as collateral and the incidence of prepayment (downpayment). Legal questions regarding firm registration and the structure of ownership assisted in providing a broad picture of the institutional environment in which small firms operate. Some findings held little surprise; for example, smaller firms were less likely to be registered or to use the courts to seek redress for unpaid orders. The analysis also produced three important findings.

First, differences in firm size may be accounted for by ownership structure; namely that firms are larger because they draw their initial investment from two or more partners. In a sector such as metal manufacturing, where investment in machinery is important for undertaking more specialized production, the added capital from multiple partners may be important for entering more lucrative segments of the market. Very small firms tend to be run as sole proprietorships and will be limited to over-crowded and highly competitive market segments. There appears to be a greater tendency for Asians to form partnerships than Africans. Thus, the disparity in firm size between Asians and Africans may be due to a reduced tendency among Africans to form partnerships.

Second, firms which do not have regular access to trade or bank credit are not limited to financing their working capital requirements from savings. Instead, they may use prepayment (i.e. downpayment) on large orders or they may use purchase orders as collateral for one-off access to trade credit. The use of prepayment on large orders was found to be common across size categories. While it does relieve the moral hazard of customers ordering but not collecting goods, it also helps to finance the purchase of inputs to complete the order. The use of purchase orders to obtain trade credit was much more common among smaller firms than larger ones. Larger firms likely already have access to trade credit and thus do not need to justify their needs to suppliers.

Third, the non-parametric tests used for the analysis were not able to confirm or deny whether Asian firms have an advantage over African firms due to the operation of stronger ethnic-information networks in credit markets. While we do find a significant association between ethnicity (Asian) and access to bank or trade credit (higher), we also find that access to credit is associated with firm size. Because Asian firms are larger, it is unclear whether access is due to size or to ethnic networks. In the next chapter, we employ stronger quantitative techniques (probit analysis) in an attempt to differentiate between the two effects.

Chapter Seven

Inter-firm, Inter-mediated and Informal Credit

We are seeking to understand the relative dominance of Asians in formal urban manufacturing and the coincident absence of Africans. A central idea is that Kenyan-Asians, as an ethnic business community, have developed strong networks which have allowed them to gain greater access to credit. Africans, excluded from these networks, are at a disadvantage in competing and indeed surviving in the urban sector. The purpose of this chapter is to specifically test for the factors which determine access to credit as a way of determining the importance of ethnic membership.

Different types of credit are supported to a greater or lesser extent by network effects. Inter-mediated credit (through banks, in the form of loans and overdrafts) are likely to be less affected because access criteria are more formalized, using collateral and credit history with the bank. In these cases, the value of the firm's assets (ability to provide collateral) and its longevity (credit history with the bank) are likely to be more important than ethnicity. Conversely, inter-firm (or trade) credit and informal credit for start up or expansion are likely to be strongly related to networks because of the informal nature of the screening and enforcement aspects of these credit contracts. The empirical results, generated from regression analysis, confirm the above intuition, except in the case of trade credit, where the value of firm assets overrides the influence of ethnicity. In addition, test results indicate that the level of starting capital is strongly correlated with firm size. Asian firms are larger, because they start larger, and they start larger because they have better access to starting capital.

These overall results support and supplement the central arguments of this study. Once established, Asian firms have no advantage over similarly sized African firms in accessing trade or bank credit. The difference is that

Asians are able to access higher levels of starting capital. This relates not only to the strength of informal networks but also to the relative wealth of the Asian community compared to those (poorer) segments of the African community from which urban proprietors are drawn. Furthermore, with higher starting capital, Asian firms can more readily meet the criteria for accessing formal credit.

This line of analysis is pursued through the two main sections of the chapter. The first sets out the institutional mechanisms which support different types of credit contracting. It also surveys key aspects of the empirical literature on small and medium enterprises in Africa. The second section then uses probit and OLS regression techniques to test for the significance of ethnicity, size and other effects in the allocation of credit. The analysis is based on the same data set employed for the two previous chapters.

INSTITUTIONAL THEORY AND FIRM CREDIT

The theoretical basis for the investigation is the institutionalism of North (1990) and its application to developing countries by Platteau (1994). They have established, at a general level, the importance of institutions, both formal and informal, in lowering the costs of transacting and supporting economic growth. Institutions reduce private transaction costs by increasing the flow of information about economic agents, thereby allowing people and firms to properly screen-in credible agents and screen-out those who less likely to be trustworthy. Furthermore, institutions provide enforcement mechanisms which ensure that agents, once they have entered into a contract, fulfill their obligations. This lowers the risks of contracting and discourages opportunism. Reducing the costs of transacting increases the frequency of transacting, thereby creating larger and denser markets. This in tern prompts specialization and an increased division of labor. In developing countries, the absence of formal screening and information mechanisms, such as credit bureaus, and the unreliability and costliness of legal procedures results in high transaction costs. Instead, reliable information flows through informal networks which are effective and low-cost but limited in their range. The enforcement mechanism works through reputation and exclusion. Firms which fail to honor commitments not only lose the chance for future contracting with the aggrieved firm but reduce their potential for contracting with other firms in the network because of the loss of reputation, transmitted through the information network (Greif 1993). These informal business networks piggyback existing social networks based on ethnicity, religion, region, etc. Information flows poorly between communities, limiting the extent of inter-group transacting and reinforcing the sectoral advantages (or disadvantages) of each group. A general reduction of inter-group barriers, either through social integration or increased business interaction and interdependence may eventually occur, however.

Networks are important for credit transactions because of the intertemporal nature of the contract in which financial (or physical) resources are provided in exchange for a promise to repay (or pay) at a future date. Firms face a number of potential options in obtaining credit which can be characterized by the institutional mechanisms which govern the transaction. While access to a bank loan may be important for expansion, other forms of credit may be key to supporting expansion, as well as the initial investment and day-to-day operations. The various options may be divided between: i) inter-mediated credit, such as loans or overdrafts, which is provided through financial institutions; ii) inter-firm credit, such as trade credit or installment credit, where the goods supplier also provides short-term credit to support the transaction; and iii) informal credit, which includes flexible loans from family or friends or even possibly business associates. While the costs of any of these forms of credit are important, the simple ability to gain access may have an important bearing on firm survival and growth.

Inter-firm credit. Trade credit and installment credit are similar in that they are not mediated through a financial institution but, as noted, the seller of goods is also the creditor. Credit in these cases is merely delayed payment for goods received and the fact that there is a transaction in the goods markets affects the nature of screening and enforcement. While these two types of credit can be classified together as inter-firm, there are differences between them. Trade credit is generally provided for component inputs and for regularly purchased supplies, over a relatively short timeframe of 30–60 days. Installment credit, however, tends to support the purchase of investment goods, such as machinery, usually involving a larger sum than trade credit and repaid in portions (installments) over a longer timeframe, usually beyond 60 days. Because installment credit involves the purchase of machinery, the goods can act as collateral. Non-payment can result in repossession which is a workable option for the creditor because he normally trades in those types of goods. Resale is thus easier and less costly than it is for a bank, for example. The same rationale about resale may hold for inputs provided on trade credit but the nature of the goods are normally less easily retrievable because they may be partly used up or embodied in finished goods. A number of small firms in my sample did repossess goods provided on trade credit, notably because of the absence of an effective and low-cost legal system.

Screening is affected through repeat dealings in cash, because the borrower and lender are also buyer and seller in the goods market. Many firms thus first need to purchase on a cash basis for a given period to build a relationship with the supplier. Furthermore, because the purchaser may have obtained credit from other firms, the supplier/creditor can assess creditworthiness by contacting other firms. As a result, the credit contract is more likely to be supported by network effects because more firms will have information to relay through the information network. For this reason, network effects are more likely to occur in inter-firm rather than inter-mediated credit (firms tend to buy supplies more often than they obtain credit from the bank). Within the category of inter-firm credit, network effects are more likely with trade credit than installments credit, again due to the greater frequency of transacting.

If networks do operate, then assessing the reputation of a member of the dominant business group will be easier than assessing the member of a non-dominant group. There is simply a greater chance that the potential creditor is known to other members of the supplier's ethnic group. In terms of Kenya, the supply of inputs and machinery is dominated by Kenyan Asians and thus Asians will find it easier to have their reputation assessed than Africans.

There are, however, ways in which a member of a non-dominant group can establish his presence. As noted, operating on a cash basis is one way, while locating in a proper industrial area, near suppliers, and maintaining a permanent business presence are others. These factors may be important in a locationally segmented manufacturing community such as the one in Nairobi.

Inter-mediated credit. Firms which access credit from financial intermediaries do so through loans and/or overdraft facilities. Loans from banks and finance companies support investment, including one-off machinery and vehicle purchases, as well as plant expansion, real estate acquisitions or takeovers. In developing countries, long term credit is commonly in short supply due to the risky economic and political environment. Bank loans tend to be secured by collateral which, given the size of the investment, makes the seizure of collateral through the legal system relatively more cost effective than for other forms of credit. On the borrower's side, the threat of collateral seizure (and the possibility of closure or housing loss) encourages repayment.

Network effects might be less important for inter-mediated credit for several reasons. Firstly, the nature of formal lending procedures, notably the use of collateral, reduces the need for checking reputation. Secondly, loan officers and managers in the banking community tend to be more representative of the country's (or a city's) ethnic composition than the heads of supplier firms. Thirdly, the existence of government-owned banks, including development banks, would tend to reduce the bias against the disadvantaged group.[1] Indeed, many of these banks were set up to deal specifically with the problem of under-financing faced by African entrepreneurs. Of the four main banks in Kenya, two are foreign controlled (Barclays and Standard Chartered), while two others (Kenya Commercial and the National Bank) were—until privatization in the mid-1990s—majority government-owned and heavily staffed by Africans.

An overdraft facility, another form of inter-mediated credit, supports both working capital requirements and the purchase of small machinery. The advantage for the firm is that the overdraft can be paid down quickly if cash flow allows and more slowly otherwise. For the bank, the advantage is that revenue earned by the firm in the normal course of business results in direct repayment.[2] As the interest charged on overdrafts is high (because credit is supplied without notice), it is expensive if the firm maintains a high overdraft. The overdraft is intimately tied to the relationship with the bank and while interim non-repayment is costly, eventual non-repayment means terminating the relationship with the bank and the loss of access to its other facilities.

Informal (or inter-personal) credit. A third category of credit is informal lending by family, friends or business associates. The latter of the three might be classified as inter-firm credit but it is included here because it is not generally available to the business public as is the case with trade credit. It involves a highly personalized element which also allows it to be depicted as 'inter-personal' credit. The institutional means for making and enforcing the contract is supported by the personal relationship. Information needed to screen is virtually costless because the parties already know each other, they know each other's past and present activities and they have a pre-existing sense of trustworthiness. Enforcement is also low-cost and highly effective because reneging on commitments results in the loss or serious downgrading of the relationship, which is cherished at a personal level; pride and good feeling are at stake.

It is unclear to what extent this type of credit may be an important source of finance for manufacturing firms but, as we will see later, there is evidence of its existence, particularly among Kenya's Asian business community. Its most important contribution may be in the provision of starting capital; before the firm has the potential to access trade or bank financing. In this regard, the relative wealth of a firm's family, friends and ethnic community will be important in determining the degree of support one might expect in starting a new business. We return to the important issues of informal credit and starting capital toward the end of the empirical section.

In summary, institutional theory suggests that ethnic network effects are more important for trade credit than for bank credit where collateral and the formal analysis of loans assumes greater importance. Whether trade credit, bank loans, overdraft credit or informal borrowing may explain the differences in firm size between Kenyan-Asian and African firms is a question we pursue latter in the chapter. The following section considers recent empirical work.

A REVIEW OF EXISTING EVIDENCE

The analysis of SME behavior in Africa has been aided since 1990 by two firm-level survey projects which have allowed for both single country and cross-country analysis on a range of issues including credit, size and growth.

The GEMINI surveys[3] are characterized by the inclusion of both rural and urban areas, the concentration on household-based firms and the preponderance of trading activities. In the Kenyan survey, for example, manufacturing firms in both the small and large industrial areas were omitted (Parker and Torres, 1994). The benefit of these surveys is that they allow for the analysis of very small firms and provide insights into the nature of African ownership (Mead and Liedholm 1998). By contrast, the surveys conducted under the World Bank's Regional Program in Enterprise Development (RPED) are notable for their focus on manufacturing across a range of firm sizes, with the exception of household-based entities. Conducted in east, southern and west Africa, the surveys are unique in that detailed questionnaires on firm activities, including credit access, were supplemented in some countries with a limited survey of the tendency for owners to socialize with suppliers and bank personnel. This was used in subsequent analytical work as an indicator of networking.

Using the RPED data, econometric analysis has been used to test for the significance of ethnic network effects on credit access. For Fafchamps (who has conducted the most detailed analysis), the purpose of the work is to understand the current size disparity between firms of different ethnic ownership and to explain why the advantage gained under colonialism by minority business groups, such as Kenya's Asians, "persists long after favorable factors and policies have been removed" (2000, p. 206). His analysis uses trade credit (measured as a proportion of total supply purchases) and overdraft and bank borrowing (measured as ever having had access) as dependent variables. Independent variables include a dummy for ethnic ownership, variables for socialization with suppliers and bank personnel, and others for size, sector, country and gender. His results from pooled data for Kenya and Zimbabwe indicate that African ownership is not significant in determining access to overdraft and banks loans when size in included in the regression. Furthermore, size is significant for overdraft access but not for bank access, a somewhat puzzling result given that size would allow for more collateral to be put forward. Socializing effects are significant in both cases, notably socializing with bank personnel during rather than after business hours. The direction of causality is not clear, however: does socializing lead to bank access (a network effect) or does bank access lead to socializing (an effect of doing business).

The results on trade credit are more difficult to interpret. They do show, however, that size as an explanatory variable loses its significance when an African dummy is included and, further, that socializing effects are significant when the African dummy is dropped (for the pooled sample and Kenya). When the African and socializing variables are included, however, the results are ambiguous. In the pooled data and Zimbabwe, the African variable remains significant suggesting that Africans receive less credit even after controlling for socializing effects. Indeed, the socializing variables are either insignificant or have the wrong sign. For Kenya, the results conform more to what is expected: African ownership is not significant when socializing variables—which are jointly but not independently significant—are included. This suggests that being an African owner does not impair credit access if the owner is socializing with suppliers and thus building networks.

What has not been tested in this work is: i) whether ethnic network effects are operating through informal credit; and ii) whether the reduced access to credit by Africans explains the skewed distribution in firm size between the two ethnic groups. Regarding this second issue, if ethnic effects are significant in determining access to trade credit (a likely scenario) and that type of credit provides a significant proportion of total firm credit (a possibility), then network effects can help to explain the skewed size distribution. On the contrary, if ethnicity is not important for facilitating trade credit or if such credit plays a relatively minor role in firm financing, then the network effect may be relatively unimportant in explaining the size distribution. The same is true of informal credit and bank credit, although in the latter case network effects are likely to be less important (as discussed above) but the proportion of such credit in total firm financing is likely to be more important.

The extent to which trade credit is important for firm survival and growth is not clearly established in the literature on SMEs in developing countries. It may be true that "only very small firms can operate on a cash-only basis" and that without trade credit agents operate a "flea-market economy" with underdeveloped market institutions (Fafchamps 2000: 209, 232). Statistics from the RPED survey suggest that in Zimbabwe, for example, trade credit from suppliers makes up 30% of external financing, with slightly lower levels for micro and small firms. Credit from formal lenders (formal bank/non-bank loans and overdrafts) account for 65% of external financing (Fafchamps, 1997: Tab. 9.2). Whether the 30% figure is considered sufficiently high to account for the skewed size distribution is open to question. Furthermore, the percentages refer to external, not total, financing (which would include reinvested profits). When the ratio of external to total financing is lower, then trade credit and the associated network effect will have less impact on the size distribution.

PREVIOUS WORK: SIZE AND STARTING CAPITAL

In addition to providing data which allows for the testing of network effects, the RPED surveys are also important for providing basic statistics on the size distribution of firms of different ethnic groups. In Tanzania and Zambia, for instance, Africans owned 93.7 and 90.5% of very small firms and only 30 and 36.4% of large firms. The presence of foreign ethnic communities in Kenya (Asians) and Zimbabwe (whites) affects the size distribution such that 79.3 and 85.0% of very small firms and only 3.6 and 8.3% of the very large firms are owned by Africans (Ramachandran and Shah 1999: 79). Of the 115 firms included in Fafchamps' study, the median size of African firms is 4 employees, while for Asian and white firms (in Kenya and Zimbabwe) it is 73. Comparing a sub-sample of African firms in which half of them are micro firms with a sub-sample including a majority of medium and large firms requires careful attention not only to the size variable, which can be controlled for, but also to the nature of firms in the two groups. Somewhat surprisingly, this size difference is not matched by a longevity difference of corresponding magnitude. African firms in the sample had a median start-up year of 1975, while Asian/white firms began on average only two years earlier. Thus, a typical African-headed firm had been in operation for just over 15 years and had four employees, while the typical Asian/white firm had been in operation for just over 17 years and had 73 employees.

Moreover, the size variable in Fafchamps' study (2000) is always significant in the regressions for trade credit access and always becomes insignificant when the African dummy is included. This suggests that a great deal of the influence of size on credit access is coming from the fact that

African firms are small. The reason that the African dummy overrides the size variable may be interpreted as African ownership implying smallness plus other elements which affect credit access. What might these other elements be?

One element may be location: many of the African firms in my survey are not located in the regular industrial areas of Nairobi. A study of firms in southern Africa indicated that location had a significant impact on firm growth (McPherson 1996: 269), although there was no test for credit access. Location may provide market opportunities, if firms are closer to customers, or technological externalities, if they are close to competitors or firms in related sectors. Furthermore, location in established commercial/industrial areas may act as a signal to creditors that the firm is a viable concern. Fafchamps (2000: 231) notes that creditworthy African firms face the problem of "distinguishing themselves from the mass of small, inexperienced micro-enterprises headed by blacks or women." In Kenya, locating in areas with Asian firms may be one way of overcoming the problem; suppliers might be more inclined to provide credit because the firm has some permanence and can be located easily if accounts are not serviced.

A second element may be the education of the entrepreneur. Studies on the RPED and GEMINI data indicate a correlation in some countries between firm growth and the owner's educational attainment (McPherson 1996; Ramachandran and Shah 1999). Education may make a difference in their conduct with suppliers, in the importance they attach to developing a credible reputation and their understanding of business arrangements. It is important to understand the causal nature of the relationship, however, and not just accept its statistical significance. As with other factors, it may provide clues to the problem of skewed distribution. One interpretation may be the following: the relatively short supply of well-trained engineers and technologists in the economy may mean that Africans with these skills enter paid employment instead of striking out on their own. Educated Asians may be less likely to follow that route because they have a family tradition of self-employment. Indeed, a higher percentage of Asian business owners had parents who ran private businesses (50.9%), as compared with Africans (8.8%) (Ramachandran and Shah 1999: Tab. 9.8). Well-trained Asians may return to run their parents' businesses or get support in establishing their own. They are less inclined to work in the public sector or for MNCs and the returns from private business, for them, may be high. Conversely, Africans know that the manufacturing sector is dominated by non-Africans and that establishing an African firm is difficult. They opt for reasonably well-paid positions in the government and with MNCs, where there is a higher probability of earning a stable income. Those with the skills and possibly better access to initial financing may not be entering self-employed manufacturing because of these high opportunity costs in paid employment. The majority of Africans who do establish businesses are therefore less educated and have lower opportunity costs. They are also likely to have little initial capital. Results from GEMINI data suggest that micro enterprises setup in "low return activities, with minimal barriers to entry, when the overall economy is languishing" (Mead and Liedholm 1998: 65). In the second section, we conduct tests of access to trade and bank credit and include variables for starting capital, location, size and education level, along with an ethnic dummy.

PURPOSE OF THIS STUDY'S EMPIRICAL WORK

The purpose of the quantitative exercise is to determine whether credit is being allocated on the basis of ethnicity rather than non-ethnic economic criteria. Ethnicity may influence the allocation of credit in two rather different ways. It may be due to statistical discrimination in which suppliers' perceptions, often based on past experience, indicate that members of one ethnic group are more creditworthy than another. Second, it may be due to informal ethnic networks which reduce the costs of obtaining the information necessary to assess reputation and make it easier to enforce contracts because of the threat to the borrower of gaining a bad reputation in the community.

The reason for undertaking this analysis is not solely to understand the nature of informal networks but to suggest how such networks may help to account for the business success of one ethnic group relative to another. In the case of Kenya, we are trying to understand whether the current skewed size distribution of manufacturing firms between Kenyan-Asians and Africans is the result of ethnic informational institutions which give advantages to Asians in assessing creditworthiness and, through reputation, enforcing credit contracts.

The firm characteristics of the two groups highlight the important differences in size, longevity, level of starting capital, location and level of formal registration. The data are provided in Table. 7.1. The only basic characteristics which are relatively similar are the years of previous experience of the owner and the years of part-time operation. There is some difference in the completion rate of secondary education but the difference is not as pronounced as many of the other indicators. What is important to note is that the difference in the median size of firms is much greater when the value of the firm (in Kenyan shillings) is used instead of the more common measure of the number of employees. This is considered in greater

Table 7.1: Descriptive Statistics: Asian-owned and African-owned firms

	African owned	Asian owned
No. of firms in sample	71	42
Size, median (value Ksh)	200,000	15,000,000
Size, median (no. of workers)	5	22
Starting capital, median (Ksh)	30,703	618,706
Firm age (years)	6	17.5
Previous experience of owner (years)	2	0
Part-time operation (years)	0	0
Completion of secondary school (%)	71	95
Registered with city council (%)	46	100
Industrial location (%)	15	100
Trade credit access (%)	10	70
Borrow from bank (%)	7	52
Overdraft with bank (%)	21	73

Table 7.2: Determinants of Firm Size

Dep. Variable: log of current value

	Coefficient	T statistic
Constant	8.41	9.13
Firm age	0.11	2.78*
Firm age2	-0.002	-2.24*
Starting capital (real, log)	0.30	4.12*
Register (1/0)	0.67	2.16*
African owner (1/0)	-0.46	-1.04
Industrial location	1.70	3.47*
Observations	98	
F (6, 91)	50.19	
R-squared	.77	
R-squared Adjusted	.75	

* significant at the 5% level

Source: Author's survey

detail below. Another important difference is in the median level of (real) starting capital, in which the African figure is only 5% of the Asian figure. Asian firms are starting off with much more capital than African firms, and, as we shall test below, this may be an important determinant of current firm size.

RESULTS ON ENTERPRISE SIZE

The statistics on firm size are supplemented with a more formal, regression analysis of the determinants of size. The results, presented in Table 7.2, are important for an understanding of the determinants of size. We hypothesize that firm size is correlated with a number of firm characteristics such that,

$$FS_i = x_1 + x_2 KS_i + x_3 R_{1\,i} + x_4 E_i + x_5 L_i + x_6 A_i + x_7 A_i^2 + e_i$$

where *FS* is firm size and the independent variables include the age of the firms (*A*), its starting capital, (*KS, logged*), whether it is registered (*R*), the ethnicity of its owner (*E*) and its location (*L*). The *x* 's are coefficients, x_1 is the constant term and *e* is the error term.

The size of the firm (*FS*) is measured by its current value (logged). Owners were asked to indicate how much money they thought they would receive if the firm were sold at that time. The reason that this indicator was used instead of the number of workers is that it accounts for the firm's possession and use of machinery. In the metalwork sub-sector, the greater use of machinery means that the firm is at a higher technological level and therefore is better able to supply more specialized and profitable market niches. More specifically, in the regression analysis we attempt to determine whether there is a correlation between firm size and the willingness of suppliers or banks to grant credit. A lender could easily see the difference between two firms, each with ten employees, if the employees of the one firm are using hammers, tin snipes and simple welders while those of the other are employed at digitally controlled lathe machines. The presence of the machinery would provide a stronger indication that the firm had had some success in accumulating capital and had the means to generate revenues in the future.

There are problems with the use of the firm's sale value, however. The figures were provided on the questionnaire by the owner and not independently verified from in-house accounting records or audited financial statements. Thus there is no way to check the reliability of the figures other than for the surveyor to make a rough judgment based on the visible size of the workshop and the quality and number of machines present. This was done in most cases.

Real starting capital (*KS*, logged) is included based on the idea that larger firms start off larger. Their owners venture into business when they have accumulated or can access the capital needed to make a proper go of it with adequate machinery. The micro firms, by contrast, are often begun by those who have few other means of personal financial support and decide to create their own employment. As a result, they have little seed capital, they start small and remain that way because they do not have the capital to invest in machinery and do not have the machinery for specialized output to generate the profits needed for expansion.

Firm registration (*R*), with Nairobi City Council, is included as a dummy to separate the very small firms from the more serious ones. The variable takes the value 1 if the firm is registered and 0 otherwise. It is expected that the variable will be positive as larger firms are likely to be registered. We include a dummy variable for ethnicity (*E*) which takes the value 1 if the firm is solely owned by an African, and 0 otherwise. This is done to suggest that there might be either a network effect which helps firms to grow bigger or there may be discrimination, in which members of the dominant business group (Asian) discriminate against African firms. We expect the variable to be negative because the descriptive statistics suggest that Asian firms tend to be larger.

From observations made during fieldwork, it was surmised that the location (*L*) of operation is strongly correlated with firm size. Firms that intend to make a more serious go of it and intend to capture business from large neighboring firms tend to locate in the more established industrial areas of Nairobi. The location variable is a dummy which takes the value of 1 if the firms is located in the two more established industrial areas (Kombo Munyiri and the Industrial Area), and 0 for the four other areas surveyed.

The final independent variable is the age of the firm (*A*). Firms are likely to be larger because they have had more time to re-invest and grow. This may be important as the general problem with micro-sized firms is that they are unable to sustain themselves in business. We use both age (number of years of operation) and age squared to test whether the relationship is linear, quadratic or both depending on the stage of a firm's development.

The results are presented in Table 7.2 and indicate a regression with an adjusted R-squared of 0.75 and with five of the six variables significant at least at the 5%-level. Of these five, all have the expected sign, with the possible exception of age squared, which is negative but is of little concern as the coefficient is very small. In other respects the variables follow the economic rationale provided above: that larger firms tend to be older, begin with a higher level of starting capital, are formally registered, and are located in the more formal industrial areas of the city. The one variable that is not significant is ethnicity and suggests that when other characteristics are fully accounted for, the ethnicity of the owner has no independent influence on firm size.

It might be noted that addition regressions were run (not shown) that included the above variables along with education variables (years of primary, secondary, technical college and university). None of these education variables were found to be significant and thus were dropped from the equation. The non-significance of these variables probably occurred because there is limited variation in the educational qualifications of the owners. If the survey had included household-based firms, at the micro end, and more medium firms and some large firms at the upper end, there might have been more variation. As it stands, most entrepreneurs have primary and secondary education. Some have technical education but this is unlikely to be correlated with firm size because such education has been more readily available recently and thus owners of new and smaller firms had greater opportunity to obtain such education, while the owners of older, slightly larger firms did not. This is an historical circumstance and thus does not suggest that education is unimportant for the development of the small-scale sector. McPherson's (1996) study, which focused on the micro end of the distribution, did find that secondary education is important for firm growth.

RESULTS ON TRADE CREDIT

To assess the possible influence of ethnicity on trade credit, three probit regressions were conducted on access to trade credit. This followed the model suggested by Fafchamps (2000) and was depicted by,

$$TC_i = v_1 + v_2E_i + v_3FS_i + v_4A_i + v_5A_i^2 + e_i.$$

TC indicates trade credit access and is defined as a dummy variable of 1 for access and 0 otherwise. The other variables have been described above with the only change being that FS is *instrumented* with predicted values from the first regression. This was done because firms with greater access to trade credit may grow faster (become larger) and therefore the use of the instrument will control for simultaneity bias.[4] TC indicates whether a firm purchased some of its steel supplies on credit. While this helps to determine whether the firm is capable of gaining access to credit, it does not measure the proportion of supplies for which credit was obtained. Such a measure

Table 7.3: Determinants of Trade Credit

Dep. Variable: access to trade credit (probit 1/0)

	Coeff.	z	Coeff.	z	Coeff.	z
Constant	0.45	2.28	-4.96	-2.06	-6.90	-2.55
African owner (1/0)	-1.75	-5.93*	-0.59	-1.06	-0.26	-0.45
Firm size, instrumented			0.33	2.18*	0.52	2.34*
Firm age					-0.18	-2.04*
Firm age2					0.01	2.15*
Observations	105		92		92	
LR chi2 (5)	39.98		33.94		41.25	
Pseudo R-squared	.30		.32		.38	

* significant at 5%

Table 7.4: Determinants of Bank Credit

Dep. Variable: access to bank loan (probit 1/0)

	Coeff.	z	Coeff.	z	Coeff.	Z
Constant	0.03	0.15	-9.24	-3.50	-9.62	-3.41
African owner (1/0)	-1.47	-4.99*	0.16	0.31	0.08	0.14
Firm size, instrumented			0.59	3.54*	0.64	3.31*
Firm age					-0.01	-0.19
Firm age2					-0.01	-0.24
Observations	112		97		97	
LR chi2 (5)	28.03		39.04		41.12	
Pseudo R-squared	.22		.37		.39	

* significant at 5% level

might have provided a more accurate picture of credit access. The statistics from Tab. 7.1 show that 10% of African firms have such access compared with 70% for the Asian firms. This is an important difference and when trade credit is regressed against ethnicity alone, there is a strong correlation. This is shown in the first two columns of Table 7.3. However, ethnicity may be a proxy for size and other characteristics which the creditor can observe. In the second regression of Table 7.3, size is included and now the ethnicity variable is insignificant, suggesting that suppliers may be granting or denying credit on the basis of firm size instead of the ethnicity of the owner. When further variables are added in the third regression of Table 7.3, the importance of size is confirmed, along with firm age.

The two age variables have different signs, which is difficult to interpret. While the positive sign on age squared would support the intuition that older firms, being more established, would have better access to credit, the negative size on age itself suggests that, up to a point, older firms receive less credit. The transition point is 9 years, after which the age-squared variable dominates the simple age variable to generate a positive correlation.[5] It is unclear why this might be.

RESULTS ON BANK LOAN AND OVERDRAFT CREDIT

Tests for the determinants of access to bank loans and overdraft credit were performed in a similar manner with probit regressions on dummy variables indicating whether any such access had been granted. These two types of credit are inter-mediated credit and thus different from the inter-firm nature of trade credit. This inter-mediated credit might be expected to be less susceptible to ethnic network or discriminatory effects and more directly related to size as a proxy for collateral. Here again it was important to properly specify the size variable based on value instead of number of employees, as valuable assets, not employees, are put forward as collateral. The models tested are similar to the one presented for trade credit:

$$BL_i = y_1 + y_2E_i + y_3FS_{1\,i} + y_4A_i + y_5A_i^2 + e_i$$

and

$$OD_i = z_1 + z_2E_i + z_3FS_{1\,i} + z_4A_i + z_5A_i^2 + e_i$$

where BL is a dummy variable for whether the firm has ever obtained a bank loan and OD is a dummy variable for whether the firm has access to an overdraft facility from its bank.

Table 7.5: Determinants of Overdraft Credit

Dep. Variable: access to overdraft facility (probit 1/0)

	Coeff.	z	Coeff.	z	Coeff.	z
Constant	.60	2.99	-8.74	-3.33	-9.98	-3.57
African owner (1/0)	-1.42	-4.93*	0.40	0.68	0.77	1.21
Firm size, instrumented			0.59	3.56*	0.69	3.70*
Firm age					-0.09	-1.21
Firm age2					0.01	1.43
Observations	92		77		77	
LR chi2 (5)	26.15		36.20		39.77	
Pseudo R-squared	.21		.34		.38	

* significant at 5% level

Table 7.6: Determinants of Starting Capital

Dep. Variable: log of real starting capital

	Coefficient	T statistic
Constant	11.02	9.52
African owner (1/0)	-2.60	-6.44*
Previous experience (yrs)	0.05	1.92***
Primary education (yrs)	0.15	1.00
Secondary education (yrs)	0.11	0.95
Technical college (yrs)	0.21	1.83***
University (yrs)	-0.03	-0.19
Observations	96	
F (6, 89)	11.58	
R-squared	.44	
Adj. R-squared	.40	

significant at * 1%; *** 10% levels

Three regressions were run for each of *BL* and *OD* and the results are presented in Tables 7.4 and 7.5. In the first regression, the ethnic variable is significant on its own. It loses significance, however, when the size variable is added in the second regression. This supports the intuition that size is a determinant factor in the assessment by banks on whether to grant bank or overdraft credit. Unlike the trade credit results, however, the firm age variables are not significant. This follows the intuition that bank credit is based more on collateral while trade credit is also dependent on the established presence of the firm as measured by its age.

Thus, the results of the quantitative analysis on access to all three types of credit leave us with little explanation as to why the size distribution, even in our limited sample of the metalwork sector, is skewed with larger Asian firms and small African ones. There appears to be no difference in the ability of firms of the two groups to gain access to at least some trade credit on their major input, steel, and to obtain loans and overdraft access.

The results do indicate, however, that firm size is an important determinant of credit access and that size is significantly related to the level of starting capital. Thus, the follow-on question is: what determines the level of starting capital?

DETERMINANTS OF STARTING CAPITAL

Factors which will determine the level of starting capital are those related to the (prospective) owner and not the characteristics of the firm after it has begun operation. We hypothesis that the determinants of starting capital (logged) might be set out as,

$$KS_i = w_1 + w_2E_i + w_3X_i + w_4PRI_i + w_5SEC_i + w_6TEC + w_7UNI + e_I$$

such that its level is determined by the ethnicity of the owner (*E*), his previous experience (X) in years, and his years of schooling in primary, secondary, technical and university education (PRI, SEC, TEC and UNI, respectively). Previous experience in the metal work sector is used as a means of making a distinction between those whose prime reason for setting up the business was not to escape from unemployment but to move from paid to self-employment. If that was the case, then the prospective owner had an opportunity to accumulate capital through savings from wage earnings. An additional variable may be the educational level of the owner. This might be based on two reasons: a more educated person may have more opportunities for employment in non-metalworking firms and therefore greater capacity to accumulate capital (as above); or he may have spent more years in school which proxies a wealthier family background which could provide financial support both for education and starting a business. A third possibility may be an ethnic variable with two possible interpretations. One, because the Asian community is relatively wealthy, there may be better access to family wealth for use as start-up capital. Two, being a member of the Asian community may make it easier to use ethnic connections to get access to informal loans from non-family members of the community (possibly on the guarantee or recommendation of a family member).

The results of regressing real starting capital (logged) on these variables are provided in Table 7.6. Ethnicity is significant at the one per cent level and possesses the largest coefficient. Previous experience is also significant, possibly highlighting the importance of generating savings from wage earnings, as suggested. Technical education is also significant at the 10% level. These results are important in that this is the first instance in which ethnicity has appeared as a significant variable in all regressions employing more than one independent variable. It suggests that Africans are starting in business with less capital and thus are establishing micro firms. Being small initially, it is much harder to access trade, loan and overdraft credit or to set up in the formal business areas. For Asian firms, the opposite holds: they start bigger, establish themselves in the formal areas and because of their size can better access various types of credit.

The next question then is: what determines access to starting capital and are ethnic network effects in operation at the start-up phase? Unfortunately, the survey did not ask questions related to the sources of starting capital. We may hypothesize that such capital is generated from savings and from formal and informal credit. Regarding formal credit, we are considering the particular situation in which the firm is not yet in operation. In that case, lending may be provided against collateral which a wealthier person (with a house, for example) may put forward. The other important area is informal lending. The survey did not directly ask questions on overall access to informal loans, much less their contribution to starting the business. It did, however, ask firms how they financed their last machine purchase and included informal loans as a response option. The results are provided in Table 7.7. Just over two-thirds of firms financed the purchase solely from business savings, while 15% had access to installment credit from the supplier, 10% relied on bank loans and 6% used informal loans. The latter is not a very high proportion (nor a high count, 5 firms) but it is interesting to note that in all five cases, they were firms which were partly or fully Asian-owned. Indeed, 11% of Asian firms supported the machine

Table 7.7: Sources of Financing Last Machine Purchase

	Savings from business	Installment from seller	Bank Loan	Informal Loan	NGO Credit	Total
African-owned						
No.	41	5	2	0	1	49
% of African firms	84	10	4	0	2	100
Asian-owned						
No.	18	7	7	4	0	36
% of Asian firms	50	19	19	11	0	100
Other	1	1	0	1	0	3
No.	33	33	0	33	0	100
% of Other						
Total by column						
No.	60	13	9	5	1	88
%	68	15	10	6	1	100

Table 7.8: Firm Growth

Dep. Variable: Growth rate of firm value

	Coeff.	T	Coeff.	T
Constant	1.35	5.53	1.35	3.80
Firm age	-0.07	-5.83*	-0.07	-4.76*
Firm age2	0.01	4.19*	0.01	3.47*
Industrial Location	0.37	3.01*	0.27	1.51
Starting capital (real, log)	-0.07	-3.31*	-0.07	-2.71*
African owner	0.12	1.03	0.14	0.81
Previous experience	0.01	0.35	0.01	0.72
Part-time operation	-0.01	-0.61	-0.02	-0.64
Trade credit			0.08	0.63
Bank loan			0.01	0.08
Overdraft			0.02	0.20
Secondary education			0.13	1.06

Continued

Table 7.8 (*Continued*)

Observations	98	68
F (7, 90), (11, 56)	11.60	4.61
R-squared	.47	.48
Adj. R-squared	.43	.37

Growth rate = [ln(value of the firm)-ln(real starting capital)]/age

significant at * 5% level

Source: Author's survey

purchase from these informal loans of friends or family. None of the African firms financed the machine purchase in this manner.

This result may at first appear odd given than many of the African firms are micro-sized and might be classified as informal enterprises. It appears odd if we associate the informal sector with informal lending but the qualitative discussions conducted with owners during the course of the surveying suggested otherwise. In the African areas, the owners were very short of cash for their own businesses and thus had little to lend to others. In addition, several African owners noted that it would be very risky to lend to others because of a high closure rate among surrounding firms. Furthermore, these African business communities did not arise from an established social community but were formed by people drawn from a variety of residential districts of the city and, in some cases, those people were recent arrivals from rural areas. The opportunity for trust to develop and for business relationships to be supported by social ones is thus reduced (Vandenberg 1997).

By contrast, the Asian business community is closely associated with the Asian social community in Nairobi and businesses are more permanently established with cash flow less of a problem. Several owners indicated that they could get access to informal loans to cover cash flow shortfalls and to help finance purchases for several weeks or months. This could be done over the phone with business colleagues. (Others indicated it would not be difficult to access large sums through Indian businessmen in London, based solely on a referral from another Kenyan Asian businessman.)

Thus there is some qualitative and quantitative evidence that Asian firms can access informal loans for machine purchases and that one in ten do so. The extent to which such lending allows Asian firms to commence business at a higher level is unknown but may be an important explanation as to why the ethnicity variable is significant in the regression on starting capital.

RESULTS ON FIRM GROWTH

Finally, we return to the question of whether access to trade and other forms of credit significantly affects the size distribution of firms. This is difficult to test for given the problem of the direction of causality: the possible influence of credit on size and the now well established impact of size on credit. With trade credit as a dummy variable, it is difficult to instrument. Instead, we have followed the work of McPherson (1996) in using the growth rate of the firm[6] and devised the following testable relationship,

$$GR_i = q_1 + q_2E_i + q_3L_i + q_4A_i + q_5A_i^2 + q_6KS_i + q_7X_i + q_8PT_i + q_9TC_i + q_{10}BL_i + q_{11}OD_i + q_{12}SEC_i + e_i$$

All variables have been defined previously except for the years of part-time experience of the owner in the metal sector (*PT*). The rationale here is that firms operated part-time would tend to grow slower because they lack the full-time commitment of the owner. The results are presented in Table 7.8 and indicate again the importance of the firm's age and its level of starting capital. While the signs on the age variables are again different, the point at which the positive relationship dominates comes much earlier, at 3.5 years. A more puzzling result is that the sign on starting capital is negative, indicating that those firms which start with high levels of capital grow more slowly that small firms. It is important to be careful in interpreting this result, given the large range of firm size in the survey. From previous results, we know that the level of starting capital is positively related to firm size and thus combined with the new results, it suggests that larger firms start larger but grow slower. This would mean that smaller firms would tend to converge to the size of larger firms but only if they could sustain themselves. Instead, it is possible that small firms grow quickly but then collapse or otherwise cannot sustain the livelihood of their owner and are forced to fold. The larger firms start larger and may be able to provide an adequate income for the owner, who is less interested in rapid expansion but keen on sustaining the operation and thus his livelihood. This may be particularly true in that many of the larger firms are older and thus had to survive the 1980s and 1990s when the general economic environment was decidedly disadvantageous.

Also included are variables for access to credit, none of which are significant. This highlights the concern expressed in the first part of the chapter that trade credit may not contribute significantly to explaining size differentials between the two groups. The result is more surprising for bank loans, which one might think would provide an important positive contribution to firm growth. These results and their interpretation must be viewed with caution, however, as the loan access variable only indicates whether a firm ever received at least one loan and does not indicate the amount of funds borrowed (over a given period, or relative to the firm's size). A more accurate measure may produce different results. The results may also suggest, however, that firms rely heavily on internal savings to finance expansion and that external finance may be seen as a means to overcome occasional cash shortfalls (notably with overdrafts) and thus contribute more to sustaining the firm than to increasing its size or rate of growth.

CONCLUSION

The empirical analysis was designed to test the importance of ethnic network effects in explaining differences in credit access. In previous chapters, we used our survey data to reveal that Asian firms had much greater access to trade, bank and overdraft credit than African firms. It was also clear, however, that Asian firms were much larger and more established in the formal sector areas of Nairobi. Thus, it was not clear whether Asian firms had better credit access due to their size or the ethnicity of their owners. Their greater size might indicate to creditors an enhanced ability to provide collateral, to accumulate capital and to generate future revenue. In contrast, their ethnicity—being Asian—might mean that they were more trusted by Asian suppliers and that these suppliers were better able to screen Asian producers by using information about creditworthiness which circulates within the ethnic community. In this way, community norms and reputation would provide a strong informal enforcement mechanism on which suppliers and other creditors might rely. It was noted that these affects were more likely to affect trade credit than bank loans because the latter relies more on collateral provision.

The test results indicate that when other measurable firm characteristics are accounted for (notably size), the ethnicity of the owner does not have a significant impact on whether a firm can access trade credit, bank loans or overdraft credit. These results suggest that Asian firms have better access to these types of credit because they are larger and more established, and not because they are Asian. These results differ from those of Fafchamps (2000) who found that ethnic effects were important for trade credit access.

We also sought to understand firms' access to starting capital. Descriptive statistics revealed that starting capital is much higher among Asian firms than African ones. In regression analysis, ethnicity was found to be a significant determinant of the level of starting capital and we also found that starting capital was strongly correlated with firm size. Thus, ethnicity affects starting capital and, in turn, starting capital affects size. With this result, we have come some way in solving the riddle presented in the Introduction: that is, why do we find that the micro, informal firms are African-owned while most of the small firms in the formal sector are Asian-owned? An important part of the answer is that Asians firms start out larger.

Does this undermine our argument that part of the secret of Asian business success is their access to informal institutions which can support credit access? Not necessarily, what it does suggest is that if informal credit institutions are at work within the Asian community they may make a stronger contribution to starting capital than to trade credit. In addition, we have provided some statistics which indicate that none of the African firms used informal loans to make machinery purchases; while about a quarter of the Asian firms did.

The correlation between starting capital and ethnicity is likely also capturing the disparity in wealth between the Asian community and those (poorer) segments of the African community which are drawn into micro-manufacturing. In other words, African networks may be present but they may connect individuals and firms which all face a severe shortage of finance. The apparent 'success' of the Asian community thus may be related to the wider questions of sectoral specialization (Asians in urban trade and manufacturing and Africans in agriculture) and to the lack of a movement of surplus African capital from agriculture into industry.

Conclusion

The predominance of Asians in urban manufacturing in Kenya is the result of a historical process of capital accumulation which was supported by informal information networks and, during colonialism, by formal institutions. A pre-colonial division of sector specialization meant that Asians focused on urban activities, while Africans specialized in agriculture. This was maintained through the colonial period and continues today. Those Africans who enter urban manufacturing tend not to be drawn from the community of successful African farmers but from poor, urban migrants and city dwellers who have entered into business with little starting capital. This has limited their ability to purchase adequate technology and to compete in more lucrative segments of the market. Their small size is a key factor in limiting their access to both trade credit and bank loans, perpetuating their difficulty in generating a surplus. This line of argument has been pursued through seven chapters of theory, history and analysis of contemporary business practices. The key points of each chapter, along with suggestions for future research, are provided in the first part of this Conclusion. The second part discusses the connections between this work on institutions and the current approaches to African development as suggested by Jeffrey Sachs' UN Millennium Development Project and Tony Blair's Commission for Africa.

At a theoretical level, the study has endeavored to define and clarify the work of Douglass North and suggest its usefulness as a framework for understanding development in Africa. His institutionalism highlights the importance of both the formal institutional environment and the micro-level institutions of governance in determining economic performance. It places contracting and property rights at the centre of the analysis. In doing so, his work overcomes the problems of standard neo-classical economics which often assumes transaction costs to be zero. Moreover, North's approach provides a more dynamic approach than old institutionalism which stresses the importance of habits and norms but lacks a notion of change. This means that North's work is more open to addressing the totality of factors that influence economic development. Much of the analysis of transaction costs is now incorporated into mainstream institutionalism. The benefit of North's work for future research lies in its application to contracting between political leaders and businessmen/citizens and the inclusion of norms in the analysis of economic behavior.

Given the existence of formal and informal institutional structures in Africa, which operate on the basis of different norms, and the problems of political behavior, the issues which North raises are germane to the study of economies in Africa. In addition, institutional analysis can be a useful tool for analyzing the range of informal institutions used by Africans and ethnic business communities. The screening and monitoring of agents is possible through easily accessible and low-cost information, while contracts are enforced though the threat of a loss of reputation. As Greif has shown, a multilateral punishment system provides a strong deterrent against opportunistic behavior. Failure to honor one (bilateral) agreement may mean the loss of access to others in a closely knit ethnic community. The institutional analysis has focused predominantly on credit contracting and land tenure, but there are other issues, such as labor contracting and contract farming, which might also be analyzed using such an approach.

While the focus has been on institutions, the author has come to realize that they provide only part of the story about economic development. A host of issues (education, health, technology, business experience and the natural environment) are critical to economic success but are not related to transacting and are only indirectly related to property rights. Furthermore, fiscal effectiveness and monetary stability are also critical factors affecting the economic environment. While these functions are performed by government *institutions*, they are not directly related to transacting and property rights. Institutionalism has a role to play in explaining economic outcomes but it does not provide an all-inclusive answer. It is one of many tools in the economist's toolkit.

Historical evidence has been used to chart the development of Kenyan Asian and African economic activities and thereby to provide a context for understanding the contemporary situation. In pre-colonial times, the two communities concentrated on difference sectors, with Africans focused on agriculture and related activities, while Asians channeled their energies into trade, notably of imports and exports, and credit provision. Within these broad categories, sub-groups also specialized: Africans in herding and cultivation for example. In addition, Europeans and Arabs sought to control political power and Asians acted as middlemen, leaving political and military affairs to others. Even the Europeans who secured control over Mombassa used different methods which resulted in greater (British) or lesser (Portuguese) success. Whatever the sub-group, people build institutions to support their specific economic activities. While this has been stressed, greater emphasis might have been given to the idea that the strength and complexity of institutions is a reflection of the density of people and economic activity. In this regard, the development of African institutions and related economic activity may have been constrained by the low population density of the interior which existed historically.

The separation of activities between Asians and Africans continued under British rule from the late 1880s to the 1960s. A host of marketing, cropping and credit restrictions constrained African expansion, while a British refusal to allow Asians access to the White Highlands led to their concentration in urban centers and to some trading in African areas. As was shown, the British developed a much stronger and more equal relationship in economic and political affairs with Asians than they did with Africans, which provided opportunities for Asian accumulation. The effort to compare African and Asian treatment by the British in one historical account is a unique feature of the chapter on colonialism. Few, if any, historical accounts of colonialism in Kenya provide this type of integration. Further research should seek to continue the process of fully integrating the histories of the people who lived and worked under British rule, and to understand differences in the latter's attitudes towards these two groups. The full incorporation of Arab and Swahili coastal activity might also be attempted.

Following independence, the state took on the role of directly supporting and creating opportunities for Africans in urban trade and manufacturing. This was done by denying some of the economic rights of Asians. Such changes in formal rules were aimed at overcoming a long historical process of accumulation based on informal institutions and expertise developed by the Asian business community. The state's assumption that Africans would be willing and able to compete in these markets was not borne out, however, and suggests that the transition of a business community from the rural to the urban sector may be a long and difficult process. Furthermore, the economic advance of Africans was not aided by a change in the control of the presidency to a non-Kikuyu. The record suggests that while many Asians decided to flee the country because of the new discriminatory policies, those who stayed have been able to maintain the Asian position. It may be that formal *institutions matter*, but that the role of informal institutions and the process of accumulation in history matter even more.

One of the larger questions which arises from both the historical analysis and the contemporary situation is the timeframe for the development of a business community. Governments in Kenya likely underestimated the time and effort needed to build a business community from the local population which could compete with Asians. A more gradual approach to business development may have been more prudent. Nevertheless, the most important impact of the post-independence period for African entrepreneurs may be the experience it provided. A new generation of Africans, schooled inter-generationally in those experiences and with greater resources behind them, may emerge in urban business and provide increased interaction, competition and co-operation with Asian firms.

Post-independence Kenya has also experienced the full implementation of the formalization of rural land tenure. Considerable research has been conducted on the transition and conflict between informal and formal arrangements with the general finding that formal tenure fails to take account of the structure of rural societies and the importance of land for family units. The processes of land transfer and land use as collateral, which are presumed by the evolutionary theory of land rights to arise from formal titling, are being constrained by the structure of the rural economy. There is some research, however, which suggests that titling assists large, productive farms. It suggests the need to match the cost and complexity of formal institutions with the underlying size and structure of productive units. The issues here do relate to transactions costs, as the large farms can more readily bear these costs because of the benefits they obtain from titling. On-going research needs to continue to assess the benefits of formal institutions for different classes of farmers. In addition, the same insights might be usefully transferred to the analysis of credit and urban business. Smaller units are unable to access formal credit because of their size (and thus higher transaction costs) and because of their inability to provide collateral. An effort to develop a full and detailed theory on the links between enterprise size, transactions costs, benefits and institutional access could yield some interesting insights.

The historical analysis provided a basis for analyzing the results of a survey conducted among small metal manufacturing firms in Nairobi. That survey confirmed the large size differential between Asian and African owned firms at the small end of the size distribution. It was hypothesized that this differential was related to credit access which depended on institutions. The key question was whether differences in credit access were related to better ethnic networks among Asian firms, or whether access was related to the size differential itself. Our regression results suggest that size was the predominant factor but that it was, in turn, not necessarily related to the capacity of firms to growth but the fact that they had better access to starting capital. Micro firms start small and stay small. The empirical results suggest that it may be the nature of firms entering the sector rather than the particular barriers within it which most account for differences in credit access.

Along with this main finding, a number of other issues were analyzed. In particular, we noted and tested for differences in location and found important contrasts between the less and the more formalized business areas of the city. These differences relate to size, starting capital and longevity but not to education levels of firm owners, their previous experience in the metal sector or the length of time in which they operated their businesses part-time. We have noted also the limited use of the legal system and the greater incidence of partnerships among the Asian community; the latter helping to explain higher levels of starting capital.

The results are based on a particular data set, which is notable for its inclusion of many micro firms, along with small ones and some medium-sized ones. Furthermore, the data provided only an indication of access to trade credit, not to the level of access. As well, a survey of other, non-metal sectors (textiles, wood, agro-processing) could yield different results. The latter two sub-sectors in particular may have a greater African presence as the activities are more closely related to the rural sector.

It is apparent that many of the Africans who do enter small scale manufacturing do so with low levels of starting capital. This is not hard to explain as many, notably the micro entrepreneurs, are migrants who are unable or otherwise disinclined to enter paid employment. Some may be genuine entrepreneurs, others not. It would be easy to suggest that they should be given start-up grants or initial loans to ensure that they can invest in adequate technology to enter more lucrative niches in the market. Efforts by UNIDO and UNDP in providing training programs may mean that they now have the technical skills to work with more advanced technology. Several micro entrepreneurs did suggest that they were interested in more specialized work than the manual fabrication in which they were currently engaged. The difficulty in providing such support relates again to institutions: adequate screening and monitoring mechanisms would be required to ensure that funds were channeled to those migrants or more long-term urban residents who were intent on making a permanent commitment to manufacturing.

The transition from agriculture to manufacturing has been highlighted. We have drawn upon a number of commentators who have suggested that local (African) populations tend not to make an immediate transition from agriculture to manufacturing, likely because they lack the necessary expertise. Instead, efforts to diversify a surplus into non-agricultural activities involve investment in land, urban real estate, transport and then commerce. Furthermore, successful farmers may re-invest in agriculture if there are adequate prospects for expansion. The whole area of African re-investment and entry into non-agricultural businesses is a grey one. It may stem from a tendency to study agriculture and manufacturing separately. An interesting follow-on study would be to locate successful African farmers who are generating a surplus to determine how they are investing it. This would include the possibility that it is being channeled into savings instruments at banks, or into other financial products such as shares, bonds or government bills. It would be interesting to know how much is channeled abroad, including into their children's education which can represent a considerable expense for middle-income farmers. Other methods by which families seek to increase and diversify their wealth inter-generationally might also be explored.

CURRENT PROPOSALS TO RESOLVE AFRICA'S ECONOMIC PROBLEMS

The exploration of the African-Asian divide in Kenya in this book was not meant to address any current policy questions regarding the problems of economic development that Africa faces. Certain policies during the colonial era did indeed contribute to the ethnic divide and efforts were made after independence to support African entry into urban business, but these policies of positive discrimination are no longer in place in Kenya. Thus, to relate this analysis of the ethnic divide to the current discussions about solutions for Africa—such as those proposed by Tony Blair's Commission for Africa or Jeffrey Sachs' UN Millennium Development Project—means stepping out of the analytical mode and thinking about policy. Here we suggest a few connections that might be made.

The discussion of what ails Africa has been going on since the continent's development problems took a negative turn in the mid-1970s. Recently these problems have been given considerable attention by the two initiatives just noted. They have arisen from two sources. One is a concern that Africa is not likely to meet the targets set out in the Millennium Development Goals, agreed by the international community in 2000. Foremost among these goals, is a reduction, by half between 1995 and 2015, of the proportion of people living on less than a dollar a day. At the half way point between the start and end dates for the calculation of the goals (2005), a team of researchers under noted economist Jeffrey Sachs undertook to study the progress and prospects of meeting the goals. In an excerpt of the main findings, Sachs and his team have focused on the problems of Africa (Sachs *et* al. 2005). At the same time, the British prime minister, Tony Blair, has made Africa a special focus of his foreign policy and along with rock starts, African leaders and others formed the Commission for Africa, which also released a set of proposals in 2005 (CFA 2005).

Neither of the reports point to a single factor impending African development. If anything, analyses of this kind in recent years have included an increasing number of factors (Collier and Gunning 1999). Nonetheless, the various elements fall into three main areas: external factors, geographic-demographic factors; and internal policy/institutional factors. Only the latter two have some connection to the private sector/institutional analysis of this book. Two key external factors are: debt, which was addressed in part at the G8 Summit in Gleneagles, Scotland in mid-2005; and trade, notably reduced developed country subsidies on agriculture and increased African access to markets. The trade issue is being address through the Doha Round of multilateral trade negotiations. The third key external factor is aid, with Sachs and the Commission for Africa both calling for large increases in aid budgets.

The analysis provided by Sachs and the UN Millennium Project is very provocative in that it does not focus on policy and governance issues, but on geography and demography and to some extent on historical factors. "Governance is a problem," according to Sachs and his team, "but Africa's development challenges run much deeper." The factors that have affected Africa include a tropical climate, limited rainfall in some areas, a lack of rivers suitable for irrigation and inland transport, high transportation costs from the coast to the interior, small market size and a high disease burden, notably malaria and HIV/AIDS. Added to this are missed opportunities arising from the "slow diffusion of technology from abroad" and the lack of suitable green revolution technology. Historically, the slave trade, resource extraction under colonialism and Cold War proxy games had a negative effect. Also, the political boundaries drawn by Europeans, which did not account for ethnic groups, were maintained at independence. This entire combination of factors resulted in Africa slipping into a poverty trap. Sachs and his colleagues explain the trap as follows:

> Our explanation is that tropical Africa, even the well-governed parts, is stuck in a poverty trap, too poor to achieve robust, high levels of economic growth and, in many parts, simply too poor to grow at all. More policy or governance reform, by itself, will not be sufficient to overcome this trap. Specifically, Africa's extreme poverty leads to low

> national saving rates, which in turn lead to low or negative economic growth rates (Sachs *et al.* 2005: 121–2).

These problems call for a "big push" in public investments that will produce, in a short period of time, a "step" increase in rural and urban productivity. Some of the key areas for public investments are health, education, agricultural extension, water and sanitation and transport infrastructure.

The Commission for Africa report, *Our Common Interest*, also accepts that substantially larger aid flows are needed and recommends that the rich world provide US$ 25 billion per year in additional aid until 2015 (CFA 2005: 14). The aid would be directed to many of the public areas suggested by the Sachs team. But the Commission has a much wider agenda that deals with the continent's current external economic relations, notably trade with the developed world; with peace and security; and with improved governance and policies. It is this latter area that relates to the issues of institutions and private sector development covered in this book.

The Commission's report makes a distinction, very similar to the one made in our first chapter, between informal institutions, that are highly resilient and necessary for people's survival, and the formal institutions of the state, which are often weak or corrupted. The informal institutions are referred to as "Africa's invisible networks" that "form much of the social capital without which many African communities could not function." They provide start-up capital for small enterprises and loans for emergencies, as well as the money needed to pay hospital and school bills (CFA 2005: 119–20). Africans rely on these networks as well as on religious and culture ones instead of government institutions because "for too many, perhaps a majority, the state is an irrelevance or a burden" (ibid.). The report sets out but does not develop the intriguing idea that these informal networks might provide the building blocks for effective state institutions in Africa. It is an idea that was previously developed by Dia (1994, 1996).

At the same time, the Commission calls for better formal institutions both to deliver services—*capacity*—and to govern the process of policy formation and service delivery—*accountability* (CFA 2005: 12). The institutions that need strengthening in these regard include the civil service but notably the bodies of representation (parliaments, local government, trade unions) as well as the justice system and the media. While much of the discussion is general, the report does focus on the specific policies and institutions needed to support private sector development; the institutions of property rights and contracting highlighted throughout this book. The Commission's strategy for economic growth is "driven by the private sector" and the need for "improved property rights, commercial justice and deregulation" (ibid.: 220). It notes that high-growth Asian countries, including China, India, South Korea, Taiwan and Singapore, as well as Africa's best performers, Mauritius and Botswana, "have promoted effective property rights, contract enforcement and macroeconomic policy" (CFA 2005: 222). Finally, the report notes that in Africa only one per cent of land is titled, making rural investment insecure (ibid.: 223). The commission recommends, among other things, support for a US$ 550 million Investment Climate Facility for use over seven years to improve the business environment (ibid.). Many of these ideas are part of the recent focus on the business environment as an important means to help the private sector expand output and employment in developing countries (see, de Soto 1989, 2000; UNDP 2004; IOE 2005; World Bank 2006).

More credible formal institutions can reduce the need for enterprises to rely on informal mechanisms to secure finance, negotiate trade and generally to conduct business. Business owners who have confidence in the justice system, for example, are more likely to agree business contracts with businesses that they are unfamiliar with, including businesses from outside of their ethnic group. Generally, as formal institutions are strengthened, the advantages of the informal networks of ethnic business communities may diminish. The increased establishment and use of credit bureaus, for example, which the Commission for Africa also endorses, make it easier to judge the creditworthiness of new and untested customers. Nonetheless, it is still unclear whether formal institutions and an improved investment climate will reduce the historical gap between Africans and ethnic business communities.

Appendix One

Survey Results of Kahawa Estates and Kariobangi

In addition to the four metalworking areas described in detail in Chapter 5, the following two areas were also surveyed.

KAHAWA ESTATES

Kahawa is a residential suburb of north-east Nairobi and its firms service that area. The firms operate either in a central market area or are run out of residential dwellings. Household-based production represents a large proportion of micro-firms in Kenya, as surveyed by Parker and Torres (1995). As is evident from the results of our survey in this area, they represent the last rung on the ladder in terms of firm size and viability. A broad survey of micro enterprise activity would need to canvass a large number of residential areas in the city. Kahawa is used here to represent that phenomenon but not in a comprehensive fashion.

A total of 12 firms completed questionnaires. Only five of these firms were actually registered and thus had a permit to conduct business, none have ever borrowed from a bank and the last machine purchase was funded solely from savings, with no use of external funds. Firm size was smallest of the six areas, with the median firm valued at Ksh 108,250 ($1,800). Starting capital was second lowest at just over Ksh 25,000 ($425), suggesting very low capital intensity. There was an average of four workers per firm, including the owner, and the average firm had been operating for just under five years. The surveying in this area was conducted by a research assistant and little in the way of personal details or firm histories was recorded.

Table A1.1 Firm characteristics – Kahawa Estates

		Median	Mean	Min.	Max.
Size					
Asset value	Ksh	108,250	199,292	45,000	500,000
Labour force (workers)	no.	4.0	4.1	2.0	7.0
Starting capital	Ksh	25,024	47,489	13,630	148,478
Age of firm	years	3.5	4.8	0.0	15.0
Part-time operation	years	0.0	0.8	0.0	6.0
Owners' previous experience	years	3.3	4.3	0.0	10.0
Education					
Total	years	13.5	12.9	9.0	19.0
Total higher	years	2.0	2.9	1.0	8.0
Technical college	years	2.0	2.4	1.0	5.0
University	years	0.0	0.5	0.0	6.0
		no.	**total.**	**%**	
Registered	no. of firms	5	12	42%	
Access to bank loan	no. of firms	0	10	0%	
Access to trade credit	no. of firms	1	12	8%	
Finance for last machine purchase	no. of firms	**no.**	**total**	**%**	
Savings		11	12	92%	
Bank loan		0	12	0%	
Installments		0	12	0%	
Informal loan		0	12	0%	
NGO		0	12	0%	

Source: author's survey, US$ 1 = 59 Ksh (Kenyan shillings)

KARIOBANGI

The Kariobangi Light Industrial Area is located along a north-south artery connecting western areas to the city centre. It is located near the Korigocho shantytown; a massive residential suburb characterized by poverty, crime and insecurity. It was visited on a Sunday with a local research assistant who initially thought that the area would be safe enough for a visit, although it later became known that he had never before visited the area. We grew increasingly concerned about our safety while walking the streets. We conducted some surveying and my assistant returned later to collect questionnaires and approach other businesses. In all, only eight firms were sampled but more importantly, it is not clear to the author how representative these are of the area. We surveyed only African firms and while it is possible that some firms here are owned by Asians, we did not see any in operation on Sunday. There are several NGOs operating in the area which focus on technology, notably the US-based Aprotech and the UN, which runs a training school (see below). This may suggest that there was more substantial activity here than covered by the survey. It could also suggest, however, that organizations went to this area because firms were small and struggling and thus in need of support. More effort would have been made to survey the area if it had been safer.

In all, only eight firms were surveyed. The median starting capital was just over Ksh 25,700, while the median current value of the firms was slightly higher at Ksh 200,000 ($3,400). The median number of employees was only 4.5 but ranged from 2 to 10; while the median number of years in operation was 4.5, ranging from 1 to 10. These figures were second lowest for the six areas surveyed, with Kahawa only slightly lower. Only one of the firms had ever accessed a bank loan and they all had financed their last machine purchase from savings. The firms sampled here can be characterized as micro.

Artisans from here, as well as those from Kamukunji, had the opportunity to enroll in the Kariobangi Technical Training School (for jua kali artisans) which was funded by UNIDO and the UNDP. According to one participant, the school operates for six hours per day, five days a week. A group of artisans is taught metal-working skills at the school for one month and then leave to work for the next two months. The entire program runs for four years and allows the trainees to earn a living, gain experience and receive skills training. There is no tuition or other costs for trainees attending the school but the loss of income during the training month makes it difficult for them to maintain their attendance. They have no money to buy food for lunch and it cuts into their other meals as well, forcing many to

Table A1.2 Firm characteristics - Kariobangi

		Median	Mean	Min.	Max.
Size					
Asset value	Ksh	200,000	273,714	36,000	1,000,000
Labour force (workers)	no.	4.5	4.6	2.0	10.0
Starting capital	Ksh	25,678	40,078	8,347	118,413
Age of firm	years	4.5	5.1	1.0	10.0
Part-time operation	years	0.0	0.1	0.0	1.0
Owners' previous experience	years	3.0	3.9	0.0	11.0
Education					
Total	years	13.5	12.5	7.0	16.0
Total higher	years	2.0	2.6	2.0	5.0
Technical college	years	2.0	2.3	2.0	3.0
University	years	0.0	0.4	0.0	3.0
		no.	**total.**	**%**	
Registered	no. of firms	3	8	38%	
Access to bank loan	no. of firms	1	7	14%	
Access to trade credit	no. of firms	0	7	0%	
Finance for last machine purchase	no. of firms	**no.**	**total**	**%**	
Savings		7	8	88%	
Bank loan		0	8	0%	
Installments		0	8	0%	
Informal loan		0	8	0%	
NGO		0	8	0%	

Source: author's survey, US$ 1 = 59 Ksh (Kenyan shillings)

drop out. As one artisan explained, "If we keep going [to the school], we suffer. It has affected so many, when we started, there was 40 [trainees] but now only eight or nine, so many have dropped out because of finances." These conditions could not be independently verified but it does indicate the tight constraints faced by poor artisans.

Appendix Two

Use of Cramer's V as a Test of Association

The use of Cramer's V in Chapter 6 as a test of association between two variables is dictated by the nature of the dependent variables; more specifically, that all the institutional variables are nominal. This involves a simple yes/no response for whether the firm uses/has access to a particular institution (i.e. type of credit or legal mechanism). Where the independent variable is also nominal (ethnicity) or has been ordinalized (size quartiles), then computing Cramer's V is appropriate for gauging the strength of association. Cramer's V is a non-parametric test which is a refinement of the more basic chi-square test. The difference between the two involves the ability to measure the strength of association, something the simple chi-square test cannot do. As Norusis notes,

> The actual value of the chi-square statistic and its associated observed significance level provide little information about the strength and type of association between two variables. All you can conclude from the observed significance level is that two variables are not independent. Nothing more. (Norusis 1998, 350).

In addition, Cramer's V is very similar to the phi test. They are both based on the chi-square statistic but the phi can only be used for 2x2 tables, whereas Cramer's V can be used for tables with larger dimensions. The phi and Cramer's V tests for any 2x2 table will produce the same result (Bryman and Cramer 1997, 186).

The presence of nominal variables precludes the use of more widely known tests used in survey work such as Pearson's R (interval x interval) or Spearman's correlation (ordinal x ordinal) (Norusis 1998: 366). A lesser-known technique, which computes an 'eta' statistic, can be used to test association between a nominal or ordinal variable and an interval variable. This might have allowed us to exploit more fully the firm-value variable without dividing it into quartiles. Unfortunately, the test requires that the interval variable be the dependent one (Bryman and Cramer 1997, 187) while in almost all of our cases we assume that firm size determines access to institutions and therefore is the independent variable. The argument is that larger firms engage in larger transactions and thus the costs of accessing or using an institution can be covered more easily by expected benefits or revenue. The use of a non-parametric test with a quartile breakdown eliminates any problem created by the non-normal distribution of some of the variables.

Cramer's V is always denoted in positive terms. Because the size variable is ordinal, we can usually determine from the descriptive statistics the direction of association between size and access. The data in Chapter 6 were analyzed using the SPSS statistical software package.

Notes

NOTES TO THE INTRODUCTION

1. The term *Asian* is used to refer to the people from the Indian subcontinent who settled in Kenya and to their descendants. The terms *Asian* and *Kenya Asian* are used synonymously. *Asian* does not refer to Japanese or Korean investors or subsidiaries. The term *African* refers to those people who have much deeper roots in Kenya and are sometimes referred to as black Africans. It might be noted that many Asians consider themselves African in the sense that they have lived in Africa their entire lives but we make the distinction for the purposes of clarity and simplicity.
2. Among others, Nicola Swainson (1977, 1980) and Michael Cowen (1981, 1982) supported Leys' revised position, while Raphael Kaplinsky (1980, 1982) and Steven Langdon (1987) supported Leys' original (dependency) position. For a full list of the contributions to the debate, see Leys (1994: footnotes 1–5).
3. Earlier but more minor contributions to the debate include those of Kaplan (1992) and Cowen and MacWilliam (1996). For a review of the debate, see Vandenberg (2003).
4. Accumulation occurs because certain persons, called entrepreneurs, use their talents and take risks with their money and that of others (banks, shareholders). Low wages certainly do contribute to profitability and a worker has a right to a decent wage, but without retained earnings, there is limited investment and investment is critical to increased output and to employment.

NOTES TO CHAPTER ONE

1. The discussion of North in this chapter is reprinted with the permission of the Cambridge Political Economy Society, from P. Vandenberg, "North's institutionalism and the prospect of combining theoretical approaches," *Cambridge Journal of Economics,* vol. 26, no. 2, March 2002, pp. 217–235.

2. The use of the term "old" may be inappropriate (if not somewhat disparaging) in depicting those contemporary theorists working in—and adding to—the long tradition of institutionalism which began with Veblen. It is used here because the distinction between new and old is commonly recognized in the literature (e.g. Samuels, 1994: 578). While the new theorists in the old tradition might be called alternative institutionalists to indicate that they do not conform to mainstream economic analysis, this would likely cause more confusion than clarity. It might also be more appropriate to refer to the older tradition simply as "institutionalism" and to consider the new institutionalism as a more recent offshoot or variant, but this makes the distinction less clear.
3. He shared the Nobel Prize for economics in 1993, for his work on institutions and economic history.
4. The importance of property rights and the legal system suggests similarities between North's work and that of the old institutionalist John Commons (Groenewegen *et al.*, 1995: 473).
5. Conversely, scholars of economic development who give some support to the new institutionalism do so on the basis of North's analysis. Thus, Platteau (1994a: 536) lends support to North in one sentence while criticizing the "crude version" of the new institutionalism—obviously not North's—in the next.
6. For a discussion of the influence of economics on political science, including North's contribution, see Miller (1997).
7. From sociology's perspective, Lindenberg (1985: 248–49) suggests that the change occurred as a result of six factors: i) an exhausted program of enquiry for sociology; ii) interest in Karl Popper sparked by Albert; iii) an article by Homans in the late 1950s on "Social behavior as exchange"; iv) the radical 1960s which revived interest in Marx; v) the 200th anniversary of *The Wealth of Nations* which renewed interest in Adam Smith; and, vi) increasing interest in game theory. For a related discussion, see Opp (1985). Others suggest that mainstream economics has exhibited imperialistic tendencies and attempted to colonize the other social sciences with its perspective and methods, see Fine (1997).
8. Changes in the perceived form and role of the state often emanate from Western capitals and institutional organization such as the World Bank. The early 1980s saw a radical swing from an active state to a minimalist one.
9. The analysis here and in the subsequent paragraph is my own, but the various aspects are often hinted at in accounts of foreign ethnic business communities. See, for example, Moore (1997), but also Mangat (1965), Marris and Somerset (1971), Manji (1975) and Zarwan (1977).

NOTES TO CHAPTER TWO

1. This was not true for the Swahili, a mixed Arab/African people, who remain along the coast.

2. This is my interpretation, in very clear and simple terms, of what the new institutional economics, in its various forms, is about.
3. Today, Bantu groups make up almost the entire population of Africa south of a rough line from Sierra Leone to the Kenya-Somali border. The major exceptions are the Khoisan peoples of south-west Africa (in and around the Kalahari Desert) and Nilotic speakers on the border areas, such as in Kenya.
4. Colonial figures are cited here because pre-colonial quantities are almost impossible to estimate.
5. It is still practiced in rural and urban areas today, as evidenced by occasional accounts in the Nairobi newspapers.
6. Mostly from the present Indian state of Gujarat.
7. A resin from various tropical trees, used as a varnish.
8. A wax-like substance with a strong smell which is secreted from the intestine of the sperm whale, is found floating in tropical seas and is used in the manufacture of perfume.
9. The mutiny in Bombay of Indian regulars in the forces supporting the (British) East Indian Company.

NOTES TO CHAPTER THREE

1. Because of heavy lending from the U.S. during the Second World War, Britain faced a crisis in maintaining the demand for and value of its currency. It tried to reduce its demand for dollars by trading more with its colonies.
2. It is also possible that the cost of wages for Indian workers was lower than that for African workers but it was probably impossible to make a direct comparison at the time, especially because there was not much of an African wage labor market in existence. Furthermore, the references given of colonial decisions make no mention of a difference in wages. Even if there was a difference it would have had to have been substantial to outweigh the costs of transport and the payment of return passage for the Asians.
3. Along with trade and production restrictions, in 1937 colonial officials also placed restrictions on the transport of goods in an effort to direct this traffic to the (financially precarious) railway. Competition came mainly from increased lorry activity in which Asians and to a lesser extent, Africans, had become increasingly involved since the 1920s (Mangat 1969: 158).
4. Box was later replaced by the Bombay-based British company, Grindlay, Groom and Co.
5. The contract was binding if it was approved by the (colonial) District Commissioner.
6. The Land Bank was formed in 1930 with a loan of £240,000, raised in London. Further increases allowed it to lend £1 million to settlers by the late 1930s. By 1936, some 542 farmers were having their mortgages refinanced through the Land Bank (Berman 1990: 167).
7. It was later replaced with the African Courts Ordinance, 1951.

8. As noted in the Introduction, the theory suggests that rights to land evolve (i.e. becoming more individualized and formalized) as a result of demographic pressure, resource scarcity and commercialization. For a detailed discussion of the theory as applied to sub-Saharan Africa, see Platteau (1995).
9. Thus making 640 acres, or one square mile.
10. The ordinance also banned the rental of land to Africans (called *kaffir* farming) and in 1919, officials began enforcing the Registration of Natives Ordinance to control the movement of people in the European-occupied areas. Even these combined regulations were ineffective and the control of squatter activity required a further strengthening of regulations in 1924 and 1925.

NOTES TO CHAPTER FOUR

1. Arable land is land suitable for growing crops.
2. All figures in this paragraph are from WDI (2004).
3. At constant 2000 prices.
4. The boards were established originally in 1960.
5. For a review of these programs, see: Ikiara 1988.
6. Personal interview with KIE/GTZ loan manager in Nairobi.
7. Agriculture fell steadily to 26% of GDP in 1998 and 16% by 2003. Services have increased from 43% in 1964 to 58% in 1998 (WDI 2004).
8. The Asian population declined by 43% between 1969 and 1979 from 176,613 to 78,600.

NOTES TO CHAPTER FIVE

1. Bryman and Cramer (1997, p. 104) cite a survey of 126 studies in the field of organizational research which found that only 21 were based on a probability sample. They note that the "requirement [of a random sample] is often not fulfilled and that even when a random sample has been used, factors like non-response may adversely affect its random qualities."
2. Notably, the Kenya Business Directory, the Kenya Association of Manufacturers Directory and the business listings of the Nairobi telephone book.
3. From an interview with a section head in the university's engineering department.
4. Because Mann-Whitney is a ranking test, all the firms for a particular location were used in a test and each location was not further sub-divided into smaller categories as would be the case in a cross-tabulation. No cross-tabulations using a location breakdown were conducted.

NOTES TO CHAPTER SIX

1. The contents of this chapter are drawn from an article previously published. Thus, basic arguments and data are reprinted from *World Development*,

volume 31, no. 11, Paul Vandenberg, "Adapting to the financial landscape: Evidence from small firms in Nairobi," pp. 1829–1843, Copyright 2003, with permission from Elsevier.

2. Personal interviews.
3. The one exception was a small African firm in the Baba Dogo area.
4. As a result of the decree, noted above.
5. We are dealing here with the security of possession or ownership, and not with the 'properties' of goods being exchanged and whether those 'properties' are being misrepresented.
6. The results are not provided in a table.
7. There were 54 firms on the Nairobi Stock Exchange when the survey was conducted, most of the firms are in the financial sector or are large, partly foreign-owned, companies.

NOTES TO CHAPTER SEVEN

1. Following independence, governments in Africa and parts of Asia tended to be controlled by the largest ethnic group, which was also the more economically disadvantaged.
2. Assuming, of course, that revenues are banked and placed in the account with the overdraft facility (not accounts with other banks).
3. The acronym stands for Growth and Equity through Microenterprise Investments and Institutions. The surveys were guided and conducted by researchers at Michigan State University.
4. For those not familiar with the use of instrumental variables in econometrics, the procedure is carried out because the regression suggests that firm size (FS) helps us to explain access to trade credit (TC). However, it might also be true that access to trade credit helps firms to group larger (i.e. affects firm size) and therefore the direction of causality runs in the opposite direction from what is suggested by the regression. *Instrumenting* the variable (starting capital) removes the possibility that trade credit is affecting firm size (what is known as simultaneity bias).
5. $TC=aA+bA^2$ where TC is trade credit, A is age and a and be are coefficients. $dTC/dA= -a + 2bA > 0$ (when there is a positive correlation), thus, $a/2b > A$ and because $a = .18$ and $b =.01$, then $A = 9$ when the correlation between age and TC is positive.
6. Growth rate = [ln(value of the firm) - ln(real starting capital)]/age, where the value of the firm is measured by the current value of assets, as discussed previously.

Bibliography

Akerlof, G. (1970). 'The market for 'lemons': Qualitative uncertainty and the market mechanism,' *Quarterly Journal of Economics*, vol. 84, no. 3

Alchian, A and Demsetz, H. (1973). 'The property rights paradigm,' *Journal of Economic History*, vol. 33, no. 1

Ambler, C. (1988). *Kenyan Communities in the Age of Imperialism* (New Haven, Conn.: Yale University Press)

Anderson, D. and Throup, D. (1985). 'Africans and agricultural production in colonial Kenya: The myth of the war as a watershed,' *Journal of African History*, vol. 26, no. 4

Aryeetey, E., Hettige, H., Nissanke, M., and Steel, W. (1998). 'Financial market fragmentation and reforms in Ghana, Malawi, Nigeria and Tanzania,' *World Bank Economic Review,* vol. 11, no. 2

Bank of England (1999). *Small Business* (London: Bank of England)

Bardhan, P. and C. Udry (1999). *Development Microeconomics* (Oxford: Oxford University Press)

Barrows, R. and Roth, M. (1990). 'Land tenure and investment in African agriculture: Theory and evidence,' *Journal of Modern African Studies*, vol. 28, no. 2

Barzel, Y. (1997). *Economic Analysis of Property Rights*, 2nd ed. (Cambridge: Cambridge University Press)

Berman, B. (1990). *Control and Crisis in Colonial Kenya* (London: James Currey).

Bhatt, P.M. (1978). *A History of Asians in Kenya, 1900–1970*, unpublished PhD thesis, Dept. of History, Howard University, Washington

Biggs, T., Raturi, M., and Srivastava, P. (1996). 'Enforcement of contracts in an African credit market: Working capital financing in Kenyan manufacturing,' World Bank, mimeo.

Bouman, F. (1995). 'Rotating and accumulating savings and credit associations: A development perspective,' *World Development*, vol. 23, no. 3

Bourdieu, P. and Coleman J., eds. (1991). *Social Theory for a Changing Society* (Boulder, Westview)

Bruce, J. and. Migot-Adholla, S.E, eds., (1994). *Searching for Land Tenure Security in Africa* (Dubuque, Iowa: Kendall/Hunt)

Bryman, A. and Cramer, D. (1997). *Quantitative Data Analysis* (London: Routledge)

Burch, E. and Ellana, L. (1994). 'Territories and territoriality: Editorial,' in Burch and Ellana, eds., *Key Issues in Hunter-Gatherer Research* (Oxford: Berg)

Carter, R., Wiebe, K., and Blarel, B. (1994). 'Tenure Security for Whom? Differential Impacts of Land Policy in Kenya, in Bruce and Migot-Adholla, eds., *Searching for Land Tenure Security in Africa* (Dubuque, Iowa: Kendall/Hunt)

———(1991). 'Tenure Security for Whom? Differential Impacts of Land Policy in Kenya,' LTC Research Paper 106 (Madison, WI: Land Tenure Centre, University of Wisconsin-Madison)

CFA—Commission for Africa (2005). *Our Common Interest: Report of the Commission for Africa* (London: Commission for Africa)

Chege, M. (1997). 'Paradigms of doom and the development management crisis in Kenya,' *Journal of Development Studies*, vol. 33, no. 4

———(1998). "Introducing race as a variable into the political economy of Kenya debate: An incendiary idea," *African Affairs*, vol. 97, no. 387

Clark, G. (1993). 'Economic growth in history and theory,' *Theory and Society*, vol. 22, no. 6

Coase, R. (1937). 'The nature of the firm,' *Economica*, vol. 4, no. 16

———(1960). 'The problem of social cost,' *Journal of Law and Economics*, vol. 3, no. 1

Coldham, S. (1979). 'Land tenure reform in Kenya: the limits of the law,' *Journal of Modern African Studies*, vol. 17, no. 4

———(1990). 'Les systèmes judicaires en Afrique anglophone,' *Afrique Contemporaine*, no. 156, 4th quarter

Collier, P. and Gunning, J. (1999). 'Explaining African economic performance,' *Journal of Economic Literature*, vol. 37, March

Commons, J. (1990, 1934). *Institutional Economics: Its Place in Political Economy*, vol. 1 (New Brunswick, USA: Transaction)

Colony and Protectorate of Kenya, *Annual Report* (London: HMSO), various years

Coughlin, P. (1988). 'Economies of scale, capacity utilisation and import substitution: A focus on dies, moulds and patterns,' in P. Coughlin and G. Ikiara, *Industrialization in Kenya* (Heinemann: Nairobi), pp. 112–125

Coughlin, P. and Ikiara, G. (1991). *Kenya's Industrialization Dilemma* (Heinemann: Nairobi)

———(1988). *Industrialization in Kenya* (Heinemann: Nairobi)

Cowen, M. and MacWilliam, S. (1996). *Indigenous Capital in Kenya: The 'Indian' dimension of the debate* (Helsinki: Interkont)

Cowen, M. (1981). 'Commodity production in Kenya's Central Province,' in J. Heyer *et al.*, eds., *Rural Development in Tropical Africa* (London: Macmillan)

———(1982). 'The British state and agrarian accumulation in Kenya,' in M. Fransman, ed., *Industry and Accumulation in Africa* (London: Heinemann)

Das Gupta, A. (1985). 'Indian merchants and the western Indian Ocean: The early seventeenth century,' *Modern Asian Studies*, vol. 19, no. 3

Degni,-Segui, R. (1995). 'L'acces a la justice et ses obstacles,' *Verfssung und Recht in Obersee*, 4th quarter,

De Soto, H. (1989). *The Other Path: The invisible revolution in the Third World* (New York: Harper and Row)

———(2000). *The Mystery of Capital: Why capitalism triumphs in the West and fails everywhere else* (New York: Basic Books)

Dia, M. (1994). 'Indigenous management practices: Lessons for Africa's management in the 1990s,' in I. Serageldin and J. Taboroff, eds., *Culture and Development in Africa* (Washington: World Bank)

———(1996). *Africa's Management in the 1990s and Beyond: Reconciling Indigenous and Transplanted Institutions* (Washington: World Bank)

Drugger, W. (1995). 'Douglass C. North's new institutionalism,' *Journal of Economic Issues*, vol. 29, no. 2

EARC (1961). *East Africa Royal Commission 1953–55 Report* (London HMSO)

Easterly, W. and Levine, R. (1997). 'Africa's growth tragedy: Policies and ethnic divisions,' *Quarterly Journal of Economics*, vol. 112, no. 4

Ehret, C. (1967). 'Cattle-keeping and milking in eastern and southern African history: The linguistic evidence,' *Journal of African History*, vol. 8, no. 1

———(1968). 'Sheep and central Sudanic peoples in southern Africa,' *Journal of African History*, vol. 9, no. 2

———'The East African interior,' in M. Elfasi, ed. ., *UNESCO General History of Africa, Vol. 3* (UNESCO: Paris).

Ellis, S. (1996). 'Africa after the Cold War: New patterns of government and politics,' *Development and Change*, vol. 27, no. 1

Elster, J. (1989a). *The Cement of Society: A study of social order* (Cambridge: Cambridge University Press)

———(1989b). 'Social norms and economic theory,' *Journal of Economic Perspectives*, vol. 3, no. 4

Ensminger, J. and Rutten, A. (1991). 'The political economy of changing property rights: Dismantling a pastoral commons,' *American Ethnologist*, vol. 18, no. 4

Fafchamps, M. (1997). 'Trade credit in Zimbabwean manufacturing,' *World Development*, vol. 25, no. 5

———(2000). 'Ethnicity and credit in African manufacturing,' *Journal of Development Economics*, vol. 61, no. 1

Feder, G., and Onchan, T. (1987). 'Land ownership security and farm investment in Thailand,' *American Journal of Agricultural Economics*, vol. 69, no. 2

———(1989). 'Land ownership security and farm investment: Reply,' *American Journal of Agricultural Economics*, vol. 71, no. 1

Field, A. (1994). 'North, Douglass C,' in G. Hodgson, W. Samuels and M. Tool, eds., *The Elgar Companion to Institutional and Evolutionary Economics*, vol. L-Z (Hants, UK/Brookfield, Ver., Edward Elgar)

———'The problem with neo-classical institutional economics: A critique with special reference to the North/Thomas model of pre-1500 Europe,' *Explorations in Economic History*, vol. 12, no. 2

Fine, B. (1997). 'The new revolution in economics,' *Capital and Class*, no. 61, spring

Forrest, T. (1994). *The Advance of African Capitalism: The growth of Nigerian enterprise* (Edinburgh: Edinburgh University Press)

Fransman, M., ed. (1982). *Industry and Accumulation in Africa* (London: Heinemann)

Freeman-Grenville, G. (1963). 'The coast: 1498–1840,' in R. Oliver and G. Mathew, eds., *History of Africa*, vol. 1 (Oxford: Clarendon Press), pp. 129–168

Fukuyama, F. (1996). *Trust: Social Virtues and the Creation of Prosperity* (New York, Penguin)

Gathii, J.T. (1994). 'The Dream of Judicial Security of Tenure and the Reality of Executive Involvement in Kenya's Judicial Process' (Nairobi: Kenya Human Rights Commission)

Ghai, Y. (1967). 'Independence and safeguards in Kenya,' *East African Law Journal*, vol. 3

Ghai, Y.P and McAuslan, J.P. (1970). *Public Law and Political Change in Kenya* (Nairobi: Oxford University Press)

Granovetter, M. (1985). 'Economic action and social structure: The problem of embeddedness,' *American Journal of Sociology*, vol. 91, no. 3

Green, J. (1987). 'Evaluating the Impact of Consolidation of Holdings, Individualisation of Tenure and Registration of Title: Lessons from Kenya,' LTC Paper 129 (Madison, WI: Land Tenure Centre, University of Wisconsin-Madison)

Greif, A. (1993). 'Contract enforceability and economic institutions in early trade: The Maghribi traders' coalition,' *American Economic Review*, vol. 83, no. 3

Groenewegen, J., Kerstholt, F. and Nagelkerke, A. (1995). 'Integrating new and old institutionalism: Douglass North building bridges,' *Journal of Economic Issues*, vol. 29, no. 2

Hakansson, N.T. (1994). 'Grain, cattle and power: Social processes of intensive cultivation and exchange in pre-colonial western Kenya,' *Journal of Anthropological Research*, vol. 50, no. 3

Harbeson, J. (1971). 'Land reform and politics in Kenya, 1954–70,' *Journal of Modern African Studies*, vol. 9, no. 2

Harriss, J., Hunter, J., and Lewis, C., eds., (1995). *The New Institutional Economics and Third World Development* (London, Routledge)

Haugerud, A. (1989). 'Land tenure and agrarian change in Kenya,' *Africa*, vol. 59, no. 1

Hilton-Young Report (1929) *Report of the Commission on Closer Union of the Dependencies in Eastern and Central Africa* (London, HMSO)

Himbara, D. (1993). 'Myths and realities of Kenyan capitalism,' *Journal of Modern African Studies*, vol. 31, no. 1

———(1994). *Kenyan Capitalists, the State and Development* (Boulder: Lynne Rienner)

———(1997). 'The 'Asian' question in East Africa: The continuing controversy on the role of Indian capitalists in accumulation and development in Kenya, Uganda and Tanzania,' *African Studies*, vol. 56, no. 1

Hodgson, G. (1988). *Economics and Institutions* (Cambridge, UK: Polity Press)

———(1992). 'The reconstruction of economics: Is there still a place for neoclassical theory?,' *Journal of Economic Issues*, vol. 26, no. 3

———(1997). 'The ubiquity of habits and rules,' *Cambridge Journal of Economics*, vol. 21. no. 6

———(1998). 'The approach of institutional economics,' *Journal of Economic Literature*, vol. 36, no. 1

Hollingsworth, L.W. (1960). *The Asians of East Africa* (London: Macmillan)

Ikiara, G. (1988). 'The role of government institutions in Kenya's industrialisation,' in P. Coughlin and G. Ikiara, eds., *Industrialization in Kenya* (Heinemann: Nairobi), pp. 218–250

Iliffe, J. (1995). *Africans: The History of a Continent* (Cambridge: Cambridge University Press)

ILO—International Labour Office (1972). *Employment, Incomes and Equality* (Geneva: ILO)

IMF: IFS—International Monetary Fund (various years). *International Financial Statistics* (Washington: IMF).

IOE—International Organisation of Employers (2005). *Approaches and Policies to Foster Entrepreneurship: A guide for employers' organizations* (Geneva: IOE)

Ingham, G. (1996). 'Some recent changes in the relationship between economics and sociology,' *Cambridge Journal of Economics*, vol. 20, no. 2

Isichei, E. (1997). *A History of African Societies* (Cambridge: Cambridge University Press)

Jensen, H.E. (1987). 'The theory of human nature,' *Journal of Economic Issues*, vol. 21, no. 3

Kanogo, T. (1987). *Squatters and the Roots of Mau Mau* (London: James Currey)

Kaplan, R. (1992). 'Continental drift: Africa's dysfunctional politics,' *The New Republic*, 28 December

Kaplinsky, R. (1980). 'Capital accumulation in the periphery: The Kenyan case re-examined,' *Review of African Political Economy*, vol. 7, no. 17

———(1982). 'Capitalist accumulation in the periphery,' in M. Fransman, ed., *Industry and Accumulation in Africa* (London: Heinemann)

Kariuki, R. (1996). 'Interest Rate Libeeralisation and the Allocation of Credit: Some Evidence from Small and Medium Scale Industry in Kenya,' unpublished DPhil thesis, IDS, University of Sussex, UK

Kelly, R. (1995). *The Foraging Spectrum* (Washington: Smithsonian)

Kenya (1965a). *African Socialism and its Application to Planning in Kenya* (Nairobi: Government Printer)

Kenya (1965b). *Development Plan for Period 1965/66 to 1969/70* (Nairobi: Government Printer)

Kenya Central Bureau of Statistics (1981). *Kenya Population Census 1979*, Vol. I (Nairobi: Government Printer)

———(1994). *Kenya Population Census 1989*, Vol. I (Nairobi: Government Printer)

KES—*Economic Survey,* (Nairobi: Government Printer), various years.

King, K. (1996). *Jua Kali Kenya* (London: Jame Currey)

Kitching, G. (1980). *Class and Economic Change in Kenya* (New Haven, Conn: Yale University Press)

Knox, A. (1998). 'Kenya country profile,' in J. Bruce , ed., *Country Profiles of Land Tenure: Africa 1996*, Land Tenure Centre, University of Wisconsin-Madison, on-line

KSA—*Statistical Abstract* (Nairobi: Government Printer), various years

Langdon, S. (1987). 'Industry and capitalism in Kenya: Contributions to a debate,' in P. Lubeck, ed., *The African Bourgeoisie: Capitalism in Nigeria, Kenya and Ivory Coast* (Boulder, Col.: Lynne Rienner)

Lawren, W. (1968). 'Masai and Kikuyu: An historical analysis of cultural transmission,' *Journal of African History*, vol. 9, no. 4

Lazonick, W. (1991). *Business Organization and the Myth of the Market Economy* (Cambridge: Cambridge University Press)

Leo, C. (1984). *Land and Class in Kenya* (Toronto: University of Toronto Press)

Levy, B. (1993). 'Obstacles to developing indigenous small and medium enterprises: An empirical assessment,' *World Bank Economic Review*, vol. 7, no. 1

Leys, C. (1975). *Underdevelopment in Kenya* (London: Heinemann)

———(1980). 'State capital in Kenya: A research note,' *Canadian Journal of African Studies*, vol. 14, no. 2

———(1982a). 'Accumulation, class formation and dependency: Kenya,' in M. Fransman, ed., *Industry and Accumulation in Africa* (London: Heinemann)

———(1982b). 'Kenya: What does 'dependency' explain,' in M. Fransman, ed., *Industry and Accumulation in Africa* (London: Heinemann)

———(1994). 'Learning from the Kenya debate,' in D. Apter and C. Rosberg, ed., *Political Development and the New Realism in sub-Saharan Africa* (London: University Press of Virginia, pp. 220–243

Lindenberg, S. (1985). 'Rational choice and sociological theory: New pressures on economics as a social science,' *Journal of Institutional and Theoretical Economics*, vol. 141, no. 2

———(1990). 'Homo Socio-oeconomicus: The emergence of a general model of man in the social sciences,' *Journal of Institutional and Theoretical Economics*, vol. 146, no. 4.

Livingstone, I. (1976). 'An evaluation of Kenya's rural industrial Development Programme,' *Journal of Modern African Studies*, vol. 14, no. 3

Lonsdale, J. and Berman, B. (1979). 'Coping with the contradictions: The development of the colonial state in Kenya, 1895–1914,' *Journal of African History*, vol. 20, no. 4

Mackenzie, F. (1989). 'Land and territory: The interface between two systems of land tenure, Murang'a District, Kenya,' *Africa*, vol. 59, no. 1

Mangat, J.S. (1969). *A History of the Asians in East Africa c. 1886–1945* (London: Oxford University Press)

Manji, M. (1995). *Memoirs of a Biscuit Baron* ((Nairobi: Kenway)

Marris, P. and Somerset, A. (1971). *African Businessmen* (London: Routledge & Kegan Paul)

Martin, C.J. (1953). 'A demographic study of an immigrant community: The Indian population of British East Africa,' *Population Studies*, vol. 6, part 3

Masinde, C. (1994). 'Report on the Metalworking and Transport Sub-sectors,' (Nairobi: USAID), Final draft report.

Mathew, G. (1963). 'The East African coast until the coming of the Portuguese,' in R. Oliver and G. Mathew, eds., *History of Africa*, vol. 1 (Oxford: Clarendon Press),

Matthews, R. (1987). 'The development of a local machinery industry in Kenya,' *Journal of Modern African Studies*, vol. 25, no. 1

Mauro, P. (1995). 'Corruption and growth,' *Quarterly Journal of Economics*, vol. 110, no. 3

Mayberry, T.C. (1969). 'Thorstein Veblen on human nature,' *American Journal of Economics and Sociology*, vol. 28, no. 3

McPherson, M. (1996). 'Growth of micro and small enterprises in southern Africa,' *Journal of Development Economics*, vol. 48, no. 2

Mead, D. and Liedholm, C. (1998). 'The dynamics of micro and small enterprises in developing countries,' *World Development*, vol. 26, no. 1

Middleton, J. (1992). *The World of the Swahili: An African Mercantile Civilization*. (New Haven, Conn.: Yale University Press)

Miller, G. (1997). 'The impact of economics on contemporary political science,' *Journal of Economic Literature*, vol. 35, no. 3

Mkandawire, T. (1998). 'Thinking about developmental states in Africa,' mimeo

Moore, M. (1997). 'Societies, polities and capitalists in developing countries: A literature survey,' *Journal of Development Studies*, vol. 33, no. 3

Mordoch, J. (1999). 'The micro finance promise,' *Journal of Economic Literature*, vol. 37, no. 4

Muriuki, G. (1974). *A History of the Kikuyu 1500–1900* (Nairobi: Oxford University Press)

Murray, R. (1978). 'The Chandarias: The development of a Kenyan multinational,' in R.

Kaplinsky, ed., *Readings on the Multinational Corporation in Kenya* (Nairobi: Oxford University Press)

Myrdal, G. (1978). 'Institutional economics,' *Journal of Economic Issues*, vol. 12, December

Newlyn, W. and Rowan, D. (1954). *Money and Banking in British Colonial Africa* (Oxford: Clarendon)

Nissanke, M. and Aryeetey, E. (1998). *Financial Integration and Development: Liberalisation and reform in sub-Saharan Africa* (London: Routledge)

North, D. (1981). *Structure and Change in Economic History* (New York: Norton)

———(1984). 'Three approaches to the study of institutions,' in D. Colander, ed., *Neoclassical Political Economy* (Cambridge, MA: Balinger)

———(1986). 'Is it worth making sense of Marx?,' *Inquiry*, vol. 29, no. 1

———(1989). 'Institutions and economic growth: An historical introduction,' *World Development*, vol. 17, no. 9

———(1990a). *Institutions, Institutional Change and Economic Performance* (Cambridge: Cambridge University Press)

———(1990b). 'A transaction cost theory of politics,' *Journal of Theoretical Politics*, vol. 12, no. 4

———(1995a). 'The new institutional economics and Third World development,' in J. Harriss, J. Hunter and C. Lewis, C., eds., *The New Institutional Economics and Third World Development* (London: Routledge)

———(1995b). 'Douglass C. North' [autobiographical sketch] in W. Breit and R. Spencer, eds., *Lives of the Laureates: Thirteen Nobel Economists* (Cambridge, MA: MIT Press)

North, D. and Thomas. R. (1973). *The Rise of the Western World: A New Economic History* (Cambridge: Cambridge University Press)

North, D. and Weingast, B. (1989). 'Constitutions and commitment: The evolution of institutions governing public choice in 17th century England,' *Journal of Economic History*, vol. 49, no. 4

Norusis, M. (1998). *SPSS 8.0 Guide to Data Analysis* (Upper Saddle River, NJ: Prentice Hall)

Ochieng,' W. (1974). *An Outline History of Nyanza up to 1914* (Nairobi: East Africa Literature Bureau)

Ogot, B.A., ed., (1976). *Kenya Before 1900* (Nairobi: East African Publishing)

Okoth-Ogendo, H. (1976). 'African land tenure reform,' in J. Heyer *et al.*, eds., *Agricultural Development in Kenya: An Economic Assessment* (Nairobi: Oxford University Press)

Oliver, R. (1966). 'The problem of the Bantu expansion,' *Journal of African History*, vol. 7, no.3

Oliver, R and Atmore, A. (2001). *Medieval Africa 1250–1800* (Cambridge, UK: Cambridge University Press)

Oliver, R. and Gervase, M., eds., (1963). *History of East Africa, Vol. 1* (Oxford: Clarendon)

Opp, K-D. (1985). 'Sociology and economic man,' *Journal of Institutional and Theoretical Economics*, vol. 141, no. 2

Paarlberg, D. (1993). 'The case for institutional economics,' *American Journal of Agricultural Economics*, vol. 75, no. 3

Parker, J. and Torres, T. (1994). 'Micro and small scale enterprises in Kenya: Results of the 1993 National Baseline Survey,' GEMINI Technical Report, No. 75 (Washington)

Phillips, A. (1945). *Report on Native Tribunals* (Nairobi: Government Printer)

Platteau, J.-P. (1994a). 'Behind the market stage where real societies exist—Part I: The role of public and private institutions,' *Journal of Development Studies*, vol. 30, no. 3

———(1994b). 'Behind the market stage where real societies exist—Part II: The role of moral norms,' *Journal of Development Studies*, vol. 30, no. 4

———(1996). 'The evolutionary theory of land rights as applied to sub-Saharan Africa: A critical assessment,' *Development and Change*, vol. 27, no. 2

Ramachandran, V. and Shah, M.K. (1999). 'Minority entrepreneurs and firm performance in sub-Saharan Africa,' *Journal of Development Studies*, vol. 36, no. 2

Rattanabirabongse, V., Eddington, R., Burns, A., and Nettle, K. (1998). 'The Thailand land titling project—thirteen years of experience,' *Land Use Policy*, vol. 15, no. 1

Raturi, M. and Swamy, A. (1998). 'Explaining ethnic differential in credit market outcomes: Evidence from Zimbabwe,' Regional Program in Enterprise Development, Paper No. 78 (Washington: World Bank)

Robinson, W. and Harbison, S. (1995). 'The fertility decline in Kenya,' *Journal of International Development*, vol. 7, no. 1

Rogers, P. (1979). 'The British and the Kikuyu 1890–1905: A Reassessment,' *Journal of African History*, vol. 20, no. 2

Ross, W. M. (1927). *Kenya from Within* (London: Allen and Unwin)

Roth, M., Barrows, R., Carter, M. and Kanel, D. (1989). 'Land ownership security and farm investment: Comments,' *American Journal of Agricultural Economics*, vol. 71, no. 1

Roth, M., Cochrane, J., and Kisamba-Mugerwa, W. (1994). 'Tenure security, credit use and farm investment in the Rujumbura pilot land registration scheme, Uganda,' in J. Bruce and S.E. Migot-Adholla, eds., *Searching for Land Tenure Security in Africa* (Dubuque, Iowa: Kendall, Hunt)

Rutherford, M. (1994). *Institutions in Economics: The Old and the New Institutionalism* (Cambridge: Cambridge University Press)

———(1995). 'The old and the new institutionalism: Can bridges be built?,' *Journal of Economic Issues*, vol. 29, no. 4

Ruttan, V. and Yujiro, H. (1984). 'Towards a theory of induced institutional innovation,' *Journal of Development Studies*, vol. 20, no. 4

Saberwal, S. (1967). 'Historical notes on the Embu of central Kenya,' *Journal of African History*, vol. 8, no.1

Sachs, J., McArthur, J., Schmidt-Traub, G., Kruk, M., Bahadur, C., Faye, M., and McCord, G. (2004). 'Ending Africa's poverty trap,' *Brookings Papers on Economic Activity*, vol. 1

Samuels, W. (1995). 'The present state of institutional economics,' *Cambridge Journal of Economics*, vol. 19, no. 4

Schoenbrun, D. (1993). 'We are what we eat: Ancient agriculture between the Great Lakes,' *Journal of African History*, vol. 34, no. 1

Sharpley, J. (1981). 'Resource transfers between the agricultural and non-agricultural sectors: 1964–1977,' in T. Killick, ed., *Papers on the Kenyan Economy* (Nariobi, Heinemann)

Shipton, P. (1995). 'Luo entrustment: Foreign finance and the soil of the spirits in Kenya,' *Africa*, vol. 65, no. 2

Sorrenson, M. (1967). *Land Reform in the Kikuyu Country* (Nairobi: Oxford University Press)

———(1968). *Origins of European Settlement in Kenya* (Nairobi: Oxford University Press)

Spear, T. (1976). 'The Mijikenda,' in B. Ogot, ed., *Kenya Before 1900* (Nairobi: East African Publishing)

———(1981). *Kenya's Past* (Harlow, UK: Longman)

Stanfield, J. (1995). 'Institutions and the significance of relative prices,' *Journal of Economic Issues*, vol. 29, no. 2

Stein, H. (1994). 'Theories of institutions and economic reform in Africa,' *World Development*, vol. 22, no 12

Subrahmanyam, S. (1988). 'Persians, pilgrims and Portuguese: The travails of Masulipatnam in the western Indian Ocean, 1590–1665,' *Modern Asian Studies*, vol. 22, no. 3

———(1995). 'Of *imarat* and *tijarat*: Asian merchants and state power in the western Indian Ocean, 1400–1750,' *Comparative Studies in Society and History*, vol. 37, no. 4

Swainson, N. (1977). 'The rise of a national bourgeoisie in Kenya,' *Review of African Political Economy*, vol. 4, no. 8

———(1980). *The Development of Corporate Capitalism in Kenya 1918–1977* (London: Heinemann)

Tate, H. (1910). 'The native law of the southern Gikuyu of British East Africa,' *Journal of the African Society*, vol. 9, no. 35

———(1911). 'Further notes on the southern Gikuyu of British East Africa,' *Journal of the African Society*, vol. 10, no. 24

Throup, D. (1987). *Economic and Social Origins of Mau Mau.* (London: James Currey)

Thurston, A. (1987). *Smallholder Agriculture in Colonial Kenya: The official mind and the Swynnerton Plan*, Cambridge African Monographs, 8, (Cambridge: African Studies Centre, University of Cambridge)

Tullock, G. (1983). 'Review: Douglass C. North, Structure and Change in Economic History,' *Public Choice*, vol. 40, no. 2

UNDP—United Nations Development Progamme (2004). *Unleashing Entrepreneurship: Making Business Work for the Poor*, Commission on the Private Sector and Development, Report to the Secretary-General of the United Nations (New York: UNDP)

UNFPA—United Nations Population Fund (1998). *The State of World Population* (New York: UNFPA)

Udry, C. (1990). 'Credit markets in northern Nigeria: Credit insurance in a rural economy,' *World Bank Economic Review*, vol. 4, no. 3

Vandenberg, P. (1997). 'Urban migration and the breakdown of credit relations,' *SOAS Economic Digest*, vol. 1, no. 3

———(1999). "Risk, ethnicity and property rights: Towards a political economy of Africa's institutions," Working Paper, Dept. of Economics, School of Oriental and African Studies, University of London, UK

———(2000). 'The evolution of SMI policy in Malaysia,' Working Paper, Visiting Researchers Series, no. 15 (Singapore: Institute of Southeast Asian Studies)

———(2002a). 'Institutions and Accumulation in Kenya: Analyzing the African-Asian divide,' PhD thesis, Department of Economics, School of Oriental and African Studies, University of London, UK.

———(2002b). 'North's institutionalism and the prospect of combining theoretical approaches,' *Cambridge Journal of Economics*, vol. 26, no. 2

———(2003a). 'Ethnic-sectoral cleavages and economic development: Reflections on the second Kenya debate,' *Journal of Modern African Studies*, vol. 41, no. 3
———(2003b). 'Adapting to the financial landscape: Evidence from small firms in Nairobi,' *World Development*, vol. 31, no. 11
Vansina, J. (1988). *Paths in the Rainforest* (London: James Currey)
———(1995). 'New linguistic evidence and the Bantu expansion,' *Journal of African* History vol. 36, no. 2
van Zwanenberg, R. and King, A. (1975). *An Economic History of Kenya and Uganda 1800–1970.* (London: Macmillan)
Veblen, T. (1899). *The Theory of the Leisure Class* (New York, Macmillan)
———(1909). 'The limitations of marginal utility,' *Journal of Political Economy*, vol. 17, no. 9
———(1914/1990). *The Instinct of Workmanship and the State of the Industrial Arts*, (New Brunswick USA/London, Transaction)
———(1994). *The Place of Science in Modern Civilization and Other Essays* (London, Routledge/Thoemmes)
Waller, R. (1976). 'The Maasai and the British 1895–1905: The origins of an alliance,' *Journal of African History*, vol. 17, no. 4
———(1985). 'Economic and social relations in the central Rift Valley: The Maa-speakers and their neighbours in the 19th century,' in B. Ogot, ed., *Kenya in the 19th Century (Hadith 8)*
WDI (2004), World Development Indicators, database (Washington: World Bank)
Williamson, O. (1975). *Markets and Hierarchy* (New York: Free Press)
———(1985). *The Economic Institutions of Capitalism* (New York: Free Press)
World Bank (2006). *Doing Business in 2006: Creating Jobs* (Washington D.C.: World Bank).
Zarwan, J. (1977). 'Indian businessmen in Kenya during the 20th century: A case study,' unpublished PhD thesis, Yale University

Index

E

F

G

K

L

M

Z

www.ingramcontent.com/pod-product-compliance
Ingram Content Group UK Ltd.
Pitfield, Milton Keynes, MK11 3LW, UK
UKHW021607240425
457818UK00018B/427